INDIAN NUMISMATICS

From the Earliest Times to the Rise of the Imperial Guptas

By

S.K. CHAKRABORTTY

BKP

BHARATIYA KALA PRAKASHAN

DELHI (INDIA)

First Edition : 2004

Published by **C.P. Gautam**
BHARATIYA KALA PRAKASHAN
3421-A, IInd Floor, Narang Colony, Tri Nagar,
Delhi-110035. Phone : 27153083 (O) , 27522129 (R)

ISBN : 81-8090-048-7

Laser Type Setting by
A-ONE GRAPHICS
JD-18C, Crystal Appartment, New Delhi-110088
Ph. : 55640278, Mob.: 9811167357

Printed by
BDH Printers at Salasar Imaging System,
Delhi-35, Ph. 31045804

DEDICATION

To

The Sacred Memory

of

My Late Father,

B. K. CHAKRABORTTY

PREFACE

The book deals with the discussion, criticism and systematic arrangement of our knowledge of the indigenous system of Ancient Indian Numismatics up to the 3rd cent. A.D. with special reference to Nothern India. It embodies the result of my work on a rather intricate and difficult subject which had not received the amount of attention from scholars which it fully deserves. I have spared no pains in making an exhaustive study of the literature on the subject and put it under a systematic and thorough criticism which had led to the discovery of new facts and the correction of many errors. The correlation of the known data thus enlightens a dark corner of Indian Archaeology and consequently tends to the advancement of knowledge of Indian Numismatics of the earliest period. I have in the footnotes given a detailed reference to the works of the scholars to whom I am indebted in this connection, and have appended at the end a list of books consulted and referred to in its preparation. My intention had been to systematise the scraps of information which lie scattered in books generally inaccessible to the public and give all the salient features of the subject in as short a compass as possible. But certain portions of this book will exhibit the result of my own research e.g., the determination of the Śatamāna unit, a new interpretation of the variations in the weight of the coins of this period, the indebtedness of India to the Greeks at a certain stage as regards the fabrication of coins, the determination of the standard coins of the different periods of Early Indian History, the chronological position in the use of the different metals for coinage, the result of the adoption of a bimetallic system in ancient times and the attempts made to grapple with the consequent difficulty, correct explanation of some of the legends in the coins and lastly attempts to throw light on the obscure points of Indian Numismatics concerning the identification of the different states, and princes and their chronological position. The eight chapters in which the work is divided give a condensed and systematic information about the important numismatic data of the period under review and a clear statement and criticism of the main theories of Cunningham, Smith and Profs. Rapson and Bhandarkar, the pioneers on the subject.

The study of the evolutionary processes of coinage in Ancient India will lead to a new orientation; and a comparison between the Indian and foreign processes and their parallel development will establish a bond of uniformity, and incidentally point out the necessary-differences. That the Indians were confronted with the problem of ratios between the different metals—the age-old difficulties of bimetallism, and their attempts to solve the difficulty and the consequential results will enable us to clearly appreciate their position. It is a record of the intellectual progress in the theory and practice of coinage in its infancy, its evolution with the progress of society and its reciprocal action on the foreign systems. It is only from the study of Numismatics that the existence of some of the states in ancient India e.g., Upagauḍa the Vimakas, etc. has been brought to our notice ; and incidentally much information about the religious, literary and political condition of that early age is brought before us and gives us a glimpse of an obscure period of Indian History. Whether I have succeeded, even partially, in my work, it is for the scholars to judge, though I owe them an apology for such an ambitious attempt.

Lastly I offer my heartfelt thanks to Rai Bahadur Jajneswar Ghosh, M.A., PH.D., and Prof. Sarat Chandra Pal, B.A. for encouragement and help, and Mr. Nalini Kanta Bhattashali, M.A., Curator, Dacca Museum for allowing me to use the Museum Library.

S. K. CHAKRABORTTY

CONTENTS

LIST OF PLATES

CHAPTER I

THE EVOLUTION OF COINAGE

In the early stage of human culture the wants of men were very limited. "The untutored Savage readily supplies his few and simple wants from the great store of Nature ; his limited requirements leave him independent even of the aid and co-operation of his fellow Savages. So long as he finds food and shelter, and the coarsest covering to shield him from the weather, he is satisfied; and his benefactress—Mother Earth—does not call upon him to return her an equivalent for her gifts."[1] When the unit of society was the family or tribe, it was generally "small and self-contained and mainly nomadic."[2] There was no necessity for exchange and the only division of labour that existed was confined to the sexes and "in the primitive form of the tribal craftsman who performed certain work for all the members of the tribe in consideration of a share of their produce."[3] But when one tribe was brought into contact with another friendly tribe, the necessity for exchange arose, because the different tribes coming from different localities had perhaps the monopoly equally of certain articles which the others desired. The transaction was surely advantageous to both the parties concerned. "Thus exchange was in the first place inter-tribal or inter-national rather than local."[4]

Barter most probably arose from the practice of "mutual propitiation by gifts"[5] among the savages and it was gradually that the idea that "the present received would be of like worth with that given" was established and the exchanged articles lost the "character of presents" Spencer refers to the gift made by European travellers to savage chiefs and shows that the initial present was at first "propitiatory" and had with it the idea of a "responsive present" which was nothing but "informal barter."[6] An account of the Andamanese, a primitive people still extant is given by Mr. Man and is quoted by Spencer in his "Principles of Sociology"—"It is customary for each family to supply itself with the chief necessaries in the shape of weapons and food." "They set no fixed value on their various properties, and rarely make or procure anything for the express purpose of bartering with it. * * * These transactions (exchanges) they are pleased to consider as presentations ; but it is tacitly understood that no present is to be accepted unless an equivalent is rendered, and as the opinions of donors and. recipients are liable to differ as to the respective value of the articles in question, a quarrel is not infrequently the result."[7] Thus according to Spencer "the savages (who invent nothing, but even in making of implements develop this or that kind by unobtrusive modifications), were led unawares, and not aforethought, into the practice of barter."[8]

When the tribes settled in fixed localities and gradually, the communities grew in size, the division of labour became more and more operative. "The artisans like smiths, carpenters, shoe-makers, etc., had enough work to keep themselves fully occupied and the wants of the hunter and the fighting men had to be satisfied. Barter was now a necessity to the community and "the exchange of the different products was essential,"[9] A picture of these exchange transactions is given by Dr. Taylor—"It is instructive to see trade in its lowest form among such tribes as the Australians. The tough greenstone, valuable for making hatchets, is carried hundreds of miles by natives who receive from other tribes in return the prized products of their districts, such as red ochre to paint their bodies with ; they have even got so far as to let peaceful traders pass unharmed through tribes at war, so that trains of youths might be met, each lad with a slab of sand-stone on his head to be carried to his distant home and shaped into a seed-crusher. When strangers visit a tribe, they are received at friendly gathering or corrobboree, and presents are given on both sides. No doubt there is a general sense that the gifts are to be fair exchanges, and if either side is not satisfied there will be grumbling and quarrelling. But in this roughest kind of barter we do not yet find that clear notion of a unit of value which is the great step in trading."[10]

The disadvantages of Barter are apparent. It necessitates, a double coincidence—the wants on the part of the seller or the buyer must be exactly of the things as offered by the other.[11] The want of coincidence is surely a great handicap in the fulfilment of social needs. There is another difficulty as regards the measure of value, —how much of one commodity is to be exchanged for a quantity of another commodity. An elaborate table of ratios between different commodities would be needed. Lastly there is the third difficulty, or sometimes the impossibility, of dividing certain kinds of goods and their number must be large *e.g.*, a coat or things of that kind have no value when cut up into sub-divisions. In spite of all the difficulties Barter is the earliest means of carrying on commerce. But with the expansion of commercial activities when it was found inadequate to meet the demands of society a new device had to be evolved. This was the employment of a medium of exchange—a common commodity serving as an intermediary in all acts of commerce. All the difficulties of Barter are thereby obviated and in spite of the fact that the use of a medium necessitates two exchanges, yet ultimately the convenience in exchange transactions is in its favour. There are surely many are original tribes that carry on trade through Barter but with the growth of commerce and intelligence, Barter would be confined to minor transactions as in the case of the civilised society. The civilised peoples had in the past to pass through the same evolutionary stages, though not surely at the same time.

Even under modern conditions, Barter has not fully gone out of use. In the United States of America, commercially one of the most advanced countries of the world Barter steps in, in modern business life. "Barter of various kinds of live-stock, of grain and hay, of fresh and cured meat and of labour, is an important feature in rural life in many sections."[12] "Much labour, specially farm and domestic labour is still paid for partly in kind."[15] Farms are sometimes exchanged for one another. And many similar cases of Barter are pointed out by

Anderson in his chapter on the subject. In Tact the present system of foreign trade is a "system of refined Barter."[14]

How business was carried on in ancient Egypt is vividly brought before us in a number of scenes of market life from a tomb at Saqqāra. "The purchasers brought with them some product of their toil—a new tool, a pair of shoes, a reed mat, pots of unguents or cordials ; often, too, rows of cowries and a small box full of rings, each weighing a "tabnu" made of copper, silver or even gold, all destined to be bartered for such things as they needed."[15] Small transactions did not lead to much complicated calculations but when a large animal or an object of considerable value had to be disposed of, there ensued a long and stormy debate and sometimes a number of various articles had to be bartered for a bull or a she-ass etc. The Phoenicians were the greatest commercial people of antiquity and the carrying trade of the Mediterranean before the advent of the Greeks was mainly in their hands. Their commerce was carried on in the same manner, that is, through Barter. The prophet Ezekiel refers to it in the following passage and the statement is confirmed by Diodorus—"Spain (Tarshish) traded with thee, because of the multitude of thy goods ; silver, iron, tin, and lead, it gave thee in exchange for thy wares." The Phoenicians exchanged the Tyrian wares, trinklets, toys and other articles of finery for the natural productions of the countries traded with and the metals changed hands not as money but merely as merchandise.[16]

A great advance is made when certain commodities are given preference to others and a higher value is attached to them. These commodities in course of time assume the character of a medium of exchange, a standard by which the value of other things is estimated. The emergence of "the notion of a unit of value" is a great step in the furtherance of commercial transactions. In the history of mankind various substances have been used as mediums of exchange. In the earliest stage of human culture, when men secured subsistence by hunting, finely worked stone implements made of hard stones were perhaps used as mediums of exchange as suggested by Boucher de Perthes. We know that furs and skins, the proceeds of the chase were used as money by various ancient nations *e.g.* the Jews, the Esthonians and others. Leather circulated in Russia upto the time of Peter the Great and traditions affirm that leather was used as the earliest currency in Rome, Sparta and Carthage. In recent times the Hudson Bay Company of North America used furs as their medium of exchange in their transactions with the Red Indians. When human society reached the pastoral stage, the herds of cattle and sheep formed their chief means of subsistence. Men live upon the milk products and the meat of their domesticated animals, go it is not at all strange that sheep and cattle were used as mediums of exchange, and their wealth consisted in the possession of these animals. A reference to the Vedic Literature of India, the Homeric Literature of Greece, the Anglo-Saxon Literature and the ancient Teutonic Code of Laws would clearly bear out the statement. As the human family advanced to the agricultural stage the products of agriculture came to be used as mediums of exchange *e.g.* corn in Europe, maize in parts of Central America and Mexico, grain in ancient China and various other articles like tobacco, olive oil, cocoanuts, cod fish, etc. in the different parts of the world.

We thus find that various articles which minister to animal wants came to function as money. But at a very early stage "a different sort of commodity comes in,"[17] namely the articles of ornament which "begin to take the place of articles which minister to mere animal wants."[18] "In warm regions, ornament has commonly preceded clothing. Very early, necklaces, bracelets, rings, ear-rings, nose-pendants etc., became objects of exceedingly great desire. And very early gold and silver were used for such purposes."[19] "Other ornaments than those made of gold and silver have also become money. Wampum, polished shells, iron ornaments, etc. have all been money. The Karoks of California were accustomed to use strings of shell ornaments as money. When this was supplanted by American silver, they used strings of silver coins as ornaments, dressing their women lavishly with rows of silver dimes, quarters and half-dollars. Ornament and money are freely interchangeable."[19a] The metals are widely used for ornaments and it has been pointed out that the position the metals have come to occupy is firmly based on "three powerful elements of human nature" which have successfully sustained the value of metals— "(1) love of approbation ; (2) the sex-impulse ; (3) the spirit of rivalry and competition."[20] The ornaments confer distinction and it is human nature that men will strive for them. It is however mainly "for the sake of the other sex that men seek ornaments"[21] and this desire to possess ornaments is in its nature competitive ; and this is due to the idea of distinction conferred.

The metals gradually supplanted all other articles in the civilised countries as mediums of exchange. They possess the requisite qualities to a greater extent than any other available commodity and all over the civilised world a time came when the metals as mediums of exchange supplanted all other articles. The necessary qualities, however, are not possessed in an equal degree by all the metals and the use of a particular metal in a country depended upon the fact whether it was available there and the extent of its supply. The various metals used by mankind for purposes of currency are iron, copper, lead, tin, silver and gold and their various alloys. Platinum was used in Russia but was given up in 1845, being found unfitted for currency; Nickel is at present only used in alloy with other metals. The order of the values of the metals changed in different ages, *e.g.* iron in the Homeric Age was more valuable than copper. In Europe silver came into use before gold, but in India in the Pre-Vedic period it was perhaps gold that came earlier in use though not as currency. This is evident from the abundance of gold and the comparative paucity of silver in the excavations of Mohenjo-daro and Harappā. But when a metal became too plentiful either from the discovery of new mines or improved mechanical process in extraction, the weight of the metal to be given in exchange increased ; consequently its cheapness was a drawback and another metal came to supplant it. The metals at first changed hands by weight and in all business transactions scales were brought into operation ; and for every commodity for sale, a certain quantity of the metal was weighed out. This became imperatively necessary in the case of the precious metals, like gold and silver, where proportionately higher value is met with side by side with small mass. Some of the civilised nations of antiquity stopped at that point ; Egypt, Babylon and Assyria did not proceed further.[22]

In Egypt the "tabnu" rings had to be weighed in scales in order to determine whether these contained the regulation amount of gold or silver[23] and there was the added chance of deception as regards the quality of the metals and this fact naturally restrained the use of precious metals among the people for a long time. For ordinary-transactions, copper "tabnu" would serve the purpose and we have to agree with Lenormant "in his conclusion that the only kind of national metal of exchange in use in Egypt was a copper wire or plate bent thus **, — this being the sign invariably used in the hieroglyphics in writing the word "tabnu."[24] In Egypt, the Theban Empire of the 18th and 19th dynasties (1635—1235 B.C.) is marked by brilliant conquests. For four hundred years, Egypt reaped the fruit of her foreign conquests and huge quantity[1] of precious metals flowed into the country. This exercised a considerable influence on the commerce of the land and though barter was the prevailing system, yet considerable modifications in business transactions were introduced. In exchange "rings" and ingots of a certain prescribed weight in "tabnu" came to be freely used "and it became more and more the custom to pay for goods by a certain number of "tabnu" of gold, silver or copper rather than by other commodities ; it was the practice even to note down in invoices or official receipts, alongside the product or manufactured articles with which payments were made, the value of the same in weighed metals."[25] The Babylonians like the Egyptians were ignorant of coins but they used the metals for purposes of exchange. The metals were not shaped like the Egyptian "tabnu" *i.e.*, flat rings or twists of wire but were "melted into small unstamped ingots which were passed from hand to hand by weight, being tested in the scales, in each transaction."[26] "To weigh" was in the ordinary language the equivalent for "payment in metal," whereas "to measure" denoted that the payment was in grain. The ingots for exchange were therefore designated by the name of the weight to which they corresponded. A shekel weighed about half an ounce, 60 shekels made a mina and 60 minas a talent. Lenormant believes that the primitive meaning of the ideogram representing the shekel is that of a "mace-head"—"globe." From this Mesparo concludes "that the ingots used by the Chaldaeans were usually of the, ovoid, slightly flattened shape of the early Lydian coins." In Babylonia silver was the principal medium in business transactions ; copper and gold were also used but very sparingly. In an inscription the price of a field is given in chariots, asses, bulls etc. and the value of these things in silver is given with each article. In the code of Khammurabi,[27] the Amraphel of the Bible and perhaps the contemporary of Abraham (2342 B.C.) the society has passed beyond barter. But the smaller payments are made in produce *e.g.* 20 Ka of gram for hiring an ox for threshing or 8 Gur of grain for hiring a harvester for a year. But for commercial transactions, metals have come into use and it is silver that is ordinarily referred to ; gold is surely known as selling of wife, son or daughter for gold is mentioned in clause 117, but there is no doubt that silver served the purpose of a currency. But wherever the metals are used as mediums of exchange, it is the weight that is referred to; the coins have not yet come into use. In the code for destroying the eye or breaking the limb of a noble man, one mina of silver had to be paid (clause 198), for striking a freeborn woman and causing her let fall what was in her womb a payment of 10 shekels of silver had to be made (clause 209) or 6 She of silver a day had to be paid for hiring a day labourer (clause 273).

The next advance in the evolution of coinage was made independently by China, Lydia and India. The metallic currency necessitated the balance and the touchstone for determining the weight and quality at every transaction but the issue of coins obviated the difficulty. A piece of metal with a recognised mark on its face, impressed upon it, by a responsible authority is a coin and has behind it the guarantee of that authority as regards its quality and weight. The impression on the coin gives it a particular shape and protects it at least to some extent from being tampered with. The advantage to the commercial community was great and business transactions were much facilitated. So it is very likely that the initiative in the matter was taken by the merchants themselves. But all merchants had not equal credit in the market and much depended on the probity of the man concerned. So in course of time the coins of private individuals were supplanted by the state issues as pointed out by M. Babelon in his Les Origines de la Monnaie. The Europeans got their coins from Asia Minor.[28] Here the oldest coins of electrum, a natural alloy of gold and silver were used most probably by the Lydians about 700 B. C. , though their claim is contested by the Greeks. But Herodotus[29] definitely singles out the Lydians as the inventors of coins.—"So far as we have any knowledge they were the first nation to introduce the use of gold and silver coins." Lydia produced gold in large quantities and received much from outside, and as the Lydians acted as middlemen in the marts of Sardis, Ephesus, Miletus and the maritime cities of Asia Minor, they soon came to employ the precious metals as a means of exchange. The large gold ingots were cut into small sections for representing the smallest values needed for ordinary daily use but at first there was no impression of a stamp guaranteeing the weight or purity of the metal and these were used like the "tabnu" of Egypt and were weighed for each transaction. At length coins were evolved when these small pieces were impressed with a common stamp in order to testify to their weight and purity. The Lydians therefore can claim the honours of being the inventors of coins in Asia Minor. The oldest coins issued by their mints were "flattened spheres more or less avoid in form." At first these were of electrum but later on of smelted gold and had "parallel striae or shallow creases impressed on them by a hammer." The heavier coins weighing 14.20 grammes—the heavy stater was perhaps of Phoenician origin but the light stater of 10.80 grammes was used as money in Lydia and both the forms had smaller subdivisions representing one-third, one-sixth, one-twelfth and one-twentyfourth of the original coin.[30] The theory favoured by M. Babelon advocates that the stamp was at first impressed by the different bankers and that the political communities followed on the footsteps of the enterprising private individuals. Though this view has been vehemently assailed, yet it is not proper to reject it altogether.[31] There surely is no improbability in the proposition that the initiative came from private citizens, and as the advantage became apparent, the state followed in the wake. We have the name of a banker in an electrum stater of Ephesus which has the stamp of a grazing stag and the legend "I am the mark of Phanes;" Phanes must have been a private individual.

The stamps at first covered one face of the coins and this is called the obverse. Several subjects were impressed in order to form the design on the obverse but each was stamped by a special punch. The complexity in design was then replaced by one, at most two figures *e.g.*, the hare under a climbing plant, a roaring lion, an antelope or a sheep etc. Gradually the legends or inscriptions on coins came into use and from these we can learn the names of the bankers or the political communities issuing them. The honour of this invention is sometimes given to Gyges, the Lydian King but there are reasons to hold that the coins of his time were nothing but small ingots of electrum with the stamp of the bankers. But with Croesus we tread on a firmer ground and to him we owe a large number of fine gold and silver coins. The Greek colonies established on the coast of Asia Minor were intelligent enough to avail themselves of the opportunity offered to them by the new invention in matters of trade and commerce ; and the Greek coins testify to the artistic faculty of the race and are masterpieces of art. By the 7th century B. C. the knowledge of the invention spread to the European side of the Aegean Sea[32] and by the 5th century B.C. minting of coins spread over the whole civilised world of the West.[33]

FOOTNOTES

1. Seyd, E.-Bullion and Foreign Exchanges, p. 8.
2. Todd, J. A.-The Mechanism of Exchange, p. 7.
3. *Ibid.*
4. *Ibid.*
5. Spencer, H.-The Principles of Sociology, Vol. II, p. 99.
6. *Ibid.*, p. 100.
7. *Ibid.*, p. 669.
8. *Ibid.*
9. Todd, J. A.-The Mechanism of Exchange, p. 8.
10. Taylor, B. B.-Anthropology, pp. 281-282.
11. Jevons, W. S.-Money and the Mechanism of Exchange, Chapter I.
12. Anderson, B. M.-The Value of Money, p, 197.
13. *Ibid.*, p. 198.
14. *Ibid.*, p. 201.
15. Maspero, G.-The Dawn of Civilization, pp. 323-326.
16. The Historians' History of the World, Vol. II, (New Edition), p. 322.
17. Anderson, B. M.—The Value of Money, p. 408.
18. *Ibid.* 19 *Ibid.*

19a. Anderson, B. M.—The Value of Money, p. 408.

20. *Ibid.*, p. 410.
21. *Ibid.*, p. 411.
22. Macdonald, G.—The Evolution of Coinage, p. 4.
23. "The observations of Chabas have established the fact that the average weight of the 'tabrm1 varied from 91 to 92 grammes (about 31/4 ozs avoirdupois)."—Maspero—Dawn of Civilization, p. 323, footnote No. 2.
24. Maspero, G.—The Dawn of Civilization, p. 324, Footnote I.
25. Maspero, G.—The Struggle of the Nations, p. 490.
26. Maspero, G.—The Dawn of Civilisation, p. 749.

27. The Historians' History of the World, Vol. I, pp. 498=514, (New Edition).
28. Gardner, P.—The Earliest Coins of Greece Proper, p. 5.
29. Rawlinson, G.—The History of Herodotus (Everyman's Library) Vol. I, p. 50.
The Cambridge Ancieut History, Vol. IV, p. 127—(For the Iono-Lydian, Controversy).
30. Maspero, G.—The Passing of Empires, pp. 605=608.
31. Head, B. V.—Historic Nommorum, p. xxxiv.
32. Gardner, P.—The Earliest Coins of Greece Proper.
33. Macdonald, G.—The Evolution of Coinage, p. 9.

CHAPTER II

THE EVOLUTION, ORIGIN AND ANTIQUITY OF COINAGE IN INDIA

The remains of the Copper Age in India were very few before the epoch-making discoveries in the Punjab, Sindh and Beluchistan. The culture of the Chalcolithic Age which is about 5000 years old has been exposed to our view by the excavations at Mahenjo-dāro, Harappā and, Nāl. It however did not remain confined to the Indus valley but extended towards the East and over Kutch and Kathiawar towards the Deccan ; and the influence of this civilization must have been felt far to the east as well as the west. Trade must have been conducted at this stage by Barter and an indirect proof of this statement is brought before us in a peculiar way. Sir John Marshall draws our attention to a tolerably well-preserved building at Harappā which is of a peculiar construction. "It covers an area of 168 ft. from north to south by 136 ft. from east to west and comprises a number of narrow halls and corridors disposed in two parallel series with a broad aisle down the middle. Its plan and the shape of the chambers recall to mind the store-rooms of the Cretan palaces and it may well be that the building at Harappā was designed for a like purpose ; for the days before the introduction of a metal currency when taxes were paid in kind and trade was done by direct barter, accommodation for the storing of merchandise on a large scale must have been indispensable." But metals have been found in large quantities in these ancient sites—gold, silver, copper, tin and lead.

The Indus people used ornaments of gold and silver and copper plated with gold. A matter which deserves special notice is the abundance of gold as compared with the paucity of silver.[1] Gold could be secured from the rivers of the Punjab and must have been more plentiful than silver which generally came from abroad. The Indus people were delichocephalic and perhaps belonged to the Mediterranean race of Southern Asia and Europe which comprised the Pre-Aryan Dravidians of India. Though no reliable conclusions can be drawn from the available data, yet that they were Non-Aryans seems to be clear.[2]

In the Ṛgvedic Age, the Aryans had already progressed from the pastoral to the agricultural stage. Their principal occupations were cattle-rearing and agriculture. Trade was carried on mainly by barter but cow has already become a medium of exchange. The Panis formed the great trading class of the community and they exchanged their merchandise for cattle.[3] "Sale appears to have regularly consisted in barter in the Ṛgveda ; (IV 24.10) ; ten cows are regarded as a possible price for an (image of) Indra."[4] The Soma plant was in great demand among the Aryans and it was usually exchanged for kine. (VIII. 32. 20). There is no reason to be surprised at the use of cattle for exchange purposes. It was a source of wealth to the Aryans and supplied them with food ; they drank the milk and ate the meat. This surely marks a further stage in development ; they had passed from the hunting stage and the possession of cattle to some extent checked their roving spirit.[5] But when they settled up as agriculturists, oxen were a necessity for agricultural work, and even the cow-dung was an article much valued as manure. Naturally when they took to agriculture the produce of this industry was exchanged for other necessities. The taxes were paid in cattle and grain.[6] "People used to contribute a definite portion of their produce and a number of cattle and horses to the king. The king therefore possessed a huge granary, besides vast herds of cattle and horses which gradually increased in number as they multiplied."[7] In the Brāhmaṇa period, the state of things as represented in the Saṁhitā texts was continued as references to the Śatapatha and Aitareya Brāhmaṇa would clearly prove. In the Aitareya, the cow was the most important source of wealth, and whenever the amount of wealth is referred to, it is estimated in cows.[8] The dakṣhiṇā[9] or the sacrificial fee to the Ṛtvika is paid in cows. The medium of exchange was the cow *e.g.* when Śunah, epa was sold by his father for being sacrificed by Hariśchandra, the price paid was 100 cows. Moreover, when no one came forward to perform the odious work of fastening the boy to the Yūpa or sacrificial post, the father offered himself and asked for a fee of 100 cows and he was even prepared to sacrifice the son for 100 cows more. It is thus conclusively proved that the cow served as a medium of exchange and payments were made in cows. The offerings to the Brāhmaṇas and the Purohitas were made in cows.[10] Niṣka is not yet elevated to a medium of exchange ; it is only once referred to in the sense of a necklace.[11] So it is evident that the society of the Aitareya Brāhmaṇa did not take up metals even by weight as mediums of exchange or at least did so very sparingly. The use of cow as a medium of exchange in the Aryan mind had become so much ingrained that even in the Sūtra period when coins had come into use, the cows are referred to as the fee to be paid to the priests for the celebration of the household festivals enjoined by the Gṛhya Sūtras.[12]

The metals gold, silver, copper and iron were known to the Vedic Aryans,[13] and it is natural to expect that the Aryans like all other civilized peoples of the time were attracted by their special qualities to serve as mediums of exchange. We have a word Niṣka[14] in the ancient literature of the country going back to the Ṛgveda. It had three different meanings. It signified "a gold ornament worn on the neck" as is shown by the epithet "Niṣkagrīva" (R. V. v-19-3), "having a gold ornament on the neck."[15] It was also used in the sense of a metallic weight equivalent to 320 ratis or 560 grains.[16] Moreover Niṣkas were used as mediums of exchange.[17] It is a difficult question to determine the gradual evolution in the meaning of this word. The interpretation, rather the supposition which is put forward, that the idea of a neck-ornament connected with Niṣka is derived from the practice of stringing together in the form of a necklace a number of Niṣka coins, is taking for granted what has got to be proved. That the ornaments came into use much earlier than coins among the peoples of antiquity goes without saying.[18] So the more correct interpretation in keeping with the evolutionary progress in society would be to take the Niṣkas in the earliest period as referring to neck-ornament only, and it would not be unreasonable to infer that these neck-ornaments were used as mediums of exchange in lieu of cow or grains,[19] just as we find even at the present time beads of cowry-shells etc. changing hands among the savages. Later on in the place of the ornament, a piece of metal equivalent to the standard weight was weighed out at each transaction. The next step would be, as in Egypt and Babylon, to have ingots of various shapes, preferably globular. In the Vedic period the Aryans had at least advanced to this stage. Whether they had these ingots stamped with symbols testifying as to the weight and the purity of the metal *i.e.* whether they had succeeded in evolving coins at that early stage is a highly debatable question. It was Mr. Edward Thomas who first pointed out the passage in the Ṛgveda (I. 126.2) where "a singer celebrates the receipt of a hundred Niṣkas and a hundred steeds ; he could hardly require the Niṣkas merely for purposes of personal adornment."[20] In another passage a Ṛṣi praises a king for giving him forty thousand Niṣkas on one occasion and eight thousand on another.[21] (R. V. VIII. 2. 41).[22] It is thus clear that Niṣkas served as a sort of currency and the question to be decided in the words of Prof. Bhandarkar is—"Were they coined money or unstamped bullion currency?"[23] The learned Professor refers to Hymn 33 of Maṇḍala II of the Ṛgveda in support of his view that the Niṣkas were coined money in the Ṛgvedic Age. His interpretation has not yet been accepted by all the scholars[24] and is against the traditional interpretation of Sāyaṇa. Moreover, it presupposes the existence of Niṣka coins - to the Niṣka ornaments ; and the fact that there is a reference to ten Hiraṇyapiṇḍas[25] (gold globules) cannot establish the proposition that the Niṣkas were coins as distinguished from pure bullion because there is no knowing that these Hiraṇyapiṇḍas were of standard weight equal to each other and circulated as mediums of exchange. So the acceptance of the bold proposition of Prof. Bhandarkar must await later investigation and so long as the greatest drawback that no gold coin of the punch-marked type had been discovered in India,[26] while thousands in silver and copper had been unearthed in various parts of the country, is removed, it would be better to suspend judgment.[27] Even when we come to later times the metallic currency seems to refer, to weight. Śatamāna is mentioned in the Taittarīya Saṁhitā of the Black Yajur Veda[28] and is given as a sacrificial fee to the priest. In the Śatapatha Brāhmaṇa also the Śatamāna is referred to as the sacrificial fee.[29] There is another word Kṛṣṇala[30] in the Taittirīya Brāhmaṇa and both the words refer to metallic currency as well as definite weights. We know that a Kṛṣṇala weighs a Guñjā berry ; Śatamāna, a hundred times the standard weight which is taken to be the Kṛṣṇala of raktika, by Prof. Keith[31] and this is also the standard weight for Niṣka and Suvarṇa as given in Manu.[32] A Niṣka is equivalent to 320 ratis and a suvarṇa 80 ratis. Prof. Bhandarkar lays much stress on the shape of the Śatamāna which was vṛtta or round.[35] From this to infer that the Śatamānas were coined money would not be fully warranted because these might be and there is no improbability, in taking the Śatamānas as round pieces of metallic ingots. Another argument of the learned Professor may also be discussed in this connection—"In India there were at least six denominations in the Jātaka and earlier periods, and they were used invariably to denote the weights of metal or money, but never of goods. It is again inconceivable that as (many as) six different denominations could be employed in one and the same country for paying money by weight. For, if money is to be paid by weight at all, one or two denominations are quite enough. The natural conclusion is that they all denoted not simply money weights but also denominations of coins."[34] The six denominations referred to in this passage are Niṣka, Kṛṣṇala, Suvarṇa, Śatamāna, Māṣaka and Kārṣāpaṇa. The learned Professor seems not to clearly appreciate the vast period of time he deals with, which cannot be less than 2000 years, and which includes the simple culture of the Vedic period and the highly civilised condition of the Buddhist Age, and also the huge extent of the country and the innumerable territorial divisions. To jumble up a number of things together cannot but fail in giving us a false perspective of the olden times. The successive periods and the successive stages of culture must be differentiated and distinguished from each other. Prof. Bhandarkar marshals out his arguments in support of his theory that "coined money must be considered to be existing in India as early as the middle of the third millennium before Christ,"[35] and he even goes to pre-historic times. But his arguments lack conviction and the acceptance of this theory would be against the experience of the evolution of coinage all over the world. But there can be no doubt that the metallic weights were in course of time replaced by coins of the standard weight. When exactly this change came in, it is difficult to determine but it would be on the side of caution, if we advance the opinion that coins in the real and correct sense of the word came into use during the later stage of the Brāhmaṇa period or in the beginning of the Sūtra period.

In the Ṛgvedic Age, Niṣka an ornament emerged as a medium of exchange but gradually it gave place to a metallic weight equivalent to that particular ornament. Here we have no reason to suspect that the Niṣka weight was in any way connected with any standard weight. We have surely in later literature Niṣka equated to a certain weight on the basis of a particular standard. But, from what we find hundreds of years afterwards, it would not be proper to go back to that early period and attribute the Niṣka weight to any particular metallic standard unit. In the Taittirīya Saṁhitā of the Black Yujur Veda a metallic weight, the Śatamāna, is referred to and there is no doubt that it is based upon a particular unit of weight, namely, the Māna and this measure we come across even in the Ṛgveda. Dr. A. C. Das's theory[36] that the Māna refers to a particular kind of coin may be so far accepted that it was a unit of metallic weight which was used for Exchange purposes. But what the unit really was, we are not in a position to determine. We may be tempted to identify it with Kṛṣṇala which is also referred to in the Brāhmaṇas and is the traditional unit of measurement as regards metals. But the weight of a Śatamāna as given in Manu is 320 Kṛṣṇalas and the unit of the Śatamāna *i.e.* 1/100 of the metallic weight is not one Kṛṣṇala and we are thus faced with an insuperable difficulty, if we try to establish Śatamāna weight on the Kṛṣṇala basis. The reference to the two words Suvarṇa and Śatamāna side by side with Hiraṇya in the two passages of the Śatapatha Brāhmaṇa[37] would clearly imply a differentiation between Hiraṇya and the two metallic pieces by weight, Suvarṇa and Śatamāna. If they be based upon the same unit of measurement, the Kṛṣṇala, their relationship might be with a great amount of pro bability one of multiple or subdivision of the other. Suvarṇa is equal to 80 raṭis or Kārṣāpaṇa and if we accept Prof. Kieth's opinion that Śatamāna was to be equated to 100 ratis, it would be a little difficult to visualise the condition of exchange with two metallic weights, one equal to 80 and the other to 100 units of a particular standard. A better position seems to be to refer the two metallic weights of exchange to two standard units—the Śatamāna to the earlier age going back at least to the Ṛgveda and the Suvarṇa to the Brāhmaṇa period when Kṛṣṇala became the recognised unit of measurement. But even here a difficulty remains,[38] and we are not in a position to determine in the scanty state of our knowledge what is exactly the unit referred to in the Śatamāna of the Brāhmaṇa period and the Māna of the Ṛgveda, though we have every reason to identify it with the Māñjāḍi as I shall try to show later on.

We have however a coin weight which is incontestably based upon the Kṛṣṇala weight of measurement and this is Karṣa which equals 80 Kṛṣṇalas or ratis.[39] The Kārṣāpaṇa weight is particularly connected with copper and when it came out as a coin, there was a strong belief in the later literature that it was of copper. "Manu takes Kārṣāpaṇa to denote a paṇa or coined money which is tamrika *i.e.* made of copper and is Karṣika *i.e.*, one Karṣa in weight";[40] or again "the Samanta-pasadika while explaining a verse from Patimokkha says about Kārṣāpaṇa as follows : "tattha Kahapano ti : Suvanna mayo va rupiyamayo va pakatiko va, here Kārṣ āpaṇa is either made of gold, or that made of silver, or the ordinary one."[41] Kārṣāpaṇa as the unit measurement of copper and not as coin must be dated back at least to the Brāhmaṇa period and it would not be unreasonable to infer that this was the national weight system of the Aryans just like the 'tabnu' of the Egyptians. In India copper might have been brought into use for the particular purpose of serving as a medium of exchange perhaps even before the Vedic period. "Some sort of money like the ring money of the Northern antiquaries were evidently used as the six rings, of which three were linked together, found from Mainipuri had been thought to be such by Dr. Oldham. They also recall the Mycenean spiral rings which are however smaller."[42] These rings may be placed side by side with the tabnu rings of Egypt which changed hands surely at first not by weight but by number andsize. Greater precision isreferred to in the Vedic period and the business transactions were closed by an appeal to weight.

That copper was the metal that ordinarily served[43] the purposes of exchange admits of no doubt. Gold embodies so much value in a little mass that for ordinary transactions of commerce it would be thoroughly unfitted, Even now India is not rich enough for gold and for the bazar transactions of the villagers the silver rupee has to he converted into smaller denominations in silver, bronze or nickel., Though we have reasons to believe that India in antiquity was rich in gold, yet it would be hazardous to infer that gold was used in exchange except on extraordinary occasions and when highly valuable things changed hands. The reference to a Hiraṇya Kṛṣ ṇala-gold Kṛṣṇala in the Kathaka Saṁhitā[44] clearly points out the difficulty in the use of a piece of gold which was only one rati in weight and surely too small for the purpose. The only reasonable inference would be that gold was used very sparingly for exchange purposes and the ordinary transactions were based upon the Kārṣāpaṇa system which embraced the Kārṣ āpaṇa and its sub-multiples. This weight system was not confined to copper only but gradually extended to gold as well as silver.[45] The Suvarṇa equals in weight a Kārṣāpaṇa[46] and a silver coin of the same weight is referred to in Kauṭilya's Artha,,āstra. The bent bars of silver which are deemed to be of high antiquity (V. Smith's Catalogue, P. 136) approximate in weight to the Kārṣāpaṇa.[47] The fact that in later times Kārṣāpaṇa referred to coins in all three metals, clearly points out that Kārṣāpaṇa, the copper coin was the earliest and the most used ; and in course of time it became the generic expression for coins ; for example in later times the Ràjataraṅgiṇī speaks of "dīnnāras of gold, silver and copper,"[48] though there is no doubt that 'Dinaras' were nothing but originally the Denarius aureus of the Romans which were imported to India in large numbers when a brisk trade was going on between Rome and India. Kārṣāpaṇa was the metallic weight for copper and gradually of gold and silver, and when the weight system gave place to coins the honour must properly belong in the first instance to copper. It extended to silver but was based upon a different standard which was peculiar to the precious metals at an earlier age, but not to gold as the total absence of early gold coins would lead us to infer.[49] The copper coins have not the same longevity as the silver and gold coins and this would explain the comparative scarcity of copper Kārṣāpaṇas and its subdivisions.[50] The large number of submultiples of copper Kārṣāpaṇa would point out that the Kārṣāpaṇa itself embodied in it so much value that its small subdivisions going down to 1/128th paṇa, the Ardha Kakini, were a necessity. Even if we accept the proposition of prof. Bhandarkar that the use of silver and copper depended upon the particular province concerned which had a predilection for one metal or the other,[51] yet we are bound to accept as a fact that copper must have preceded silver even in those parts of the country where it was discarded in favour of the other metal. Vincent Smith hazards the proposition that "in some parts of the country the use of silver preceded that of copper."[52] India was never known for her production of silver and the paucity of this metal as compared with gold and copper in the excavations of the Indus valley would clearly indicate that silver was at best mainly secured from foreign lands and was not in common use ; and the argument that the silver coins are extremely old would not put out of court the claim of copper to a higher antiquity. V. Smith refers the bent bars of silver to 500 to 600 B. C. on account of their "extremely archaic appearance,"[53] and he thinks that the solid silver ingots "marked with 3 dots only" must be very ancient. The acceptance of this view cannot establish the proposition that the use of silver preceded that of copper. The Kārṣāpaṇa as the medium of exchange was the oldest and the most common, and became in course of time the generic expression not only for metallic weight but also for coined money. Of gold coins of a primitive type (punch-marked) we have no knowledge and India cannot boast of any gold coinage of a native dynasty before the Imperial Guptas. So the presumption is and this is strengthened by reference to the case of silver that the gold pieces circulated in the form of solid ingots, sometimes as globules[54] or as bent bars chipped into pieces to approximate to the standard weight. After the introduction of silver the necessity of gold as a circulating medium was greatly obviated and the gold pieces did not come up to the same stage of finish and manufacture as the silver and copper punch-marked coins. This is clearly testified to by the entire absence of gold punch-marked coins in India. The two thin pieces, one of gold and the other of silver found in the Piprawa Stūpa of about the 6th century B. C. cannot be satisfactorily identified with the Kṛṣṇala coin of 1.83 grains, as they weigh only one grain, though they are impressed with symbols. These symbols might as well be connected with funerary rites of which we have no definite knowledge nor can it be asserted that coins had been discovered in all the Buddhist Stūpas.[55]

The foregoing discussion would surely raise a strong presumption that coinage was evolved in India in the Brāhmaṇa period. "The interpretation which recognises punch-marked coins in the signatum argentum presented by Ambhi (Omphis) to Alexander at Taxila in 326 B. C., as related by Quintus Curtius"[56] fixes the currency of these coins to the 4th century B. C. "That Pāṇini knew coined MONEY is plainly borne out by his Sūtra, V. 2, 119, rupad ahata ....where he says, "the word rupya, is in the sense of "struck" (ahata), derived from rupa., "form, nape" with the taddhita affix, ya, here implying possession ; when rupya would literally mean "struck (money), having a form."[57] Pāṇini has been "assigned to the middle of the 6th century B. C. at the latest" by Prof. Bhandarkar, though Sir Ramkrishna and Goldsticker would place him even earlier.[58] So we can accept without the least hesitation the view of Prof. Bhandarkar that "the beginning of the art of coin-making in this country must be placed earlier than 700 B.C."[59]. The consensus of opinions among scholars would place the Brāhmaṇa period at about 800 B. C. Prof. Keith's view is that "it is not likely that the Brāhmaṇa period began later than 800 B. C."[60] and Mr. Pargiter thinks that the Vedic Age closed roundly about 1000 B. C.[61] and Prof. Winternitz opines that the Vedic period extended up to 800 B. C.[62] So it can safely be asserted that coinage in India was evolved at about 800 B. C. and if we fix the approximate date at 1000 B. C. and accept the view of Sir Alexander Cunningham, we are not likely to go wrong;[63] at least the margin of error would be very small.

The claim of India having evolved an indigenous system of coinage has now been fully and conclusively established. The opinions of some of the European scholars who advocated a foreign origin have now been fully disproved. Prof. Bhandarkar has successfully combated their views and has fixed the last nail on the theories that wanted to prove the indebtedness of India to Babylon, Bactria or Persia for her earliest system of coinage. Their opinions have been summarised by Prof. Bhandarkar in his Carmichael Lectures, 1921 and by Prof. Rapson in J. R. A. S., 1895, P- 869. James Princep held the view that "the Hindus derived their knowledge of coinage from the Greeks of Bactria"[64] and Wilson in his Ariana Antiqua asserted that "the Hindus had learned the usefulness of money from their Bactrian neighbours and from their commerce specially with Rome."[65] James Kennedy held the view that the punch-marked coins, the oldest coins of the country "were copied from Babylonian originals"[66] as a result of the active maritime trade in the sixth century B.C. This view is supported by Vincent Smith and according to him the coins came into use in the 7th. century B.C. when the foreign maritime trade seems to have begun.[67] The Bactrian theory is thoroughly disproved by the discovery of two hoards of coins, one in 1853 in the Punjab by Sir E. C. Bay ley[68] and the other at Taxila in 1912-13 by Sir John Marshall.[69] Bayley found a number of coins, punch-marked as well as Indo-Greek,[70] the punch-marked coins were much worn while the others were comparatively fresh. The exacavation at Taxila unearthed a hoard of coins, 175 punch-marked coins with "a gold coin of Diodotus struck in the name of Antiochus II of Syria."[71] Diodotus was a satrap of Antiochus before he declared the independence of Bactria in about 250 B.C. So the punch-marked coins might be earlier than Bactrian ones. In another hoard discovered at Taxila the coin of Alexander the Great and a Persian *siglos* were found mixed up with punch-marked coins.[72] Moreover the controversy is set at rest by the reference of Quintus

Curtius to the presentation to Alexander the Great of a number of coins which are evidently referred to in his *Signati Argenti.*[73] Cunningham thinks that the attribution of the epithet purāṇa to the Kārṣāpaṇa or the punch-marked coins is the result of a contemporaneous currency of two kinds—the indigenous Kārṣāpaṇas and the Bactrian coins ; the Kārṣāpaṇas are therefore referred to as compared with the Indo-Greek coins as puraṇa or old.[74] The Babylonian theory has got a crushing reply from Prof. Bhandarkar who asserts that no coin "of a type closely corresponding to the Kārṣāpaṇas," 'of a period prior to 600 or 700 B.C.'[75] has been found outside India ; nor "is there any evidence at all to show that there was foreign coinage, of a date anterior to 600 or 700 B.C.—the earliest date assigned by them, to the Kārṣāpaṇas which through identity or at any rate extreme similarity of type couldj rightly be called to be their prototype." The position, therefore, taken up by him is unassailable and this is supported by great scholars like Cunningham and Thomas. As pointed out by Cunningham "the types, the shape and the standard of the earliest Indian money" are throughout indigenous.[76] The punch-marked coins are mostly rectangular in form and the weight is based upon the rati and unlike the Indo-Bactrian coins there are no inscriptions or busts of gods and goddesses. Another theory "that the punch-marked coins, whether of silver or copper, constitute simply a Hindu variety of Akhaemenid Persian coinage" was started a few years ago by a French scholar M. Decourdemanche.[77] In his opinion the Persian Emperor issued "the punch-marked coins with Hindu symbols side by side with the Persian *sigloi.*" He mainly depended, upon the weight of the coins to prove his theory, the hollowness of which has been clearly demonstrated by Prof. Bhandarkar and most probably the last word about it has been said. The consensus of opinions among the scholars all over the world has now fully accepted the Indian origin of the earliest coinage of this country which had served the commercial necessity of the people for centuries.

FOOTNOTES

1. Mr. Rakhaldas Banerjee in the Annual Basumati of 1333 B.S. p. 127.
2. Sir John Marshall's Statement to the Press on the Pre-historic Civilization of the Indus valley.
3. Dr. A. C. Das— Rigvedic Culture, p. 130.
4. *Ibid.*, p. 145.
5. "Like the aborigines, the Vedic Indians were primarily pastoral" but "Agriculture was already an important part of the Vedic economy."—The Cambridge History of India, Vol. I, p. 99.
6. "A commodity which is useful to every member of a tribe fulfils the primary condition of a 'money', and is naturally adopted as such when the need for a money arises. Thus it is that skins are found to be used as money in hunting communities, cattle in pastoral, and corn or other grains in agricultural communities." —D. A. Barker—The Theory of Money, p. 12.
7. Dr. A. C. Das—Ṛgvedic Culture, p. 320.
8. Aitareya Brāhmaṇa—V, xxii, 9.
9. "The name of the sacrificial fee, dakṣiṇā, is explained as referring originally to cow placed 'on the right hand' of the singer for his reward."—The Cambridge History of India, Vol. I, p. 99.

10. Aitareya Brāhmaṇa—VII, xxxiii, 6; VIII. xxxvii, 7; VIII. xxxix, 8.
11. Aitareya Brāhmaṇa—VIII, xxxix, 8.
12. Gobhila Gṛhya Sūtra. Hiraṇyakeśi Gṛhya Sūtra.
13. The Cambridge History of India, Vol. I, pp. 100, 101, 137.
14. Ṛgveda—II, 33, 10; VIII, 47, 15.
15. Vedic Index quoted by Dr. A. C. Das— Ṛgvedic Culture, p. 140.
16. Bhandarkar—Carmichael Lectures, 1921, pp. 61 & 212.
17. Dr. A. C. Das— Ṛgvedic Culture, p. 140. References given by him—A.V.—XX, 127, 3; Lat. Śra. Sut. IX, 9, 20; Sat. Bra. XI, 4, 1, 1, 8; Gop. Brah. I. 3, 6 etc.; Vedic Index I, pp. 454-55.
18. "It is practically certain that the precious metals, also, have come into use as money only because they were first used as ornaments."—D. A. Barker—The Theory of Money.
19. "The Niṣka, originally a gold ornament, was also at this time a unit of value; and the cow as a unit was probably in course of supersession." The passage refers to the Brāhmaṇa period. —The Cambridge History of India, Vol. I, p. 137.
20. Quoted by Prof. Bhandarkar from the Vedic Index— Carmichael Lectures, 1921.
21. "* * * we may reasonably infer that the niṣka of the Vedas had, even then, attained so much of a definite and unvarying form, and partial fashioning, as to be suitable for decorative purposes in its current shape,—a deduction which would further imply that the piece itself was understood or admitted to be of a constant and uniform make, and that, in effect, carried its description in its name."—Edward Thomas—Ancient Indian Weights, p. 34.
22. A. C. Das— Ṛgvedic Culture, page 140.
    Dr. Das here takes the Niṣkas to be coins pure and simple. The inference is however a little overdrawn.
23. Carmichael Lectures, 1921, p. 65.
24. Bhandarkar—Carmichael Lectures, 1921, p. 67.
25. *Ibid*, p. 69.
26. Rapson—Indian Coins, p. 2.
27. "There is an allusion to Indian money in the record of Alexander's invasion of the Punjab. Quintus Curtins, describing the reception of Alexander by Omphis, King of Taxila, says that the Indian ruler presented golden crowns to Alexander and his friends in addition to eight talents of coined silver." Gold was available but while silver coins are referred to there is no mention of a gold coin. This is sure to raise a strong presumption, if not conviction, that the standard currency of the 4th cent. B.C. in Taxila was of silver.—R. B. Whitehead—The Pre-Mohamadan' Coinage of North-Western India, p. 42. Edward Thomas—Ancient Indian Weights, p. 43.
28. Bhandarkar—Carmichael Lectures, 1921, p. 58. T. Brāh.— I. 7. 6. 2; I. 2. 7. 7.
29. Quoted by Bhandarkar-Carmichael Lectures, 1921, p. 57; Sat. Brāh.—V. 5. 5. 16 etc.
30. Tait. Brāh. I. 3. 6. 7. (Bhandarkar, p. 60).
31. The Cambridge History of India, Vol. I, p. 137.
32. Bhandarkar—Carmichael Lectures, 1921, p. 212.
33. *Ibid*, p. 57.
34. *Ibid*, p. 62.
35. *Ibid*, p. 71.
36. A. C. Das— Ṛgvedic Culture, p. 140.
37. XII. 7. 2. 13; XIII. 2. 3. 2.
38. "But it is difficult to divine the object or the meaning of 'one hundred measures' (Śatamāna), which do not fit in with either of the national metric schemes"—B. Thomas—The Ancient Indian Weights, p. 12.

39. Bhandarkar—The Carmichael Lectures, 1921, p. 86.
40. *Ibid*, p. 81.
41. *Ibid*. Edward Thomas—Ancient Indian Weights, p. 42, footnote 2.
42. P. Mitra—Pre-historic India, p. 192.
43. "The tenor of the entire text of Mann conclusively demonstrates that the primitive standard . . . of the currencies of the Indians, like that of the Romans and those independent originators of their own proper civilization, the Egyptians, was based upon copper, a lower metal, which, however it may revolt the gold predilections of modern times, was clearly in so far preferable in the early conception of inter-changeable metallic equivalents, that it constituted the most widely distributed and diffused representative of value, brought home to the simplest man's comprehension, and obviously in its very spread remained the least liable to sudden fluctuation from external causes, such as would more readily affect the comparatively limited available amounts of either of the higher metals. Hence in remote ages, under an imperfect philosophy of exchange, copper may be said to have been the safest and most equable basis for the determination of all relative values";—E. Thomas—Ancient Indian Weights, p. 53.
44. Bhandarkar, p. 60.
45. Carmichael Lectures, pp. 77, 81.
    "In short, the weight of 80 ratis .... was immutable, and it was employed, without regard to metals, to measure gold, silver or copper, down the whole western coast." E. Thomas— Ancient Indian Weights, p. 22; footnote 5.
46. Carmichael Lectures, 1921, p. 90.
    "The duties of ancient coins were . . . dual, as authorised weights and current money,"—Edward Thomas—Ancient Indian Weights, p. 29.
47. Vincent Smith—Catalogue of Coins in the Indian Museum, Calcutta, p. 136.
48. Carmichael Lectures, 1921, p. 204.
49. *Ibid.*, 1921, pp. 91, 94.
50. "That the silver coins should have been preserved to the present time, in larger numbers than their more perishable and less esteemed copper equivalents, was to be anticipated, especially considering the greater wear and tear and easy reconversion of the latter into either new dynastic mintages or their proverbial absorption by all classes for the construction of domestic utensils." —E. Thomas—The Ancient Indian Weights, page 53.
51. Carmichael Lectures, 1921, p. 84.
52. V. Smith—Catalogue of Coins in the Indian Museum, p. 133.
53. *Ibid.*
54. See Plate I, No. 2—'a spherule of gold'; Blliot—"Coins of Southern India."
55. The Carmichael Lectures, 1921, p. 179.
56. V. Smith—Catalogue of Coins in the Indian Museum, p. 135. E. Thomas—Ancient Indian Weights, p. 43.
57. Numismata Orientalia, Vol. I. E. Thomas—Ancient Indian Weights, p. 39: footnote 3.
58. *Ibid*, footnote 4.
59. Carmichael Lectures, 1921, pp. 45, 46.
60. The Cambridge History of India, Vol. I, p. 113.
61. F. E. Pargiter—Ancient Indian Historical Tradition, p. 321.
62. Carmichael Lectures, 1921, p. 71.
63. Cunningham—The Coins of Ancient India, p. 43.
64. The Carmichael Lectures, 1921, p. 38.

65. *Ibid.*
66. *Ibid.*, p. 39.
67. *Ibid.*
68. Cunningham—The Coins of Ancient India, p. 54.
69. The Carmichael Lectures, 1921, p. 40.
70. General Cunningham—Num. Chron. 1873 XIII, 209— The silver coins of "Antimachus II, Philoxenes, Lysias, Antialkidas, and Menander, together with a few punch-marked pieces, the last being much worn whilst all the Greek coins were comparatively fresh.
71. The Carmichael Lectures, 1921, p. 41.
72. Archaeological Survey of India, 1924-25, pp. 47 & 48.
73. Cunningham — Coins of Ancient India, p. 52.
74. *Ibid.*, p. 53.
75. Carmichael Lectures, 1921, p. 43.
76. Cunningham—Coins of Ancient India, p. 52.
77. Cannichael Lectures, 1921, pp. 118 and 120-22.

CHAPTER III

COINS : A GREAT SOURCE OF VALUE IN INDIA

Coins are a great source of value in understanding the trend of events in history and supplement in no small measure the valuable material gathered from inscriptions. Both these, and particularly coins, with their short legends and suggestive artistic rendering of portraiture, iconographic forms or revealing symbols, are best understood by a reference to appropriate passages from literature that throw a flood of light on their significance.

There are several early coins that have legends in Brāhmī and Kharoṣṭhī to proclaim the ruler that issued them apart from a constant factor in all of them, the humped bull and the elephant on the obverse and reverse . One of these is an Indo-Greek silver coin of Apollodotus of the second century before Christ (Fig. 58) with the legend in Greek on obverse *Basileos Apollodotus Soteros* around the figure of an elephant and with the legend in Kharoṣṭhī on the reverse around a humped bull *Maharajasa Apaladatasa tratarasa*. Another, a tribal silver coin of Audumbara Mahādeva of the 2nd-1st centuries B.C., with obverse showing the humped bull, the legend in Kharoṣṭhī running round it *Bhagavata Mahādevasa* and below *rājaraña,* the reverse with legend in Brāhmī around an elephant with raised trunk *Bhagavata Mahādevasa* and *Rājarāja,* below. Yet another is again a Tribal potin coin of the Yaudheyas (Fig. 59), also of the 2nd-1st centuries B.C. with legend in Brāhmī *Yaudheyānām* above the bull and the usual elephant on the reverse without any legend.

The reason for showing these two animals repeatedly in coins of different dates and different sovereigns is indeed interesting to know. It is the pride of growth in stature politically represented by the stadure of the two most important examples of the highest worth.

In India the words *vṛṣabha* and *kuñjara,* the bull and the elephant are appended to any class of beings to indicate the best of the class. Pāṇini has a special injunction for such usage. The mighty personality of the king that ranks with the majesty of the full-grown elephant and the bull is the significance sought to be conveyed. Kālidāsa in describing the increased physical power and overpowering personality of Raghu, the noblest of his race, remarks that as a young calf grows into a mighty bull or as a baby elephant becomes a noble tusker in due course, so Raghu passed from childhood to youth and maintained a body at once noble and beautiful : *mahokṣatām vatsataras spṛsanniva dvipendrabhāvam kalabhas śrayanniva raghuḥ kramād yauvanabhinnaśaiśavaḥ puposa gāmbhiyramanoharam vapuḥ. Raghuvaṁśa* 3, 32.

Another early coin of the second century before Christ hailing from Avanti shows a king almost like a deity standing wearing a short-tailed coat and high crown. (Fig. 60*)* To his right is a standard surmounted by the Sun with fierce rays radiating. To the left is the solar symbol composed of alternating arrowheads and *nandipādas* Above the figure are the *svastika* and *nandipāda*. The solar standard motif in later coins like the Kāca type of Gupta coin is to be derived from this early example. The true significance of this Avanti coin, specially when we take into consideration the place of its find, is well understood when we read Sunandā's description of the king of Avanti. Kālidāsa describes him as of beautiful chiselled features and lustrous like the Sun after he was properly trimmed by Tvaṣṭā on the rotating wheel used for the purpose. The fierce-rayed Sun on standard beside the king and the Solar wheel are thus significant when we consider Kālidāsa's verse: *avantināthoyam udagrabāhur viśālavakṣās tanuvrittamadhyaḥ āropya cakrabhramam ushṇatejās tvastreva śāṇollikhito vibhāti, Raghu-vaṁśa* 6, 32.

On a coin of king Parvata of Kauśāmbī of the second century before Christ there is a representation of a mountain and a tree in railing (Fig. 61*)*. This symbol occurs also on the Kuṇinda coin of Amoghabhūti. The significance of this is not quite clear though it may be understood as comparison to the best of each class, Meru or Himavān among mountains and *Kalpavṛkṣa* among trees. Rama was like the Himavān in fortitude, like the Meru in strength and deep in nobility like the ocean. *dhalryena himavān iva meruṇā sadṛśo vīrye gāmbhīryāt sāgaropamaḥ. Rāmāyaṇa* 1, L 17. Rāvaṇa though bejewelled like the *Kalpavṛkṣa* was frightful: *sa kalpavṛkṣapratimo bhūṣitopi bhayankaraḥ, Rāmāyaṇa* 5, 22, 29. The king liberal in giving is always likened to the *Kalpavṛkṣa, strībhiḥ kāmo 'rthibhiḥ svardruḥ kālaḥ, śatrubhir aikṣi saḥ, Kuvalayānanda,* p. 22.

But it is a verse from the *Raghuvaṁśa* describing king Atithi before a mirror decked in all his jewels and the best of apparel and reflected in all his glory like the *Kalpavṛkṣa* loaded with jewels and silks mirrored on the slopes of the Meru mountain that gives a clue to understand this coin: *nepathyadarśinas cāyā tasyādarśe hiraṇmaye virarājodite sūrye merau kalpataror iva, Raghuvaṁśa* 17, 26. The idea of the mountain reflecting as a mirror is common in poetic parlance as in Kālidāsa's *kailāsasya tridaśavanitādarpaṇasyātithis syāḥ, Meghadūta* I, 61. It is this idea of a king in all his glory that is sought to be suggested in the representation on these coins.

An early silver Tribal coin of Amoghabhūti of the first century B. C. is extremely interesting for its superb suggestive content (Fig. 62*)*. It represents a cow and a damsel standing holding a lotus, the *śrīvatsa* mark above and in between the horns of the animal and a small figure of the *Kalpavṛkṣa* to suggest celestial associations for all the objects delineated. The inscription in Brāhmī running all around gives *rājñaḥ kuṇindasa amoghabhūtisa mahārājasa*. The sense of this peculiar combination of figures and symbols becomes clear when we read the line of

Kālidāsa that refers to Pṛthvī or the earth as *gorūpadharā* or in the form of a cow, with the four oceans as her udder, meaning thereby a mighty expanse of empire reaching the oceans. It is clear from inscriptions like those of the Guptas that it was the ambition of every king to rule the earth upto the shores of the oceans: *caturudadhisalilāsvāditayaśasaḥ, C. Inscr. Ind.* 3, p. 26. This was the ideal limit of the empire; but a certain element of vanity in some cases excusable, always drove even kings in their limited territories to style themselves as ruling a realm extending to the seas.

This coin of Kuṇinda Amoghabhūti suggests his unfailing fortune symbolized by the cow of plenty, with the damsel close by suggesting Pṛthvī or earth personified, who assumed the form of a cow : *payodharībhūtacatussamudrām jugopa gorūpadharām ivorvīm, Raghuvaṁśa* 2,3. The cow is also the celestial cow of plenty in the proximity of the *Kalpavṛkṣa* and answers Kālidāsa's line *āsīt kalpataruccāyām aśritā surabhiḥ pathi, Raghuvaṁśa* 1,75.

There is even greater significance. Pṛthvī here is not just the damsel of earth. She is Rājyaśrī, the goddess of the empire on earth, Royal prosperity personified. Hence she significantly holds the lotus, the emblem of Lakṣmī : *lakṣmīs tathā padmini padmahastā, Rāmāyaṇa* 5, 7, 14; *nityam sā padmahastā mama vasatu gṛhe sarvamāṅgalyayuktā, Śrīsūkta.* The *Śrīvatsa* symbol above the horns of the cow is Lakṣmī shown symbolically, while the cow is the zoomorphic form of Lakṣmī. In the *Mahābhārata* there is an elaborate description of the cow representing Lakṣmī in particular while embodying in herself all the other celestials as well in the different limbs composing her body (*Mahābhārata*). The name Amoghabhūti itself suggesets limitless fortune; and the trebly emphasized form of Lakṣmī, Rājyalakṣmī in this case, in anthropomorphic, zoomorphic and symbolic representations of her, makes the name significant *anvartha*.

Among Indo-Parthian coins there is a silver one of the Satrap Jihunia or Zionises of Taxila of the first century A.D., with the reverse showing the *satrap* standing facing a goddess carrying a cornucopia in her left hand and crowning him with a wreath held in her right hand (Fig. 63). The legend around runs in Kharoṣṭhī *managulasa catrapasa putrasa catrapasa jihuniasa*. Vincent Smith suggests that this is probably a respresentation of the Fortune of a vanquished city. We know that in one of the Gupta inscriptions Lakṣmī is described as having chosen the king as her lord: *vyapetya sarvān manujendraputrān lakṣmīs svayam yam varayāṁcakāra, C. Inscr. Ind.* 3, p. 59. Surely it should remind one of similar idea repeated so often by Kālidāsa : *bheje'bhisārikāvṛttim jayaśrīr vīragāminī, Raghuvaṁśa* 17, 69; *aṣīd atiśayaprekṣyas sa rājyaśrīvadhūvaraḥ, Raghuvaṁśa* 17, 25; *narendramūlāyatanād anantaram tadāspadam śrīr yuva-rājasamjñitam agaccad aṁśena guṇābhilāṣiṇī navāvatāram kamalād ivotpalam, Raghuvaṁśa* 3, 36; *upāttavidyam vidhivad gurubhyas tam yauvanodbhedaviśeṣ akāntam śrīḥ sābhilāshāpi guror anujñām dhīreva kanyā pitur ācakāṅkṣa, Raghuvaṁśa* 5, 38.

Whether it is the goddess of Royal fortune, Rājyalakṣmī, or the Goddess of the fortune of a city that woos the valorous king as her Lord, there is a certain picturesque effect in it as in

Kālidāsa's description of the Goddess of the City of Ayodhyā personally come for wooing her Lord Kuśa that caused great joy among the learned Brāhmaṇas assembled in the king's court: *tad adbhutam samsadi rātr-ivṛttam prātar dviiebhyo nṛpatis śaśamsa śrutvā ta etam kularājadhānyā sākṣāt patitve vṛtam abhyanandan, Raghuvaṁśa* 16, 24.

The idea of City goddesses was also greatly in vogue, and, like the example of the goddess of Ayodhyā just mentioned, there are others particularly known through the legends on coins as for instance *Pukhalavadi devatā (Skt. Puṣkalāvatī devatā)* from Puṣkhalāvatī or modern Charsadda and *Kavisiya nagaradevatā (Skt. Kdpiśāyā naga-radevatā)* from Kāpiśā or modern Begram.

The motif of Lakṣmī, as just Lakṣmī on lotus or as Gajalakṣmī or Lakṣmī with *nidhis* around her, is a favourite one that has survived through the centuries both as a sculptural theme to decorate architectural monuments and as a theme on royal seals and on the obverse of a huge variety of coins. She occurs as early as the second century before Christ on a rare Śuṅga coin (Fig. 64*)* of Sujyeṣṭha (*J. N.S. I.* 16, p. 59.60*)* and on Sodāsa's coins from Mathurā as Gajalakṣmī standing on a lotus and bathed by elephants answering the description of Vālmīki *niyujyamānā ca gajais suhastā lakṣmīs tathā padmini padmahastā, Rāmāyaṇa,* 5, 7,14. She appears in similar form on some Tribal coins like those of the Kuṇindas but not necessarily always as Gajalakṣmī. She occurs on the obverse of the Sātavāhana coin of Siri Yajña Sātakarṇī. Though the figures are not very clear this is Lakṣmī surrounded by *nidhis*. To understand this coin better a gold coin of Kumāragupta comes to our help (Fig. 65*)*. Here on the obverse of the elephant rider type, she is clearly flanked by the lotus and conch representing *Padma* and *Saṅkha-nidhis,* the two principal ones that in themselves represent the rest of the nine *nidhis, mahāpadma, makara, kaccapa, mukun-da, kunda, nīla* and *kharva*. Kālidāsa describes the two *nidhis* as flanking the doorway of the Yakṣa's mansion: *dvaropānte likhitavapuṣau śaṅkhapadmau ca dṛṣṭvā, Meghadūta* 2, 20. This is a feature in all *prāsādas* and temples. Like the *pūrṇaghatas* suggesting Gaṅgā and Yamunā the lotus and conch suggest all treasures and prosperity. Even in Tamil classics *Saṅkha* and *Padamanidhis* are described flanking deities. In the description of the various celestial *sabhās* in the *Mahābhārata,* Lakṣmī fianked by *Saṅkha* and *Padma* is mentioned ever present in Ku Sera's *sabhā*. It is thus that Lakṣmī on the Gupta coin has to be understood.

The elephant-rider type is prominent because of the extremely suggestive theme chosen and portrayed by Kumāragupta on the obverse of the coin (Fig. 66*)*. It represents the emperor as a charming prince riding the state elephant in all his glory with the single parasol on earth raised over his head. To understand this we should peep into the *Rāmāyaṇa* in which the picture painted by Vālmīki inspired Kumāragupta to choose this theme for depiction on his coin. In the *Rāmāyaṇa,* the citizens of Ayodhyā with one accord express their mind to Dasaratha, on hearing from him his intention to anoint Rāma as Yuvarāja, that nothing would give them greater joy than to see their beloved prince, the noble and mighty Rāma, in royal movement galore on the lofty state elephant. with his head screened from the sun by the umbrella held aloft: *iccāmo hi mahābāhum raghuvīram mahābalam gajena mahatā yāntam rāmam* *catrāvṛtāna-nam, Rāmayaṇa* 2, 2, 22. Kālidāsa describes King Atithi, the son of Kuśa and Kumudvatī, riding the elephant in all splendour with parasol held over his head, parasol denied to all others and vouch-safed for him alone, making him emperor of all the domain on earth like Indra in heaven: *sa puram puruhūtaśrīḥ kalpadrumanibhadhvajām kramamāṇas cakāra dyām nāgenairāvataujasā tasyaikasyoccṛtam catram mūrdhni tenāmalatvishā pūrvarājaviyogauṣmyam kṛtsnasya jagato hṛtam, Raghuvaṁśa* 17, 32. 33.

There is another variety of the same coin found in the Bayana hoard which, by the addition of a lion trampled under, makes it the elephant-rider lion-trampler type. In this the parasol, being only for him and none else, making him the suzerain lord, conveys the sense of the second verse quoted above and also brings to our mind the tribute paid by Sītā to Daśaratha in introducing herself to Hanumān as his daughter-in-law, Daśaratha who was the foremost among all the lion-like kings on earth devastating the armies of all his foes: *prithivyām rājasiṁhanām mukhyasya viditātmanaḥ suushā daśaratha-syāham śatrusainyapramāthinaḥ, Rāmāyaṇa* 5, 33, 16.

All the opponent kings of Kumāragupta are thus made the lion below, himself the mightiest royal lion riding the elephant, the umbrella of suzerainty held over him. It also shows him as a charming prince like Rāma whom his subjects loved to picture thus on elephant-back.

There is no doubt an earlier version of king on elephant in Huvishka's copper issues (Fig. 67*)*, which shows him just seated on the animal without the umbrella held over him, which makes an ocean of difference between this and the coin of Kumāragupta, which is a faithful picture of a prince, the beloved of his people, so pictured by them in their minds. This however shows him as rivalling Indra on his Airāvata. A poet, who composed an early Eastern Chaḷukyan *praśasti,* remarks that as the king Amma mounted his elephant his foes climbed up the hill-top and as he grasped his sword the princesses of his enemy kings held up the *caurīs,* meaning thereby that as he overcome his enemy forces mounted on elephant in battle, driven from their kingdoms his foes had to seek shelter on hill slopes, just as when his sword played havoc bringing victory, the princesses of the vanquished realms had to humble themselves before the victor: *yasmin ārūḍhadantinyarikulam akhilam rohati kṣmābhṛdagram yatpāṇā-vdttāśastre ripuyuvatikarā gṛhṇate cāmarāṇi, Epigraph. Ind.* 5, p. 122.

On the reverse of this coin is shown Sūrya called in the legend in Greek letters *Mioro* for Sanskrit *Mihira.* The deity is shown standing with radiating halo around his head, right hand extended and the left resting on sword fastened to his left, and wearing long coat, trousers and top boots, exactly as in similar earlier coins of Kaniṣka who does not however ride an elephant on the obverse. To understand this type of Kuṣāṇa Sūrya, which has tremendously influenced the iconography of Sūrya all over North India through all subsequent centuries, making him always wear *udīcyavesha* or northern apparel, meaning thereby the Central Asian type from further north, we should refer to the description of Sūrya's form given by Varāhamihira : *kuryād udīcyavesham gūdham pādād uro yāvat kañcukaguptaḥ smitaprasannamukhaḥ, Bṛhatsamhitā* 57, 46-48.

It is thus observed that the Kuṣāṇa kings display a rare form of early Hindu iconography, which it requires a careful study to under-stand. The early indigenous type of turbaned, barebodied, garland-decorated Sūrya, completely Indian in concept, becomes a transformed and almost Central Asian type, which became such a norm, at least in North India, that Varāhamihira has no other description of the Solar deity except this. Buddha as known from Kaniṣka's picture of the Master on his coin is also understood by us better from the recorded description in the *Bṛhatsamhitā*. Vāyu or Vāta on the coin of Kaniṣka is shown running fast almost as fast as Atalanta in her race (Fig. 68). Never has Vāyu been represented so in any later sculpture of his. There is none of his earlier either, either similar or dissimilar. It is a unique form of the wind god, fresh and natural in concept and execution. The banner fluttering in his hand symbolizes him, and his vehicle the swift deer distinguishes him in medieval sculpture. Here, however the speed of Vāyu is directly marked in the figure of the deity itself. In the *Kenopanishad* Agni, Vāyu and Indra approach the highest spirit Brahman to know all about it and Vāyu announces himself and his powers to prove which he runs in all his speed towards the blade of grass held out. *tad udapreyāya sarvajavena, Kenopanishad* 3, 10. In the *Rāmāyaṇa,* Sītā, asked by Hanumān to permit him to fetch her on his shoulder to Rāma, shudders at the idea, and expresses how she would not stand the velocity of his speed equal only to that of Vāyu. *vāyuvegasavegasya vego mām mohayet tava, Rāmāyaṇa* 5, 37, 43.

It is interesting that on the Kuṣāṇa coin of Vāyu, two-armed, and running with hair dishevelled, he holds the terminals of his *uttarīya* or upper garment filled with wind indicating swift movement just as directed for pictorial representation in the *Viṣṇudharmottara*. *vayvāpūritavastraśca dvibhujo rūpasamyutaḥ kāryo gṛhītavastrāntaḥ karābhyām pavano dviia vyāvrittāsyas tathā kāryo devo vyākulamūrdha-jaḥ, Viṣṇudharmottara* 3, 58, 1-3. The *Viṣṇu-dharmottara,* an early Gupta text, has no doubt recorded faithfully existing forms of deities as known from earlier times and this is a happy instance.

A rare coin of Huviṣka shows the King on the obverse rising an elephant, the reverse showing the figure of an archer holding a bow of his own length (Fig. 69) with legend in Brāhmī *gaṇeśa* (*Coins of Anc. Ind.* p. 81). This figure with a single pair of arms, tall and imposing, with no elephant head or pot belly or dwarfish stature appears to pose a problem. J.N. Banerjea has discussed it under Śiva and explained *ganeśa* as an epithet of Śiva, quoting from the *Rāmāyaṇa, Development of Early Hindu Iconography* p. 125). To understand this there are two important things to be considered. The first is that the Kuṣāṇas had a great veneration for Śiva and clearly expressed it by representing him with a single pair of arms or with four arms, with a single head or with three faces, with a variety of weapons, associating him with weapons of other deities like Viṣṇu, Indra, Brahmā, Skanda, Gaṇeśa, Sūrya and so fourth. On the coins of Kadphises there is not only Śiva on the reverse but almost identifying himself or composing himself with Śiva gives the legend in Kharoṣṭhī *mahārājasa rājātirājasa sarvaloga īśvarasa maheśvarasa wima kathphisasa tratarasa, Coins of Anc. Ind.* p. 68. This shows the spirit of importance attached to the Śiva concept by the Kuṣāṇas. The second point is the early text giving the *vibhūti* of Śiva, the *Śatarudrīya,* the importance of which for Śiva iconographic concept is comparable only to the *Puruṣasūkta* that gives the *vibhūti* of Viṣṇu. It cannot be that the Kuṣāṇas did not think of this most important text in their ardour for Śiva. In the *Śatarudrīya,* Śiva with his great bow, arrows and quiver is the form pervading throughout the text: *namas te astu dhanvane bāhubhyām uta te namaḥ* is an exact picture of this figure. In the same text Rudra is adored as the lord of *gaṇas, gaṇebhyo gaṇapatibhyas ca vo namaḥ*. Similarly he is the Lord of the armies and the Commander of *ugaṇas* or the Mātṛkās, *nama ugaṇābhyas trimhatibhyas ca*. The idea that he is lvIahadeva, the great Lord and that Ganeśa or Senānī or Mahāsena or the Mātṛkās are after him, deriving their attributes from him, is made clear by this coin and thes coin with the legend Mahāsena.

A silver coin of Kṣatrapa Nahapāna of the second century A.D., has two emblems on its reverse, the arrow and the thunder-bolt, both weapons of war (Fig. 70). The legend in Brāhmī and Kharoṣṭhī run all around *rājño kṣaharātasa nahapaṇasa*. A passage from the *Abhijñānaṛākuntalam* makes it clear that the bow of the ruling king and the thunderbolt of Indra were the two weapons that effectively protected their respective realms from the onslaught of enemies: *āśamsante surayuvatayo baddhavairā hi daityair asyādhijye dhanuṣi vijayam pauruhūte ca vajre, Abhijñānaśākuntalam* 2, 16. But the true significance of the thunderbolt is clearly understood from the verse of Kālidāsa that describes the might of the king as comparable to that of the weilder of the thunderbolt: *tataḥ param vajradhara-prabhāvas tadātmajas samyati vajraghoṣaḥ babhūva vajrākarabhūṣaṇāyāḥ patiḥ prithivyāḥ kila vajraṇābhaḥ, Raghuvaṁśa* 18, 21. The special power of the thunderbolt is also clear when we see the description of the battle between Raghu and Indra, where finally the latter throws away his bow and takes the thunderbot as the supreme weapon: *sa cāpam utsṛjya vivṛddhamatsaraḥ praṇāśanāya prabalasya vidvishaḥ mahīdhrapakṣavyaparopaṇocitam sphuratprahāmaṇdalam astram ādade, Raghuvaṁśa* 3, 60.

The ideal of a mortal king was the celestial one. While Indra wielded the *vajra*, the king on earth was the best bowman, both to protect their respective realms. The highest power on earth lying in the bow, here signified by the arrow, to shoot which it was used, is in juxtaposition with the thunderbolt of the Lord of heaven.

The might of the bowman, the only bowman to be reckoned on earth, is admirably illustrated in a lead coin of Gautamīputra Śātakarṇī (Fig.71). This shows a single large bow strung and fitted with arrow marked on the obverse with legend in Brāhmī *Raño Gotamīputasa Vilivayakurasa*. Gautamīputra Śātakarṇī is one of the most remarkable kings in Indian history. The figure of the bow naturally leads us to the question of what it connotes. The answer is to be sought in the line of the famous inscription of Balasiri, the mother of Gautamīputra, who gifted an excavated cave to Buddhist monks at Nāsik and recorded the donation. There is a long glowing description of the noble qualities of Gautmīputra recounted by the fond mother Balasiri sorrowing for her great son during the reign of her grandson Vāsiṣṭhī-putra Pulumāvi, worthy son of Gautamīputra. A line in this *praśasti* describes Gautamīputra Śātakarṇī as *ekadhanudharasa, Epigraph. Ind.* 8, p. 60. He had no rival bowman on earth. In describing Dilīpa, Kalidāsa uses the identical expression in his verse *na kevalam tadgurur ekapārthivaḥ kṣitāvabhūd ekadhanurdharo'pi saḥ. Raghuvaṁśa 3,* 31. The sense of the coin is thus made clear in unequivocal terms. Further, as it is strung with arrow fitted on it, it also conveys the sense, as in Kālidāsa's verse, that there was nothing that the king could not obtain even in heaven when he tightened the string of his bow: *na hīṣṭam asya tridlve'pl bhūpater abhūd anāsādhyam adhijya-dhanvanaḥ, Raghuvaṁśa,* 3, 6.

It is in this context that several later coins, particularly the archer type of coins of the Guptas, of Chandragupta II, Kumāragupta, Skandagupta and others are to be understood.

The battle axe type of Samudragupta is an important coin with the axe as a destroying weapon emphasized as the very personification of death as the legend would have it *kṛtāntaparaśuḥ* (Fig. 72*).* This has an allusion to the axe of Paraśurāma that gave a death blow to the entire Kṣatriya race twentyone times and not to Yama, as Yama has either his *daṇḍa* or *pāśa* for inflication and not the *paraśu.* But in the case of the Kṣatriya race it was the axe of Jāmadagnya that acted as death personified. No doubt a powerful king was a terror to his foes appearing kāla or death in his form as in the verse from the *Kuvalayānanda, strībhiḥ kāmorthibis svardruḥ kālas śatrubhir aikṣi saḥ.* But the term *paraśu* at once brings to our mind the famous line of Kālidāsa where Pratīpa, a scion of the race of Kārtavīryārjuna, is described as on the friendliest terms with the god of Fire, which enabled him to look on the sharp edge of Rāma's axe, the very night of deluge for all Kṣatriyas, as just a smooth lotus petal : *āyodhane kṛṣṇa-gatim sahāyam avāpya yaḥ kṣatrryakālarātrim dhārām sitām rāmaparaśvadhasya sambhāvayatyutpalapatrasāṛām, Raghuvaṁśa* 6. 42. The word *kālarātri* is the most terrible aspect of death. Hence the word *kṛtāntaparaśu* on the coin. *Kṛtāntaparaśu* should be understood in the sense of *kṛtānta iva paraśuḥ* or *kṛtānta-ścāsau paraśus' ca i.e.* axe dreadful like death and not as *kṛtāntasya paraśuh,* the axe of Death or Yama, as Yama does not carry an axe. Kālidāsa has correctly spelt it out. The axe of Paraśurāma distingui-shes Rāma with the axe from Rāma with the bow and it is that which is *kṣatriyakālarātri.* Samudragupta's axe was thus another such to his foes.

On some silver coins of Gautamīputra Yajña Śātakarṇī (Fig. 73*)* is imprinted on the obverse a youthful head with sidelocks known as *kākapakṣa.* The side locks like the *vyāghranakha* or tiger claw pendent for necklace were the special features of juvenile adorn-ment, the former a characteristic mode of hair-dress for princes in their boyhood in ancient India. Rāma, when he sallied forth with Viśvāmitra to protect his sacrifice from the onslaught of evil demons, is described as wearing side-locks: *viśvāmitro yayāvagre tato rāmo mahāyaśāḥ kākapakṣadharo dhanvt tam ca saumitrir anvagāt, Rāmāyaṇa* 1, 12, 6.

Kṛṣṇa and Balarāma are shown as little boys fighting the wrestlers Muṣṭika and Chāṇūra in a carved panel from Pahārpur where this juvenile decoration specially marks them as children. A scul-pture of the child-warrior Kārtikeya wearing *kākapakṣas* and the tiger's claws in the Bharat Kala Bhavan is an exquisite Gupta piece.

The figure of the coin shows the *kākapakṣa* associated with princely youth but its significance is understood only from the verse of Kālidāsa emphasizing the fact that age is of no consideration in the case of the powerful: *kauśikena sa kila kṣitīśvaro rāmam adhva-*

ravigātaśāntaye kākapakṣadharam etya yācitas tejasām hi na vayas samīkṣyate, Raghuvaṁśa 11, 1. Again Kālidāsa has it that the appellation *mahānīla* cannot be false in the case of even a small sapphire owing to its splendour, so the renowned title *mahārāja* befitted him even though he was but a child. Word of command coming from his mouth, on whose cheeks were waving the side-locks and beside whom *cauris* were waved, never failed even on the shores of the oceans: *maṇau mahānīla iti prabhāvād alprapamaṇopi yathā na mithyā śabdo mahārāja iti pratītas tathaiva tasmin yuyuje' rbhake' pi paryantasañcaritacāmarasya kapolalolobhayakākāpakṣāt tasyānanād uccarito vivādas casāla velāsvapi nārṇavānām, Raghuvaṁśa* 18, 42, 43.

In the light of this we understand that though still Yajña Śātakarṇī was in his youth, his prowess and power was immense and his tender age suggested by his side-locks should not underrate his might.

On the reverse of this coin there are symbols whose meaning is obscure (Fig 73). The individual symbols are quite clear though the connotation of the group as such is far from clear. On this coin there are what is called by Numismatists the Ujjain symbol, a cross with circlets at the terminals, one of them topped by a crescent, a symbol of *caitya* or more correctly a hill surmounted by a crescent, a star or a circle of stars and a zigzag symbol connoting a river or stream as it is usually believed. It is amazing how the connotation of this group of symbols is made quite clear by a verse of Kālidāsa describing the spread of the fame of Raghu that ascended mountains, crossed the oceans, entered the abode of the snakes *i.e.* the netherworld, went up to heaven, and being still expansive was too much to be measured by any standard : *ārūḍham adrīn udadhīn vitīrṇam bhujaṅgamānām vasatim praviṣṭam ūrdhvam gatam yasya na cḥānuban-dhi yaśaḥ paricchettum iyattayālam, Raghuvaṁśa* 6, 77. Fame has always been regarded in India as white in colour and has been compared to the moon. This accounts for the representation of the moon as a crescent above the hill as in no otherwise can an abstract object like fame be represented. The line *ārūḍham adrīn* is thus substantiated. The rest of the line *udadhīn vitīrṇam* and *bhujaṅgamānām vasatim praviṣṭm* is suggested, fame again crossing the four oceans implied in the four circlets of the Ujjain symbol, and zigzag effec-tively symbolizing the snake or *bhujaṅga i.e.* that which goes zigzag, whose dwelling is in the deep and down below, the netherworld. The sky or heaven can be represented only by the stars and the symbol of the star or a cluster of stars clearly points to that sphere where fame travelled and substantiates *ūrdhvam gatam.*

Herein lies the beauty of symbolic representation of the great fame of a mighty king from a single verse of a gifted poet adopted by a mighty ruler of later day on his coin Raghu the hero of the family *Raghuvaṁśa* which forms the theme of the poet's song in epic glory, was enough to inspire not only Śātakarṇī but a host of successive rulers thereafter. This fascinating theme did not disappear after its appearance on this Sātavāhana coin. So attractive and so full of significance was it, that the Kṣatrapas who finally overcame and dispossessed the Sātavāhanas of their Western dominions, still did not refrain from adopting this symbolic representation of fame originated by the Sātavāhanas on the model of Kālidāsa's verse (Fig. 74). To show clearer that fame climbed the mountain the crescent was now shown on the slopes, *kaṭaka* and then on the top of the hill as in the original, and the circle of stars was sometimes replaced by a circle of rays symbolizing the sun to suggest the sky and the Ujjain symbol omitted. This is the type found on the coins of Western Kṣatrapa rulers like Rudradāman, Dāmasena, Vīradāman and others. It occurs on some issues of the Traikūṭakas of the third and fourth centuries A.D., though however by this time the symbols degenerate, the sense getting confused and almost lost.

It is interesting that the coin of an earlier ruler Vāsiṣṭhīputra Śrī Śātakarṇī is a bilingual variety, a very rare type, of which only three surviving examples are known (Fig. 75). It has on its obverse the earliest Sātavāhana portrait on a coin which precedes that of Śrī Yajña Śātakarṇī in this feature of a portrait and the four significant symbols on the reverse as well. The portrait however lacks *kākapakṣas* that can be only for a juvenile figure. It has the usual Brāhmī legend on the obverse showing the portrait name .*Vāsiṭhiputasa siri satakanisa,* with the additional legend repeated not in Brāhmī but in Tamil. The Tamil word *tiru* replaces *siri* and *makan* the word *putra, rajño* being substituted by *aracan,* the whole reading *aracanuku vaciṭṭmakanuku tiru Chaṭakaniku.* The Sātavāhanas were great patrons of literature, Sanskrit and Prakrit, particularly the latter. It is interesting that this Śātakarṇī encouraged the use of one of the oldest venaculars in India, Tamil, along with Prākṛt by making his coins bilingual. The marking of '*pulli*' or a dot over a consonent to indicate it as a pure consonent is exclusive to Tamil and its very early occurrence in this legend is most interesting (*Seminar on Inscriptions* 1966, Madras 1968, pp. 200-202).

The Yaudheyas were a warlike tribe and they were distinguished for their valour and prowess in battle. Naturally they prided in this and chose Kārtikeya as their war-lord, and on their coins showing Skanda standing holding a spear in his hand (Fig. 76) with the legend in Brāhmī *yaudheya gaṇasya jaya or brahmaṇyadevasya yaudheyagaṇa-syajaya* this choice of theirs to have the celestial war-lord as their patron deity and ideal in military glory is clearly pronounced. They were fully conscious of the importance of Kārtikeya as the glowing power of Śiva himself exceeding even solar effulgence conserved in flaming fire to be the protector of the celestial army itself : *rakṣāhe-tor navaśaśibhṛtā vāsavīnām camūnām atyādityam hutavahamukhe sambhṛtam taddhi tejaḥ, Meghadūta* 1, 46. When Kālidāsa mentions Kumāra as the appropriate comparison of a warlike prince born, *Kumārakalpam suṣuve kumāram,* it is to emphasize his worth as a Kṣatriya prince.

The name Brahmaṇyadeva for Kārtikeya appears to create a puzzle as Kṛṣṇa is also Brahmaṇyadeva according to the famous verse *namo brahmaṇyadevāya gobrāhmaṇahitāya ca jagaddhitāya kṛṣṇāya govindāya namo namaḥ.* But it is Kārtikeya with six heads on Yaudheya coins that is styled Brahmaṇyadeva, Ṣkaṇmukha nurtured by the six Kṛttikās who has significantly six heads. Skanda Kārtikeya is well known to the Guptas as Brahmaṇyadeva and is so called in the Bilsad inscription of Kumāragupta : *bhagavatas trailokyatejassambhārasamudbhūtamūrter brahmaṇyadevasya svāmimahāsenasyāyatane, C. Inscr. Ind.* pp. 44-45. In South India during *sandhyā* the verse *namo brahmaṇyadevāya gobrāhmaṇahitāya ca* is daily repeated. Along with this the salutation to Narmadā is offered by a group of *smārtas*.

called *Vaḍamas* or northerners. It is a known fact that serveral Vedic families moved from North India to the South and settled down wherever they were given some land as *agrahāra* by the rulers in recognition of their Vedic learning. The memory of the movement of one such group, *Aṣṭasahasram,* is preserved in the name of the village Eṇṇāyiram in South Arcot district. The Brahmaṇyadeva of this prayer is Kārttikeya Brahmaṇyadeva of the Yaudheyas. Brahmaṇyadeva is the god of righteousness. That is how to emphasis the opposite of *abrahmaṇya,* Brahmaṇyadeva was styled Subraḥmaṇya in South India, a synonym for Skanda more popular than the term Skanda or Kārtikeya.

In the context of the choice of Kartikeya as the ideal for a warlike prince intended to establish his might on earth everything associated with Skanda, the cock, the peacock, the spear, all appealed, the peacock specially. So there was a special type of coin of Kumāragupta, the peacock type, showing Skanda or Kumāra on the bird. It is interesting to recall that Kumāragupta was named after Kumāra himself even as Kālidāsa would put it *Kumārakalpam sushuve kumāram, Raghuvaṁśa* 5, 36. This was an age when Kumāra as Kārtikeya, Ṣaḍānana and Brahmaṇyadeva was highly venerated. We have noticed that the Yaudheya coins of the first-second centuries A.D., showing a six-headed deity, eulogise Kārttikeya and Shadānana like some others with Brahmaṇyadeva. In the so called warrior type of Yaudheya coins of sligntly later date, Kārtikeya is shown with his spear as in the previous coin, but with a single face and with his cock beside him. Kumāra was the warrior god *par excellence* and was the type kings tried to emulate which explains why Kālidāsa often compares several distinguished princes to Kumāra: *brāhme muhūrte kila tasya devt kumārakalpam suṣuve kumāram, Raghuvaṁśa* 5, 36. *athopayantrā sadriśenav yuktām skandena sākṣād iva devasenām, Raghuvaṁśa* 7, 1; *hareḥ kumāropi kumāra vikramaḥ, Raghuvaṁśa* 3, 55, meaningrespectively 'his queen gave birth at dawn to a prince equal to Kumāra','with bridegroom befitting her, like Devasenā herself with Skanda' and 'the prince mighty like Kumāra'. The figure on the obverse of the coin of Kumāragupta is fully understood in this sense of comparison (Fig. 77a) when we re-call the description of the prince looking exceedingly beautiful comparable to Guha seated on the back of the peacock : *bhūyiṣṭham āsīd upameyakāntir mayūrapriṣṭhāśrayiṇā guhena, Raghuvaṁśa* 6, 4.

On the reverse also of this coin there is the peacock glorified. The goddess of Prosperity or Devasenā personified tries to fondle the vehicle of Skanda by offering a fruit (Fig. 77b). In this case the goddess is erect and not bent and the peacock with spread tail is dancing before her in great joy. The legend is *mahendra Kumāraḥ.* In the tiger-slayer type of coin with the legend *śrīmahendro vyāghrabala-parākramo jayati.* There is again on the reverse the goddess fondling the peacock but here she is bent towards the bird and all the more solicitous towards it. Does it not remind one of the Yakṣī in the *Meghadūta* playing with the peacock and coaxing it to dance with its tail spread picturesquely colourful: *tālais śiñjāvalayasubhagaiḥ kāntayā nartito me yām adhyāste divasavigame ntlakaṇthaḥ suhṛd vaḥ,Meghadūta* 2, 19.

The might of the warrior becomes the theme of a category of coins. Power is associated with the king of the beasts, the lion, the sniff of the lions in the Himālayan caves, that just turned their head a little, without the least concern as the tumultous mighty host of victorious troops marched past, conscious of the fact that they were equally powerful, brings out this fact clearly : *śaśamsa tulyasatvānām sainyaghoṣe'pyasambhramam guhāśayānām siṁhānām parivṛtyāvaloknam, Raghuvaṁśa* 4, 72. Naturally the king asserted his own power by vanquishing the lion; and the poet's fancy enlightens us on the king's attitude of fight with the lord of the beasts by explaining that the king cleared himself of his obligation to the mighty elephants that helped him in his battles by killing their dreaded enemy: *tān hatvā gajakulabaddhatīvravairān kākutsthaḥ kuṭilanakhāgralagnamuktān ātmā-nam raṇakṛtakarmaṇām gajānām ānṛṇyam gatam iva mārgaṇair amamsta, Raghuvaṁśa* 9, 65. And in this combat his might is proved to be equal to that of the lion. It is this fight with the lion and the establishing of his superior power and leonine strength that is sought in the figure of the king slaying the lion on the obverse of the lion-slayer type of gold coin of Chandragupta II. The use of arrows *mārgaṇaiḥ* to kill the lion answers the description of Kālidāsa. On the reverse is the legend *siṁhavikramaḥ* which is a repeat of the last word of the legend on the obverse *narendracandraḥ prathita...divam jayatyajeyo bhuvi siṁhavikramaḥ*. and it is a clear echo of Kālidāsa's *simhorusatvam niiagāda simhaḥ, Raghuvaṁśa* 2, 33.

The beautiful warrior pose in which the archer with his drawn bow engages his opponent, and famous both in *nāṭya* and *śilpa* to represent the best of warriors, *ālīḍha* or *pratyālīḍha,* is again immortalized in another variety of coin of Chandragupta II on which the king appears attacking the lion, his right leg bent and left leg drawn to trample the animal even as he shoots him with his bow and arrow. This is the *ālīḍha* posture, one of the five warrior poses. It does remind one of the lines of Kālidāsa where he describes Raghu in the majestic warrior stance of *ālīḍha* to attack Indra: *sa evam uktvā maghavantam unmukhaḥ kariṣyamāṇas saśaram śarāsanam atiṣthad ālīḍhaviśeshaśobhinā vapuḥprakarsheṇa viḍambiteśvaraḥ. Raghuvaṁśa* 3, 52. It also brings to our mind the picture of prince Sudarśana wielding the bow standing with the forepart of his body stretched a little, with his hair tied up, with his left leg contracted, and with the bow to which the arrow was added drawn up to the ear: *vyūhya sthitaḥ kiñcid ivottarārdham unnaddhacūḍo 'ñcitasavyaiānuḥ ākarṇam ākṛṣṭasabāṇadhanvā vyarocatāgre sa vinīyamānaḥ Raghuvaṁśa* 18, 51.

One of the most important of varieties of coin of Samudragupta is the *Aśvamedha* type (Fig. 78) which has on its obverse the horse shown near the sacrificial post decorated with flying pennons with legend *rādhirājaḥ pṛthlvīm avitvā divamjayatyapratlvāryavīryaḥ*. On the reverse is a damsel standing with fiywhisk in her left hand, a staff adorned with pennons in front of her. The legend behind her is *aśvamedha-parākramaḥ* meaning mighty by the performance of the *Aśvamedha* sacrifice. In the dialogue between prince Raghu and Indra, the latter justifies his carrying away the sacrificial horse in the care of Raghu as he had to act so to save his own glory by carrying away the sacrificial horse and prevent the accomplishment of a hundred horse sacrifices by his sire: *yaśas tu rakṣyam parato yaśodhanaiḥ jagatprakāśamtad aśesham ijyayā bhavadgurur langhayitum mamodyataḥ, Raghu-vaṁśa* 3, 48. The performance of the *Aśvamedha* established the sovereign's *parākrama* and the legend on the coin is pregnant with meaning. The horse itself is mentioned by Kālidāsa as the first and foremost accessory of the sacrifice *tad aṅgam agryam maghavan mahākrator amum turaṅgam pratimoktum arhasi, Raghuvaṁśa* 3, 46. Hence the sacrificial horse is prominently figured on the coin. The performer of Aśvamedha becomes a *samrāṭ* or suzereign sovereign over other rulers. Hence the goddess of Royal Fortune is shown *caurī* in her hand waiting on the mighty emperor even as Kālidāsa would have it *padmā padmātapatreṇa bheje sā nrājyadīkṣitam, Raghuvaṁśa* 4,5. This coin has a long history behind it as it is not a first innovation. It is itself based on similar earlier types. The Sātavāhanas were emperors in their own right. In the early Sātavāhana inscription of Śātakarṇī in the Nānāghāṭ cave he is described as the sacrificer of two *Aśvamedhas* giving sacrificial fees composed of a horse with silver trappings, twelve golden. .... 24000 *kārṣāpaṇas*, a village. . .an elephant. . . milch cows, a cart for conveying a mountain of grain etc. *asamedho bitiyo yitho dakhiṇāyo dinā rūpalamkāro suvamna. . .ni 12 dakhiṇā dinā kahāpanā 240000 gamo I hathi dakhiṇā dināgāvo... sakatam dhamnagiritamsapayutam. . . Arc. Sur. West Ind., V,* p. 60. In Ayodhyā inscription, Puṣyamitra Śuṅga is credited with the performance of two *Aśvamedhas*: *dvir aśvamedhayājinaḥ senāpateḥ pushyamitrasya shashthena, Epigraph. Ind.* 20, p. 57. The Nāgārjunakoṇḍa inscriptions of the Ikṣvāku king Siri Cantamūla mention the *Aśvamedha* among other sacrifices performe by him: *agihotāgiṭhomavājapeyāsamedhayājisa. . . ikhākusa siricantamūlasa, Epigraph. Ind.* 20, p. 20. Pravarasena I, ancestor of Rudrasena, the consort of Prabhāva-tīguptā, has a large variety of sacrifices including four *aśvamedhas : pravarapurād agnishtomāptoryāmokthyaśodaśyatirātravāiapeyabṛhas-patlsavādyaskracaturaśvamedhayājino viṣṇuvṛdadhasago trasya samrājo vākātakānām mahārāja śrīpravarasenasya, C. Inscr. Ind.* 3, p. 236. The same inscription mentions the Bhāraśivas, connected with the Vākātakas by matrimony, as the performers of ten *aśvamedhas, daśāśvamedhāvabhṛtasnātānām bhāraśivānām, C. Inscr. Ind.* 3, p. 236. The Hirahadgalli Prākṛt grant of Śivaskandavarman brings in the early Pallavas among sacrificers of *Aśvamedha*: *kāñcīpurāaggitthoma-vājapeyassamedhayāji dhammamahārājādhirājo. Epigraph. Ind.* I. p. 5. The most remarkable find in recent excavations, inscribed sacrificial altar bricks from Kalsi, have one with a verse in Brāhmī letters of the third century A.D. mentioning four sacrifices performed by king Śīla-varman probably of the Yaudheyas in eastern Punjab, in Jagatgrām close to Dehra Dun, sixth in descent from king Pona, whose name is still fresh in the minds of that neighbourhood by the existence of an early medieval portrait statue in metal of king Pona in the Chambā area. The legend on the brick reads *nṛpater varṣagaṇḍasya ponaṣaṣṭhasya dhīmataḥ caturthasyāśvamedhasya caityoyam Sīlavarmaṇaḥ J.O.R.* 21, p. 28. Kālidāsa is well aware of the sacrifices performed by the earliest Pāṇḍyas, of whom one was styled Palyāgaśālai Mudukudumi Peruvaludi long before the Kalabhra interregnum, and makes Sunandā describe the Pāṇḍya come for the *svayamvara* of Indumatī as one who had performed many sacrifices and eulogizes him as wet with the bath after *Aśvamedha* sacrifices, with Agastya himself to hail him after successful completion of each of them: *prītyāśvamedhā-vabhṛtārdlramūrtes sausnātiko yasya bhavatyagastyaḥ, Raghuvaṁśa* 6,61. The larger Sinnamannur plates mention that the early rulers of the Pāṇḍya family performed several *rājasūya* and *aśvamedha* sacrifices: *yatrotpannā rājasūyāśvamedhair ishtvānekair devabhūyam prapannāḥ, S. Ind. Insc.* 3, p. 45 L This is actually substantiated by the representa-tion of the sacrificial horse on some of the earliest Pāṇḍyan coins (Fig. 79*)* of the second or third century A.D. Even so late as the thirteenth century when the great Sundara Pāṇḍya triumphed over the whole of South India, a copper issue with the horse and the royal umbrella shown above to signify his suzerainty was issued, though unfortunately the back of the legend prevents its definite attribution to a particular sovereign. But it is a Pāṇḍyan issue and Sundara Pāṇḍya who was the most distinguished has the best claim for such an ambitious position.

There are two coins of the Sātavāhanas one of Śrī Candra Śātakarṇī and Śrī Yajña Śātakarṇī with the sacrificial horse of the *Aśvamedha* imprinted on them, the legend giving their names encircling the animal in each case (Fig. 80). The legends in the order of the kings named above are *raño siri cada satisa* (*Rapson* p. 32) and *raño gotamīputasa siri yaña satakamnisa* (*Rapson* p. 38). This last was the last great Śātakarṇī king and his empire was still to be reckoned. He hence could boast of this sacrifice and feel confident that he was not weak to be scattered, enabling his enemies to capture the horse, which could render his sacrifice, symbolic of empire, nullified, as the *Taittīrīya Brāhmaṇa* would put it: *rāshtram vā āsvamedhaḥ parā va esha sicyate yobalo'śvamedhena yajate yad amitrā aśvam vinderan hanyetaśya yajñaḥ.*

Aśvamedha and *Rājasūya* were sacrifices that established the title of a sovereign to the position of a *samrāṭ* or emperor. This entitled the king to enjoy *ekacchatra* or the only umbrella on earth, even as the poet has put it, that over his head alone was raised an umbrella, and by that umbrella of spotless lustre the affliction of the entire world on account of separation from the former kings was removed: *tasyaikasyocchṛtam chatram mūrdhni tenāmalatvishā pūrvarājaviyo-gaushmyam kṛtsnasya jagato hṛltam, Raghuvaṁśa* 17, 33.

Ambition at its highest in every king in ancient India has been to subdue all contemporary princes and rule an empire with a royal umbrella raised over his head alone, denying this privilege to every other prince. The ambition of sovereignty of a single parasol *ekacchatrādhipatya* has caused all the wars that history records, and loss of life has been counted as nothing by kings and emperors in the achieving of this object. A prize so coveted should naturally be expected to be properly displayed. And how best can it be shown except as it is given on one of the Gupta coins' Chandragupta II, the great emperor, is shown standing and a *vāmana* dwarf attendant raises an umbrella over his head (Fig. 81). No greater significance can there be in this figure than that conveyed by Kālidāsa in his lines picturing a heroic scion of Raghu's race with arms long like the bolt of a city-gate enjoying the earth on which was raised only one single umbrella, or another in whom were combined sovereignty of the earth with only a single umbrella raised on him, the charm of youth and the splendour of beauty of form: *ekātapatrām bhuvam ekavīraḥ purārgalā-dīṛghabhujo bubhoja, Raghuvaṁśa* 17, 4; *ekātapatram jagataḥ prabhu-tvam navam vayaḥ kāntam idam vapuś ca, Raghuvaṁśa* 2, 47.

The might and majesty of the sovereign as given in the line *sālaprāmśur mahābhujaḥ, Raghuvaṁśa* 1, 12, is sought to be conveyed with emphasis by showing the king standing, a *vāmana* attendant being specially chosen to lift so lofty a parasol, only for an effective contrast.

The idea of the single umbrella so appealed to so many subse-quent sovereigns that along with the *caurīs* or fiywhisks this became the emblem of suzerainty for many great later emperors. On the coins of one of the greatest emperors of medieval India, Rājendra Chola, son of Rājarāja who was an equally great sovereign, is found the emblem of the Cholas, the tiger, seated triumphantly with emblems of the two principal vanquished neighbours in front and behind, the bow of the Cheras and the fish of the Pāṇḍyas (Fig. 82). At the bottom is the Nāgarī legend *rajendraḥ* giving the name of the king. To the top is a parasol with fiywhisks on either side. There are similar coins of Uttamachola and Rājarāja. The importance of the parasol and fey-whisks as royal emblems *par excellence* is quite dear in Kālidāsa's verse describing the generosity of a king who could refrain from giving away to the announcer of the sweet tidings of a long-awaited prince's birth only the royal umbrella, radiant like the moon, and the pair of feywhiks: *janāya śudhāṅtacarāya śamsate kumārajanmāmṛ-tasammitākasharam adeyam āsīt trayam eva bhūpates śaśiprabham chatram ubhe ca cāmare, Raghuvaṁśa* 3, 16.

The tiger is substituted by a boar in the case of the gold coins of Rājarāja, the Eastern Chālukyan king who was the daughter's son of Rājarāja Chola and son-in-law of Rājendra Chola whose daughter Ammaṇgā he married, and who was not slow in emulating the Chola expression of royal might (Fig. 83). The Pāṇḍyas also found this expression of sovereignty so satisfying to their sense of self-esteem that the umbrella and feywhisks were raised over the pair of fish, emblem of the Pāṇḍyas. During the time of the greatest of the later Pāṇḍyas, Sundara Pāṇḍya, in the thirteenth century, the parasol was raised over a horse signifying suzerainty established by a horse sacrifice like *Aśvamedha* or *Rājasūya.*

The dominion of a king on earth, however much a *dharmavijgī-ṣu,* righteous victor, he may be, is only conquered by force. The ambition of man being unlimited, conquests lead on to further conquests. The next sphere of conquest after the subjugation of the earth is heaven. To occupy the seat of Indra as almost his equal was the desire that all great kings evinced in ancient India. Conquest of heaven was not possible by force. It was only by one's own good deeds and the performance of difficult sacrifices like the *Rājasūya* and *Aśvamedha.* Gupta coins abound in legends recording this great accomplishment of the king. The winning of heaven by good deeds is given in so many words. In the archer type of Samudragupta's coin it is *apratiratho viiyitya kṣitim sucaritair divam jayati Cat. Ind. Coins, Cupta* p. 6, meaning having conquered the earth without an opponent, he wins heaven by his good deeds. The legend on the *chatra* type of Chandragupta II is *kṣitim avajitya sucaritair divam wyati vikramādityaḥ, Cat. Ind. Coms, Cupta* p. 35, which means 'Vikramāditya having conquered the earth wins heaven by good deeds'. Kumāragupta's swordsman type of coins give the legend *gām avajitya sucaritair divam jayati vikramādityaḥ, Cat. Ind. Coins, Cupta* p. 67 purporting that 'Vikramāditya having conquered the earth wins heaven by good deeds'. The legend differs however on his archer, horseman and other types: *viitāvanir avanipatiḥ kumāragupto divam jayati, Cat. Ind. Coins, Gupta* p. 61 and *kṣitipatir ajito vijayī kumāragupto divam jayati, Cat. Ind. Coins, Cupta,* p. 71 etc. respectively connoting 'king Kumāragupta, after conquering the earth, wins heaven' and 'king Kumāragupta, unconquered and victorious wins heaven.'

The idea of winning heaven is still present in these legends as well. In the verse from the Mandasor inscription of Yaśodharman *gāmevonmātum ūrdhvam vigaṇayitum ivajyotishām* *cakravālam nirdeṣtum mārgam uccair diva iva sukṛtopārjitāyās svakīrteḥ tenākalpānt-akālāvadhir avanibhujā śrīyaśodharmaṇāyam stambhas stambhābhirāma-sthirabhujaparig-heṇocchritim nāyitotṛa, C. Inscr.Ind.*3,p. 147, the line *nirdeṣtum mārgam uccair diva iva sukṛtopārjitāyās svakīrteḥ* suggesting the way up for his fame to reach heaven won by his good deeds is indeed a noble echo of this legend on Gupta coins. And the source of this legend by *sukṛta* or *sucarita* is clearly given in Kālidāsa's line *tasmin gate dyām sukṛto-palabdhām, Raghuvaṁśa* 18, 22. The term *karmabhiḥ* is sometimes used in the coin legends as on the Kāca type of Samudragupta's coins *kāco gām avajitya divam karmabhir uttamairjayati, Cat. Ind. Coins, Cupta* p. 15. This is found given in exactly the same manner in the line of Kālidāsa *kaumudvateyaḥ kumudāvadātair dyām ārjitām karmabhir āruroha, Raghuvaṁṣa* 18, 3.

The ideal of the king in ancient India was not to live for himself but for the weal and welfare of his people. All his great quali-ties were for the good of others *sarve tasyāsan parārthaikaphalā guṇāḥ, Raghuvaṁśa* 1 , 24, Thus he was a parent to his subjects who were almost his offspring: *sa pitā pitaras tāsām kevālam janmahetavaḥ, Raghuvaṁśa* 1, 24. The words used in India were *prajā* meaning offspring and *rājā* one who gladdened *tathaiva so'bhud anvartho rājā prakṛtirañjanāt, Raghuvaṁśa,* 4, 12. The king milked the earth of her resources to perform such sacrifices as would bring welfare for his subjects and, in turn, the celestials pleased, Indra sent timely showers to assure him agricultural prosperity; both the terrestrial and celestial lords thus exchanging their resources with a great good will: *dudoha gām sayajñyāya sasyāya maghavā divam sampadvini-mayenobhau dadhatur bhuvanadvayam, Raghuvaṁśa* 1, 26.

The king as a sacrificer, mainly for the good of his people, is shown prominently making offerings in the holy fire. This aspect of the king is indicated in the *chatra* type of coin of Chandragupta II where the stress is more on the suzerainty of the sovereign who had made himself the sole enjoyer of the only umbrella on earth. The king is making offerings in the fire with three fiames leaping up from the fire altar, *dakṣiṇāgni*, *āhavanīyāgni* and *gārhapatyāgni*. The inspirers of this motif, the earlier coins of the Kuṣāṇas like Kaniṣka (Fig. 84*)*, Huviṣka and Vāsudeva, show only this aspect of the king as a sacrificer, introducing to us an interesting chapter in history where the foreign Scythians, completely acclimatized to Hindu religion and ritual, take a pride in performing Vedic sacrifices, apart from their indicating their mind towards deities which include Hindu, both Brahmanical and Buddhist, Iranian and Greek, a rare spirit of assimilation of ideas and ideals.

On the coins of Chandragupta I there is a rare representation, the king and queen together on the obverse (Fig. 85*)*. It is usually the king that is shown and the imprinting of the queen's figure is rather rare. There are instances known but of very rare occurrence. Hermaios, the last of the Indo-Greek kings, has a special silver issue showing the bust of his queen Kalliope along with his on the obverse. It is interesting that Kumāragupta revived the practice of showing the king and queen on the coin which was continued by Skandagupta also. This type however is so rare that there is only one known of Kumāragupta from the Bayana hoard, though there are a few of Skandagupta that have survived.

Chandragupta I took pride in his Licchavi alliance and the princess of that family that gave him dignity was pictured along with him on his coin. The legends give both their names. On the reverse is Lakṣmī with her feet resting on lotus, carrying the cornucopia or the horn of plenty, and seated on lion signifying thereby that she is on a *siṁhāsana* and is Rājyalakṣmī. Here in the concept of Rājyalakṣmī is a fusion of Śrī, goddess of Fortune and Bhū, goddess of the Earth making up Rājyaśrī or Royal Fortune. In her right hand is a noose the instrument of *daṇḍa* or power, enabling punishment where required, and in her left the cornucopia, the receptacle of *kośa* or treasure and remind us of Kālidāsa's description of Kṣiti or Pṛthvī as producing a full treasure and army complete in every respect in the context of Sītā's giving birth to Kuśa and Lava: *sutāvasūta sampannau kośadaṇḍāviva kṣitiḥ. Raghuvaṁśa* 15, 13. The coin as a whole is in the fullest sense intended to convey the spirit of Kālidāsa's ideal of the principal queens of a king, who considered himself truly wedded only by his noblest anointed queen and the goddess of Royal Fortune, though his harem abounded in damsels: *kalatravantam ātmānam avarodhe mahatyapi tayā mene manasvinyā lakṣmyā cha vasudhādhipaḥ, Raghuvaṁśa* 1, 32. The principal queen and the lady of Royal Fortune are clearly represented on the coin, one on the obverse and the other on the reverse. The queen in flesh and blood being the *manasvinī* is shown in close contact with the king being present on the same side opposite him. In the king and queen type of coin of Skandagupta this is repeated except that Lakṣmī on the reverse is seated on a lotus in this case and carries the lotus in her left hand instead of the cornucopia, which does not alter the sense in any way, as the lotus symbolizes the *Padmanidhi,* the most important of the nine principal treasures.

Yet another coin introduces a third consort for the king. It a gold coin from Jessore (Fig. 86*)* which has not been definitely attributed to any Gupta monarch and is tenatively given under the coins of Śaṛāṅka. It bears very interesting figures on both the obverse and reverse and on the latter the legend *narendrāditya.* On the obverse the king is shown seated on a lion throne attended by a damsel on either side. On the reverse goddess Lakṣmī stands with lotus in her hand and surrounded by lotuses in bud and bloom beside her; in front of her near her feet is a swan. To correctly understand this coin one has to remember Kālidāsa's verse giving Sunandā's description of the prince of Aṅga who was at once the abode of the goddess of Prosperity and of Learning *nisargabhinnāspadam ekasamstham asmin dvayam śrīśca sarasvatī ca kāntyā girā sūnṛtayā ca yogyā tvam eva kalyāṇi tayos tritīyā, Raghuvaṁśa* 6, 29. The presence of Sarasvatī and Lakṣmī together is so rare and difficult that the poet of the Khajuraho inscription of Dhangadeva expresses amazement that Chandella Harsha should combine in himself such opposites: *yatra śris ca sarasvatī ca sahite. . . tasyānantaguṇasya vismayanidheḥ kim nāma vastustumaḥ, Epigraph Ind.* 1, p. 122f. The reverse explains the second half of Kālidāsa's verse wherein Sunandā asks princess Indu-matī to be his third spouse along with the other two goddesses as she was well fitted by her sweet address and beauty of form. The lotuses and the swan symbolize beauty and sweet address: and through the figure of the goddess there is the suggestion that the form of the queen is comparable to the goddess of Royal Fortune herself.

In this context Kālidāsa aptly remarks that Śrī and Sarasvatī who usually dwell apart have come together in the case of the gifted prince. That is how the queen could be a third to them. The idea of an accomplished prince basking in the sunshine of royal prosperity is used to advantage by Bāṇa who describes Harṣavardhana eulogi-zingly as being the abode of the two goddesses, to whom he has apportioned their spheres by a boundary line, formed as it were, by the pearl necklace on his neck indicating the face or rather the mouth as Sarasvatī, seat of learning, the broad chest being the sphere of Lakṣmī or Royal Prosperity: *śri sarasvatyor urovadanopabhogavi-bhāgasūtreṇeva pātitena śesheṇeva ca tadbhujastambhavinyastasama-stabhūbhāralabdhaviśrāntisukhaprasuptena hāradaṇdena parivalitakan-dharam, Harshacarita* 2, p.73. The prince seated on the lion throne flanked by the two goddesses wears a pearl necklace exactly answering this description.

A unique coin of Chandragupta II, of which only one example was found in the Bayana hoard, is an excellent example of a numismatic commentary on the emperorhood of the Guptas. It shows the emperor receiving three pellets from the *puruṣa* on the *cakra,* Sudarśana, the wheel of Kṛṣna personifiied (Fig 87*)*. Here again it is a suggestion of the suzerain king receiving the blessing of ernperorhood from the Sudarśana *cakra.* The three *śaktis,* most important for a king, are the essentials that build up his power and majesty. They are great *sampattis.* The birth of Raghu in all his glory is described by Kālidāsa as the reassurance of *sampatti* of Rājyalakśmī or royal Prosperity. The *śaktis* are *prabhu, mantra* and *utsāha*: *asūta putram samaye śacīsamā trisādhanā śaktir ivārtham akṣayam, Raghuvaṁśa* 3,13. The three pellets offered by the *Cakra-puruṣa* are these.

One of the greatest medieval emperors who was styled *sakalada-kṣiṇāpatheśvara,* contemporary of Harshavardhana who was *uttarāpatheśvara,* was Pulakeśn who by his abundance in the three *śaktis prabhu, mantra* and *utsāha* conquered and reestablished the kings in all directions, adored the gods and learned *dviias* and ruled from his city of Vātāpī the entire earth with the ocean as its moat: *utsāha-prabhumantraśaktisahite yasmin samastā diśo jitvā bhūmipatīn visṛjya mahitān arādhya devadviiān vātāpīm nagarīm praviśya nagarīm ekām ivorvīm imām cañcanniradhinīlanīraparikhām satyāśraye śāsati, Epi-graph. Ind.* 6 p. 6.

The legend on the reverse of the coin is *cakravikrama* which is pregnant with meaning in the context of Chandragupta's vast empire and power. The *Ahirbudhnya Samhitā* as Agrawala has pointed out (*J.S.S. I.* 16, p. 97-101*)* assures the status of an emperor to one that worships *Cakra purusha*: *asya cakrasya madhye yad vartate puruṣaḥ paraḥ tasmānnigaayate loke cakravartīti sūribhiḥ tasmād abhyarcayed etat yo rājā bhaktisamyutaḥ śocireṇaiva kālena cakrāvartitvam āpnuyāt, Ahirbudhnya Samhitā* 36, 23-25.

In the context of the *cakra* and the so-called Ujjain symbol indicating te conquest of the earth up to the snores of the four oceans, enabling the victor to set in motion his wheel of power as *cakravar-tin*, exactly like the ideal mythical emperor Māndhātā, ahead of whom ever moved the *cakra* from one *dvīpa* to another according to the *Mandhātu jātaka* up to heaven itself, *mandhātā cakkaratnam abbhukkiritvā attano parisāya parivito tāvātimsābhimukho pāyāsi,* the die-struck rectangular copper coin of Sujyeshtha, third king of the Śunga family (Fig. 64*)* from the Ajit Ghose collection is interesting *(J.N.S.I.* 16, p. 59-60*)*. On the obverse is shown the king riding a prancing horse preceded by one holding a *gharghari* or water vessel. On the top between the Ujjain symbol and an eight-petalled lotus-shaped *cakra* is a Brāhmī legend *sujeṭhasa* in characters of the second century B.C. On the reverse is a graceful figure of *Cajalakṣmī* standing on lotus, holding a lotus in her right hand and bathed by a pair of elephants bringing to our mind *niyujyamānā ca gajais suhastā lakṣmīs tathā padmini padmahastā, Rāmāyaṇa* 5,7,14. The line of the *Srisūkta, lakṣmīr divyair gajcndrair maṇigaṇakhacitais snāpitā hemakumbhair nityam sā padmahastā mama vasatu gṛhe sarvamāṅgalyayuktā* is also admirably answered. In the *Jātaka* there was always one who led the way as the wheel moved. The generosity of the *dharmavijayī* emperor who was free from greed and gave lavishly establishing opposing kings in greater pomp after vanquishing them is all conveyed by the monarch on horseback with the attendant holding water vessel preceding him, the water vessel for pouring water on the donee's palm to solemnize every gift made.

There is a category of coins that reveals the personality of the sovereign. The special qualities and accomplishments in which the prince prided are stressed individually in each variety of coins. Princes were given a liberal education in literature and all the fine arts like music, dance, painting, sculpting. In the *Rāmāyaṇa* Rāma is described as well-versed in *vaihārika śilpas* and as an adept in music: *vaihārikāṇām śilpānām vet tā, Rāmāyaṇa* 2, 1, 27; *gāndharve ca bhuvi śreṣṭhaḥ, Rāmāyaṇa* 2, 12, 35. The word *vaihārika śilpa* connotes the sense of hobby, an art for amusing oneself. It was also called *vinodasthāna*. Dushyanta remarks that the *vinodasthāna,* the picture of Śakuntalā painted by him, is only half done: *ardhalikhitam idam vinodasthānam asmābhiḥ., Abhijñanaśākuntalam* 6. In the *Mṛcchakatika* Cārudatta remarks that the lyre is a gem but only it is not from the ocean: *viṇā hi nāmāsamudrotthitam ratnam, Mṛcchakatika* I . It is a *vinodasthāna* as it beguiles the mind. In the *Kathāsaritsāgara* is the description of Naravāhanadatta playing the harp as his consort the princess danced. A greater musician than Udayana is unknown to Sanskrit literature. Mahendravarman was an adept in music and his Kudimiāmalai inscription reveals this, as also his titles like *saṅkīrnajāti*, *citrakārapuli*, *mattavilāsa* and *vicitracitta* proclaiming his proficiency respectively in music, painting, poetic skill and versatile accomplishments. Harsha mentions himself an accomplished poet *śrīharsho nipuṇaḥ kaviḥ parishad apyeshā guṇagrāhiṇi Nāgānanda* 1,3. In the Girnār inscription the accomplishment of Mahākṣtrapa Rudradāman in literature, music and other noble arts is mentioned: *śabdārthagāndharvanyāyādyānām vidyānām mahatīnām pāraṇadhāraṇaviiñānaprayogāvāptavipulakīrtinā rudradāmnā* (*Epigraph. Ind.* 8, p. 36f*)* In the famous Allāhābād inscription of Śamudragupta, the great emperor's proficiency in music is described as putting to shame the preceptor of the celestial king, Tumburu, Nārada and others by his keen trained intellect, and subtle variations in musical modes: *niśitavidagdhamatigāndharvalalitalr vrīḍitatridaśapatigurutumburunāradādeḥ, C. Inscr. Ind.* 3, p. 8.

This is substantiated by the picture on the obverse of the lyrist type of coin of Samudragupta (Fig. 88*)* where the king is shown seated on a couch with the lyre in his lap, his fingers thrumming the strings of the instruments, and legend clearly giving his name *mahārājādhirājaśrīsamudraguptaḥ*. The lyre resting on the king's lap does certainly recall Kālidāsa's verse: *aṅkam aṅkaparivartanocite tasya ninyatur aśūnyatām ubhe vallakī ca hṛdayaṅgamasvanā valguvāg api ca vāmalocanā, Raghuvaṁśa* 19, 13. Kumāragupta emulated his grandfather in this and his lyrist coin, a rare one found in the Bayana hoard, is interesting.

On the couch type of coin of Chandragupta II, the king is shown seated on a couch with a lotus in his right hand, the left resting on the seat, one leg tucked up and the other resting on the bejewelled footstool. (Fig. 89). The legend *rūpākṛti* given below the couch is very significant as it emphasises his beauty. The main legend gives him as Chandragupta II, *devaśrīmahārājādhirāja śrī candraguptasya.* No better picture can be found to answer the description of the sportive prince, prince charming, with the lotus in his hand. The lotus in his hand and his leisurely attitude symbolize his aesthetic taste and his life of ease and pleasure.

To understand this we have only to turn to the description of one of the lovely princes assembled at the *svayamvara* of Indumatī, who gently turns a sportive lotus held in his hand by its long stalk, its moving petals warding off the bees around and its pollen inside *kaścid karābhyām upagūḍhanālam ālolapatrābhihatadvirepham rajobhir antaḥ pariveṣabandhi lilāravindam bhramayāmcakāra, Raghuvaṁśa* 6, 13. This was almost to indicate to the princess his sportive spirit and aesthetic taste.

Every prince in India was a trained warrior and a fearless sportsman. We know of how Ulysses, so fond of hunting, was gored by a boar and bore a scar through which, even when he was in disguise when back home after ever so long, he could be recognized by his aged nurse.

A graphic description of Daśaratha's hunt in the *Raghuvaṁśa* and of Chandrāpīḍa in the *Kādambarī* are classical examples. There is a picturesque account of the special dress of the prince in green, even his hair tied up with a sylvan garland, which so camouflaged him to throw the wild animals off their scent: *grathitamaulir asau vanamālayā tarupalāśasavarṇatanuccadaḥ, Raghuvaṁśa* 9, 51. The king, as the poet puts it, lightened the head of the rhinoceros by cutting and relieving it of its horn, and being gracious even allowed it to run away, as he was unable to endure the towering horn of a proud opponent whom he would just subdue without any intention on his span of life: *prāyo viṣāṇaparimokṣalaghūttamāṅgān khaḍgāmśca-kāra nṛpatlr niśitaiḥ kṣurapraiḥ śṛṅgam sa dṛptavinayādhikṛtaḥ pareshām atyucchritam na mamṛshe na tu dīrgham āyuḥ, Raghu-vaṁśa* 9, 62. The attitude of the hunting prince bent forward from his horse as he engaged the wild animal is also again given vividly in a revealing line *tam vāhanād avanatottarakāyam īshad vidhyantam uddhatasaṭāḥ pratihantum iṣuḥ, Raghuvaṁśa* 9, 60.

When studied with the vivid description in mind the *khaḍga* coin of Kumāragupta (Fig. 90), a rare issue found in the Bayana hoard, fully reveals its import where the royal hunter has the forepart of his body bent as he attacks the rhino that turns back to face his opponent cutting his horn. The legend *bhartā khadgatrātā kumāragupto jayatyaniśam, Cat. Cupta*

Coins, Bayana Hoard, p. 296. is equally illuminating. *Khadgatrātā* does not mean protecting from the rhino. The rhinoceros is not so potential a danger to his subjects that it should be so understood. It is rather the sense of his cutting only its horn and allowing it to live, though he is a hunting, that is as Kālidāsa has put it, just symbolic of his destroying the pride of his foes with no intent on their life. Apart from the praise of the prince as an able sportsman it individually proclaims him a subduer of the proud but a benevolent restorer of territory and giver of a long lease of life to the humbled ones. The region of the rhino, Assam and eastern India is indicated as subdued and included in his empire, a subtle suggestion.

On the reverse is imprinted the form of personified Gaṅgā standing on her vehicle, the *makara,* with her right hand in *abhaya* and with an attendant woman holding up a *chatra* or umbrella for her as it is held for the king in the *chatra* type of coin of Chandragupta II. This is again very significant. The king suggests his empire extended up to the region of Assam by the representation of the rhino on the obverse. The figure of Gaṅgā shows his pride and joy in bringing under his sway the entire region of the Gaṅgā beyond which comes Assam. The hand of the river goddess in *abhaya* shows the emperor's attitude towards Gangā as to a mother. We have to bring to our mind the feeling of Rāma approaching Sarayū mentioning her as the common mother of all the children of their riverine area : *yām saikatotsaṅganiveśitānām prājyaiḥ payobhiḥ pariva-rdhitānām sāmānyadhātrīm iva mānasam me sambhāvayatyu-ttarakosalā-nām, Raghuvaṁśa,* 13, 62. As she is almost a mother, nourishing the children of the soil on her dunes with an abundance of water (*payobhiḥ*) like a mother her child on her lap with abundant breast-milk, the river-fed area is called *nadīmātṛka*. Amarasiṁha clearly defines *deśo nadyambuvṛshtyambusampannavrīhipālitaḥ syānnadīmātṛko deva-mātṛkaśca yathākramam, Amarakośa* 2, 1, 13. Another emperor who brought abundant water of Gaṅgā to his capital to justify his title *Caṅgaikoṇḍa* similarly expressed his joy by the issue of a commemorative coin with the title he assumed *Caṅgaikoṇda* spelt on it.

The well known silver coin of Mihira Bhoja of the Gurjara Pratīhāra family (Fig. 91*),* with the boar incarnation of Viṣṇu imp-rinted on the reverse and with the legend *śrimadādivarāha* on the obverse, is interesting, when we find that the king compared himself to Viṣṇu himself and assumed the title of *Ādivarāha*, satisfied that he upheld the earth just like Varāha. The Kuṣāṇa king Kadphises II, who compared himself and even identified himself with Śiva, represented on his coin, reveals the extent to which fondness to glorify oneself could go. It is no wonder Bāna laughs at kings or princes, flattered by sycophants, that imagine themselves to be the very celestials named and look for the additional pair of arms as somewhere hidden inside their shoulders : *manasā devatādhyāropaṇād asadbhūtā-sambhāvanopahatās cāntaḥpravishtāparabhujadvayam ivātmabāhuyugalam sambhāvayanti*, *Kādambarī*, p. 178. But the idea of kings emulating Varāha was all the time present. That is how the Guptas, great devotees of Viṣṇu, sought to represent the most monumental sculpture of Varāha at Udayagiri at the heyday of their power. There are many allusions to Varāha lifting up Pṛthvī and the kings succeeding in acting exactly like him in delivering the earth almost from a deluge. Even rescuing of Sītā from Rāvaṇa is so compared : *tām iśvareṇa jagatām pralayād ịvorvīm varṣ-ātyayena rucam abhraghanād iṇvendoḥ rāmeṇamaithilasutām daṛakaṇthakṛcchrāt pratyudd-*

hṛtām dhṛtimatīm bharato vavande, Raghuvaṁśa 13, 77. Udayāditya, that succeeded Paramāra Bhoja, when the kingdom was overrun by floods as it were, in which the sovereign was submerged and delivered the earth again from the mighty ocean of troublous kings, and Karna aided by the Karṇātas that lorded over for a while, did indeed act like the Varāha: *tasmin vāsavabandhutām upagete rājye ca kulyākule magnasvāmini tasya bandhur udayādityobhavad bhūpatiḥ yenoddhṛtya mahārṇavopa-mamilatkarṇātakarṇaprabhum urvīpālakadarthitām bhuvam imām śrīma-dvarāhāyitam, Epigraph. Ind.* 2, p. 185.

On the 16th of February 1515 a beautiful image of seated Bāla-kṛṣṇa in greenish black granite was installed in a temple specially built for it by Kṛṣṇadevarāya at Hampi, his capital. It was a trophy brought from Udayagiri near Nellore after his victory over the Gajapati. A lengthy inscription has recorded this great event. The famous king Kṛṣṇarāya conquered Udayagiri and from there tact-fully brought away to his city an image of the deity Kṛṣṇa and consecrated it in a jewelled *maṇḍapa* according to Śāstraic rules in the year Bhava, (corresponding to) Saka 1436. Hail Prosperity. In the prosperous Śālivāhana Śaka 1436, the year Bhava, on Friday the third day of the bright fortnight of the month of Phālguna Mahārājādhirāja Rājaparameśvara Śrī Vīrapratāpa Śrī Vīra Kṛṣṇarāya Mahārāja brought victoriously from Udayagiri and consecrated the image of Śrī Bālakṛṣṇa. At the time of the consecration he presented it with a variety of jewels inlaid with the nine kinds of gems and other articles (vessels) in silver and gold. For the worship of the deity, for waving of lamps, offering of fruits, cakes and other daily offerings, Pañcaparva car festival and offerings for Brāhmanas, for *aṅgaraṅgavibhoga,* the following villages are given, *S. Ind. Inscr. No. 254, 255 soyam śrīvarakṛṣṇarāyanṛpatir jitvodayādrim tataḥ kṛṣṇam devam upāyatas svanagarīm nītvā maṇīmaṇtape śālīyābdara-sāgnivedavidhuyugbhāve tavasye site tārtīye divase vṛṣepi vṛdhival pau-ṣṇe pratiṣṭhām vyadhāt, S. Ind. Inscr.* 4, p. 47.

The historic image dug out of the debris of the temple and now in the Madras Museum can be understood in all its significance only through this long contemporary record and the empty ruined Kṛṣṇa temple at Udayagiri itself whence it was brought.

But there is another and more interesting evidence of the gen-uineness of this find. A gold coin with this Bālakṛṣṇa's figure imprinted on it (Fig. 92) and with the legend giving his name *pratāpa kṛṣṇarāya* was issued by the emperor for distribution on that occasion and later several reprints of it have been issued. For a long time the figure on this coin was wrongly identified as Durgā and it was styled *durgi* pagoda. The inscription that mentions the circumstances of the consecretion of the image and the complete figure of Bālakṛṣṇa on the coin compared with the image with broken arms reveals the identity of both the coin and the sculpture.

There are two rare gold coins of Akbar. One shows a hawk on the obverse with ornamental design all around (Fig. 93) and the *ilāhi* year, the divine epoch of Akbar, on the reverse reading, *Allāhu Akbar 45 Isjandarmeez Ilāhi Zarb Azir.* This is a rare innovation in Muslim coinage where so far there had been no portrayal of bird, animal or portrait of man. The hawk is only a symbol of Akbar's passion for hunting. Abul-Fazl has recorded in his *Āin-i-Akbarī* any number of hunting expeditions of Akbar where he had bravely fought tigers, lions, cheetas, elephants, buffaloes, not to talk of the lesser denizens of the forest. Akbar's fondness for hawks and hawk-hunting has also been faithfully recorded by Abu-l-Fazl. He says 'His Majesty is very fond of the remarkable animals, and often uses them for hunting purposes. Though he trains the *baz, shahen, shungar* and *burkat* falcons, and makes them perform wonderful deeds, His Majesty prefers the *basha,* to which class of hawks he gives various names' (*Ain-i-Akbarī* p. 304). After describing at length the special attention paid by the emperor to these varieties of the hunting bird, Abu-l-Fazl explains that 'His Majesty, from motives of generosity and from a wish to add splendour to his Court, is fond of hunting with falcons, though superficial observers think that merely hunting is his object' (*Ainṣi Akbarī* p. 305). He goes on to elaborate the department of huntsmen engaged for this, their pay and food, allowances, prices of falcons and so on. The representation of the hawk on the coin is to be understood in a suggestive sense of the emperor's general enthusiasm for hunting and not just hawk-hunting, as the hawk itself as a symbol of hunting added splendour to the Court as Abu-l-Fazl puts it.

The coin showing the duck (Fig. 94), an equally interesting and beautiful one aesthetically, shows as in the earlier one the bird on the obverse in an ornamental field and the *ilāhi* year on the reverse reading *Allāhu Akbar 50 KhurdadIlāhi Zarb Agrah*. Akbar was as we know from the *Ain-i-Akbarī* the most appreciative of God's creation. In fact he justifies his encouragement of artists against the accepted orthodox forbidding of imitating the forms of God's creation. His plea has been wonderfully put by Abu-l-Fazl 'One day at a private party of friends, His Majesty, who had conferred on several the pleasure of drawing near him remarked: 'There are many that hate painting; but such men I dislike. It appears to me as if a painter had quite a peculiar means of recognising God; for a painter in sketching anything that has life, and in devising its limbs, one after the other, must come to feel that he cannot bestow individuality upon his work, and is thus forced to think of God, the giver of life, and will thus increase in knowledge' (*Ain-i-Akbarī* p. 115),

It is seen thus that he appreciated the best work done of birds, animals, even plants and flowering shrubs. The duck, the hawk, the elephant, the goat and several other birds and animals have been portrayed by the famous galaxy of painters in the Court of Akbar and Jehāngir. The duck is only a symbol of the emperor's appreciation of painting from nature.

Jehāngir has a type of gold coin that is unparalleled in Muslim coinage. It has a portrait of his (Fig. 95,96). It is not only one, but the type has been issued in more than one form. One variety shows the emperor's bust in profile, another almost facing the spectator, and a third again in profile but more elaborate and up to the waist in a square frame in the circular coin. The emperor here holds a wine cup. It is not surprising that Jehāngir had issued this. It correctly represents him as a candid and truthful monarch who made no pretence of what he was not. It is indeed touching to read the frank confessions of a monarch so good as to admit his weakness for drink and his attempt to overcome the passion at least to an extent.

In his *Tuzuk-i-Jahāngirī,* the emperor says, he has given twelve orders to be observed as rules of conduct in all his dominions. The fifth of these is 'they should not make wine or rice spirit (*dilbahra*) 'exhilarating drink,' or any kind of intoxicating drug or sell them; although I myself drink wine, and from the age of eighteen years till now, when I am thirtyeight, have persisted in it, when I first took a liking to drinking, I sometimes took as much as twenty cups of double-distilled spirit, when by degrees it acquired a great influence over me. I endeavoured to lessen the quantity, and in the period of seven years I have brought myself from fifteen cups to five or six. My times for drinking were varied; sometimes when three or four sidereal hours of the day remained I would begin to drink, and sometimes at night and partly by day. This went on till I was thirty years old. After that I took to drinking always at night. Now I drink only to digest my food.'

The other and the most spectacular series of coins issued by Jehāngir is the Zodiacal ones (Fig. 97). We know from *Akbar Nāma* that Akbar had great faith in stars. The planetary position at the time of the birth of Akbar and also at the time of his ascension to the throne is elaborately discussed by Abu-1-Fazl. Similarly the auspicious moment of the birth of Jehāngir has been elaborated. It is no wonder that born under such influences .Jehāngir took a delight in glorifying the signs of the zodiac during the twelve months as the Sun moved from one to another and in a way extolled the *ilāhi* started by his father. These are also, as examples of art, aesthetically perfect. As a great patron of art it is not at all a wonder that Jehāngir envisaged the form of each one of the zodiacal signs. The zodiacal sign against the radiating solar disc on each of the twelve varieties, the lion and the rising sun on the reverse of the portrait type (Fig. 96) are superb examples of numismatic excellence in aesthetic representation.

FOOTNOTES

1. O-C. Sivaramamurty: Sourecces g Hstory. Illumined by luteratune, pp. 44-78, 1979 Delhi

CHAPTER IV

WEIGHTS AND COIN DENOMINATIONS

A piece of coin does an important service to the community ; it is a mark of its high economic development and embodies in it three definite ideas. It is a piece of metal of definite weight, has a mark or marks of authorisation preferably of the state, testifying to the weight and purity of the metal and serves the purpose of a medium of exchange. The evolutionary process by which this stage is reached is a long one and it is a strange fact that some of the highly civilised nations of antiquity did not reach this stage.[1]

The evolution in the connotation of the term Niṣka will exemplify the different steps by which coinage came to be established in India. It is one of the oldest words and perhaps may be pre-Vedic. At first it signified a necklace, and we know that ornaments came into use at a very early stage in the civilisation of man and surely before the Vedic culture which is mainly agricultural.[2] Its use was very general as can be well-expected, and in the early society, Niṣka, the necklace[3] served as a medium of exchange like cow, rice and wampum beads. When this early stage was passed, the difference in weight of different Niṣkas had to be taken into account, and the necessity arose for the standardisation of the Niṣka which was now equated to a definite weight of metal. The necklace as a medium of exchange was replaced by a lump of metal which was one Niṣka in weight. Gradually sub-multiples came into use and exchange transactions were conducted with the help of lumps of metals weighing a Niṣka or its sub-multiples. The metal was surely gold which India produced in profusion in an early period and which must have attracted the admiration of primitive men by its bright yellow colour. That in the Vedic period, the Niṣka had progressed to weight,[4] there cannot be the least shadow of doubt. But the next stage in the evolution of coinage at so early state of culture is a. highly debatable one. Prof. Bhandarkar puts forward a strong claim that the Niṣka as a coin is the product of the Vedic period.[5] His arguments cannot be taken as conclusive in the total absence of any extant piece of gold coin of an early age,[6] and much depends upon what he takes to be the connotation of the term. That the Niṣkas were subdivided into pādas[7] and that they were round in shape[8] can very well be conceded ; but the rotundity cannot prove much ; lumps of metals in the shape of globules or spherules may well have changed hands as mediums of exchange. Moreover, we cannot suppose that gold, however plentiful it might be in the Vedic period, served as a medium of exchange, at least for ordinary purposes. Even at a late period we find the cow[9] or a measure of grain[10] to be the common medium for business purposes and even in the 20th century A.D. in India, silver coin is the standard and gold

Mohurs are nothing but curiosities to the common people. So Niṣka had only one characteristic of a coin, namely, it was a piece of metal of definite weight ; there might have been some signs like dots etc. either impressed by the shroffs or by the king guaranteeing the weight and purity, but there can be no doubt that the economic condition of the time precluded the idea of using it as a medium of exchange, at least for ordinary purposes. When coinage was evolved, it was copper which was requisitioned for the purpose and the seeming absurdity of the statement disappears when we consider its comparative paucity in those early days and the high value which was consequently attached to it. Prof. Bhandarkar shows "that copper in early times had comparatively much greater value than it possessel at present,"[11] and he points out that a Kārṣāpaṇa, the standard coin at Vidiśā was "equivalent to 20 modern pice, that is, five annas, although its weight is not even double that of a pice."[12] The process of depreciation must have been very gradual and the price of copper was surely at an earlier period high enough for the ordinary purposes of exchange. If it is once conceded that gold coinage in the ordinary sense of the word was preceded by copper, a consideration of the weight system will clearly prove that silver was requisitioned at a later period when a higher economic development had been secured. Silver was mainly imported from abroad[13] and so its paucity stood in the way of its use for the manufacture of coins. Some of the states in ancient India—Vidiśā, the Mālavas etc., retained copper coins only even though silver had come into use in the neighbouring states.[14] The early Buddhist Literature dating from the 6th and 7th cent. B.C. knows nothing of the silver coins, the Dharaṇas or the Purāṇas.[15] Taking all these things together, the inference that copper came earlier into use than silver in India for coinage is practically irresistible.

The weight of the Niṣkas, the necklaces naturally varied, but when a greater nicety was demanded with the progress of civilisation, the Niṣka weight had to be standardised. Niṣka weight was the original unit of measurement but such a big lump of gold equivalent in weight to a neck-ornament must have a value too high for purposes of exchange. It had to be sub-divided into sections and sub-sections and the whole system had to be based upon a unit of measurement, small and convenient enough for the economic state of the society. A clue to it is supplied by the Tables of Ancient Indian Weights in Manu and Yājñavalkya.[16] A Niṣka of gold is equated to 320 ratis which is also the weight of a Śatamāna of silver. Śatamāna was of gold in the Śatapatha Brāhmaṇa[17] and is referred to not only in the Taittirīya Brāhmaṇa but also in the Taittiriya Saṁhitā which forms the Saṁhitā text of the, Kṛṣṇa Yajur-Veda.[18] Śatamāna is evidently 100 times the unit of measurement which is therefore 3.2 ratis or 5.6 grains in weight taking a Sata-Māna equal to 320 ratis as given by Manu. This is in opposition to the views of Prof. Keith and others who want to identify the Māna, the unit of Śatamāna to a rati which weighs only 1.8 grains.[19] This is surely not reasonable when we find that the first mention of the Raktika or Kṛṣṇala occurs in the Brāhmaṇa period only, in the Taittiriya Brāhmaṇa.[20] As would be natural for us to expect the old unit, the Māna of 5.6 grains would surely be deemed too heavy with the progress of society and a smaller one would be necessary for a nicer discrimination ; and I shall try to show that this smaller unit of rati was adopted when coins for the first time, mainly of copper, came to be issued to the people.

We know that "in all countries the common measures have been derived from natural objects ;"[21] and that the Indian measures of weight are all based on seeds and beans—the Raktika, the barley-corn, the Māṣa bean etc. Now our position will be almost unassailable if we can identify any such natural object which was used as a unit of measurement in ancient India equal in weight to a Māna. In Northern India Rati as the unit had established itself at the time of Manu but in Southern India it "did not come into use till a later period,"[22] and there the Māṇjāḍi occupied the same position in the system of weights. According to Elliot "Māṇjāḍi claims the first notice, as being the earliest used as a measure of weight. It is the seed of the Adenanthera pavonina, a tree common in most parts of India and the Eastern Archipelago."[23] The weight of a Māṇjāḍi has been shown by elaborate estimates to be a little less than 5.7 grains as opined by Cunningham and somewhat higher than Elliot's own average of 4.8 grains.[24] So we can be practically sure that the Māṇjāḍi would approximate to 5.6 grains and 100 Māṇjāḍi would give us the Śatamāna of 560 grains or a little less—the closest approximation that we can have, dependent upon the size and the 'condition of the Māṇjāḍi seeds. The Niṣka or Śatamāna system of measurement affords the clue to the satisfactory solution of the mystery in the employment of Dharaṇas of 32 ratis side by side with the copper Kārṣāpaṇa of 80 ratis, and in the two separate Tables of Weights—one for the precious metals, gold and silver, and the other for copper.[25] The Māna unit of 5.6 grains is applicable only to the precious metals ; it is older in origin and heavier in weight, while the rati unit of 1.8 grains came into use later and gradually supplanted the older unit in Northern India and pushed itself to the South also. But already in the North, the subdivisions of the precious metals were based upon the Māna unit and when silver coins were issued these were equated in weight to the submultiples of the Śatamāna which had been used from an earlier time. Thus there was a silver Dharaṇa of 32 ratis weight, 56 grains which is exactly 1/10th of Śatamāna, while half a Dharaṇa would be equal to 1/20th of a Śatamāna. Such a low subdivision was necessitated by the economic condition of the country ; the heavier weights would have been too valuable for common exchange purposes. The silver punch-marked coins of this weight and their sub-multiples had been unearthed in thousands in all parts of India. Gold coins of approximately the weight of a Dharaṇa are the Kaḷanju of the South which is theoretically 10 Māṇjāḍis in weight but actually a little less, 52 grains ; and these are "spherules quite plain and smooth, save for a single very minute punch-mark too small to be identified."[26]

While discussing the weight of the silver Dharaṇa and trying to identify it with Kārṣāpaṇa weight of ratis Prof. Bhandarkar is confronted with a serious difficulty—"No rational objection can therefore be raised to Dharaṇa of Kauṭilya's description denoting the real silver Kārṣāpaṇa. But here we are confronted with another question. If Dharaṇa was up till the time of Kauṭilya equal to one Karṣa, why did it suffer a diminution shortly after as is clearly evinced by the actual specimens of Purāṇas we have obtained which weigh not 146 grains like a karṣa but 58 grains only. Those who have read Cunningham's book entitled "Coins of Ancient India" must be familiar with his remark that India produced little or no silver. Kauṭilya, on the other hand, speaks of many varieties of silver, and in no place gives us the impression that it was scarce in his time. Is it possible that shortly after Kauṭilya the sources of producing silver in India began to fail and that consequently as silver became scarce and increased in value, the Purana had to be diminished in weight?"[27] But we have to bear in mind that no extant piece of silver coin of 146 grains in weight, anterior to the time of Kauṭilya had been discovered or identified in India ; and there is no reason assigned why this arbitrary standard of 32 ratis, and not a sub-multiple of 80 ratis *e.g.*, 40 or 20 ratis came to be accepted. Moreover India was never noted for its production of silver ; she had always to depend mainly on foreign countries for her supply of this metal,[28] and there is no conceivable reason why all on a sudden her small supply of indigenous silver should dry up immediately after Kauṭilya. It was exactly at this period that the foreign supply increased in volume as the trade with the West must have been accelerated by the Greek invasion of Alexander which opened up routes hitherto unknown or little used.[29] That foreign trade was an important feature in Chandragupta Maurya's administration is evident from the existence of a Board which was in charge of foreigners. "The members of the Board were required to find lodgings for foreigners, to keep them under observation, to escort them out of the country ; and in case of sickness or death to provide for the treatment or burial of the stranger, whose property they were obliged protect or account for. The existence of such officials and regulations affords conclusive proof that the Maurya Empire was in constant intercourse with foreign states and that many strangers visited the capital on business."[30] This trade with the West went on increasing and "during the early centuries of the Christian era, the Roman trade with India increased to such an extent that the annual balance in favour of India amounted to nearly half a million pounds sterling. This was made good by sending actual cash, both in gold and silver to India,"[31] and this drain of specie was bitterly condemned by Pliny.[32] So after all, the argument that after Kauṭilya the supply of silver indigenous and foreign dwindled away must be rejected and the explanation of the issue of silver coins, the Dharaṇas of 32 ratis, may properly be taken to be that it was based upon the traditional weight system for the precious metals, dependent upon the old and bigger unit of Māna. The Table of Weights that we have, may be arranged as follows : —

GOLD AND SILVER

1 Niṣka or Śatamāna	— 100 Mānas	— 560 grains.
½ Niṣka	— 50 Mānas	— 280 grains.
¼ Niṣka or pàda	— 25 Mānas	— 140 grains,
1/10 Niṣka or Dharaṇa (Purana, Salaka, Kalanju).	— 10 Mānas	— 56 grains.
1/20 Niṣka or ½Dharaṇa	— 5 Mānas	— 28 grains.
1/100 Niṣka, or Māna, or Fanam (a variant of Mānam or paṇam?)	— 1 Māna	— 5.6 grains.

The pādas are referred to in the Śatapatha Brāhmaṇa and Bohtlingk and Roth suggest that "the word pāda-denotes the fourth part of a certain gold weight but not a coin."[33] Prof. Bhandarkar assails this opinion and thinks it preposterous that on the spur of the moment 20,000 pādas of definite weight were hammered out to meet the needs of the occasion. So far this is true that the pàdas were separate pieces of metal, approximating to a certain standard weight but there is nothing to prove that these pieces bore the marks of authentication from an organised authority or that these were the common mediums of exchange; and also the number of the pieces must have been much augmented to give us an exaggerated idea of the importance attached to the matter referred to in the Śatapatha. Of the sub-division the one-tenth Śatamāna weight, we have innumerable examples—the Dharaṇas and Purāṇas of silver and the Kalanju of gold which circulated only in the South. In the early centuries of the Christian era the demand for gold coins in Northern India was met by the foreign types of the Kuṣāṇas[34] and others and later on by the Gupta coins, at first in the Kuṣāṇa standard[35] and then on the Indian standard weight. In the South, however, the foreign coins were issued to the people as these were imported to the country[36] or gold coins of indigenous origin based on the traditional weight system (the one-tenth of the Śatamāna, or a Kalanju)[37] were minted to meet the exchange demands. The oldest specimens of the extant indigenous coins of gold in Southern India weigh about 52 grains and according to Elliot they are "evidently derived from the kalanju, their original name being *pon*, which simply means gold in Tamil, becoming *hon* in Canarese, and the origin of the Mahommedan *hun* ;"[38] and he also opines that "the Purāṇa is simply a silver Kalanju."[39] The gold fanams are the Southern variant, of the "tenths" of the original "gold Karṣa" of 57.6 grains,[40] as pointed out by Cunningham and these average 5.75 grains. This is approximately the weight of a Māna —the one-hundredth part of a Niṣka. As the ratio of gold to silver under the Kuṣāṇas was 1 : 10, we find that the fanam of 5.75 grains of gold is equal in value to 57 grains of silver, the approximate weight of Karṣapaṇa. It is however to be clearly marked that no claim can be put forward about the contemporaneity of the weight denominations—the Śatamāna, the Dharaṇa, the Kalanju, the fanam etc., but that it is only pointed out that the measures of weight, the Śatamāna and its sub-multiples are constant, though the names might differ in the various parts of the country in the different periods of its history.

The smaller unit of measurement was necessitated by the economic advancement of the country which now required a finer unit in the place of bigger and necessarily the cruder unit, the Māna. This is the Rati—"The red-and-black berry of the Guñja plant (*Abrus precatorius* or wild liquorice), which is usually called *Rati* or *Raktika*, the "Red," and is also known as the Kṛṣṇala, or the "Black", from a black spot at one end."[41] Its weight varies according to the computation of the different scholars. Cunningham takes a rati as equal to 1.83 gr.[42] Elliot as 1.68 gr.[43]; Bhandarkar as 1.75[44] and Smith as 1.825.[45] The standard weight of the rati is never actually attained by the extant coins and this deficiency has to be accounted for by the wear and tear of the centuries during which these were in circulation. But a careful examination inclines me to accept Prof. Bhandarkar's weight of 1.75 grains for a rati. Eighty of these seeds came to be equated to a Karṣa, "the seed of the Belleric Myrobolan (*Terminalia Bellerica*), known as *amalaka or Karṣa-phala*, that is the "Karṣa-fruit."[46] This was the new standard and it was more convenient because it was smaller than the Śatamāna and based upon a finer unit of measurement, exactly suited to the more advanced society of the Brāhmaṇa period. This new standard unit was gradually applied to all the metals used for monetary purpose, When adopted for gold, it was called Suvarṇa—the gold Kārṣāpaṇa. But ordinarily Kārṣāpaṇa was restricted to copper., though in course of time, it became the generic expression for standard coins in all metals—gold,[47] silver,[48] copper,[49] or lead.[50] As pointed out by Prof. Rapson—"Manu seems to imply that the term was properly applied to the copper paṇa weighing a karṣa.—'*Kārṣ āpaṇas tu vijñeyas tāmrikaḥ Kārṣikaḥ paṇaḥ,*"[51] while "Nārada, quoted in the Vacaspatya, states that the silver Kārṣāpaṇa was current in the "South" "Kārṣāpaṇo dakṣiṇasyām diśi raupyah pravarttate."[52] The gold coins of the Guptas were known as the Suvarṇas and from the time of Skandagupta, coins were issued approximating to the standard weight of 80 ratis or 146 grains.[53] in Southern India "the smallest denomination of the copper currency was the *Kāsu*"[54] and "it has also the peneral significance of money, wealth and likewise of coin, as *pon-kāsu*=gold coin, *vella-kāsu*= silver coin, *semba-*(or red) *kāsu*=copper coin."[54] "The kāsu has been identified by Mr. Ellis with the Sanscrit Karṣa, and they are probably both derived from the same original source ; for according to the law-books "a karṣa or eighty ratis (raktikas) of copper is called a paṇa or karṣa paṇa"[55] Afterwards it came to be restricted to "a weight of gold or silver equal to 180 grains troy."[56]

The attempt to superimpose the new system of measurement on the older the Śatamāna system was successful when four Suvarṇas came to be definitely equated to a Śatamāna.[57] This period of transition is marked by uncertainty as regards the number of Suvarṇas that would go to a Śatamāna or Niṣka.[58] But in the time of Manu at the latest, the two systems had been equated to the new unit the rati ; though this change must have begun long before his time. The new standard, the karsha and its sub-multiples were originally restricted to copper but when silver coins also came into use, attempts were made to bring the measures peculiar to the precious metals gold and silver (Śatamāna) in a line with the prevalent and readily understandable newer system of Karṣa weight and its sub-divisions, all based on the rati.

We shall now try to determine the position of the measure Māṣaka, in the weight systems of the different metals. Cunningham points out that the Māṣaka is equated to 8, 5, 3 or 2 ratis.[59] From Manu and Yajñavalkya, we find that a silver Māṣaka is equated to a ratis.[60] But it is clear that Māṣaka is the one-sixteenth of the standard coin for the time being, whether Suvarṇa, Dharaṇa or Karṣahaṇa. Two ratis of silver is equal in weight to one Māṣa when we have the Dharaṇa of 32 ratis under discussion while it is 5 ratis when referred to the Kārṣāpaṇa of 80 ratis. The multiples of Māṣaka are Chatur-Māṣaka, Dvi-Māṣaka and the sub-multiples are the Ardha-Māṣaka and the Kakanika.[61] The standard coins where the monometallism of copper prevailed were the Kārṣāpaṇa, its multiples and sub-multiples.

THE TABLE OF WEIGHTS FOR COPPER COINS

1 Kārṣāpaṇa . . .	= 80 ratis	= 140 grains or 146 according to Cunningham.
½ Kārṣāpaṇa . . .	= 40 ratis	= 70 or 72 grains.
¼ Kārṣāpaṇa, Pada or Chatur-Māṣaka .	= 20 ratis	=35 or 36 grains.
1/8 Kārṣāpaṇa or Dvi-Māṣaka	= 10 ratis	= 17.5 or 18 grs.
1/16 Kārṣāpaṇa or Māṣaka	= 5 ratis	=8.75 or 9 grs.
1/32 Kārṣāpaṇa or ½ Māṣaka	=2½ ratis	=4.37 or 4.5 grs.
1/64 Kārṣāpaṇa or ¼ Māṣaka or 1 Kakanika	= 1¼ rati	= 2.25 grs.
1/128 Kārṣāpaṇa=1/8 Māṣaka = ½ Kakanika	= 0.62 rati	=1.12 gr.

This Table of Weights can be applicable only to those states where coins of copper were in circulation *e.g.*, in Vidiśā, among the Mālavas etc. But when silver came into use, bimetallism would necessarily require certain consequential changes, in the Artha śāstra we have the weight system of a bimetallic state with silver and copper in circulation, one linked to the other. Kauṭilya "speaks of Paṇa, Half-Paṇa, Quarter-Paṇa and One-eighth-Paṇa as silver coins, and Māṣaka, Half-Māṣaka, Kakani and Half-Kakam as copper coins."[62] From this statement Prof. Bhandarkar draws certain conclusions. Firstly he opines "that the smallest silver coin in Kauṭilya's time was One-eighth Paṇa or Kārṣāpaṇa."[63] Though there is nothing improbable in it, yet we have no extant specimens of a silver coin of this weight ; specially as Cunningham with his long experience of these coins, came definitely to the conclusion that "the tale of silver coins is limited to three sizes, the Kārṣāpaṇa, with its half and its quarter"[64] But the other conclusion that the learned Professor arrives at seems to be based on misapprehension. He goes on to prove that as a Māṣaka is equal to five ratis in weight a Half-Kakani which is 1/8th the Māṣaka must be equal to 5/8ths of a rati, that is 1.14 grain. He himself is astonished at his conclusion—"Such a thing is almost inconceivable in the present age."[65] Surely it is inconceivable for all ages. A coin weighing only 1.14 grain of copper would be too small a size for exchange purposes, and no such coin had yet been discovered in India. The natural conclusion would be that it was a nominal coin or a coin of account only which was paid not in copper but in cowries (like a ganda which is 1/5th of a pice in Bengal at present) ; but as there is no doubt about the existence of such copper coins, so these are likely to be of a heavier weight ; and this will be evident from a close examination of Kauṭilya's statement. Kauṭilya's arrangement would clearly point to the employment of the two metals, silver and copper, in which copper was linked up with silver and the copper coins were the sub-multiples of the silver coins in value only and not in weight. The Māṣaka, if it is to be connected with the silver Kārṣāpaṇa, is evidently its, 1/16th in value *i.e.* it is equal to 2 ratis of silver ; but it is a copper coin as stated by Kauṭilya. So this can be explained by taking the Māṣaka as equal to a certain weight of copper valued at two ratis of silver. The weight of copper would surely vary with the change in the ratio of two metals. Cunningham tried to establish a tentative equation in the two Tables of Weights given by him in pages 46 and 47 of his "Coins of Ancient India." We find that a silver Kārṣāpaṇa or Dharaṇa of 32 ratis is equated by him in value to 16 Kārṣāpaṇas of copper, each equalling go ratis in weight. So the ratio of silver to copper is 32: 1280 *i.e.*, 1:40. This was surely not the ratio of the two metals at the time of Kauṭilya as I shall try to prove in the Chapter on Metrology of the Indian Coins. Cunningham's ratio is even lower than the present one which approximates 1 : 36 ; and so long as the exact ratio between copper and silver at the time of Kauṭilya cannot be determined, it would be impossible for us to estimate the weight of the copper Māṣakas and Kakanis. But there can be no doubt that the Half-Kakani was much heavier than 1.14 grain, the estimate of Prof. Bhandarkar. The Māṣaka and its sub-multiples would be the token coins of copper and their weight would be dependent upon the variation in the price of the metal. This will help us in unravelling some of the intricacies in the weights of the extant coins and would be a justification for the use of the heavier weights, the multiples of copper Kārṣāpaṇa which were nothing but sub-multiples in value of the standard silver Dharaṇa *e.g.*, the Chatur-Māṣaka, Tri-Māṣaka, and Dvi-Māṣaka. Conversely if copper be accepted as the metal for the standard coin, a rise in its price would lead to the appreciation in the weight of the silver coins. Otherwise a scope for profit would be given to the forgers who would find it very easy to manipulate the rude pieces of olden times. It was to the interest of the state to keep the metallic ratio of the coins on the market level of the two metals ; as otherwise the whole system of coinage would be thrown out of gear by a few clever forgers.

The Kārṣāpaṇa weight of silver referred to by Kauṭilya is one of 80 ratis as proved by Prof. Bhandarkar.[66] But there is nothing strange in this as the Kārṣāpaṇa standard of copper was extended to the other metals for the purposes of weight only. Not a single silver punch-marked coin of 80 ratis (*i.e.* a Purāṇa or Dharaṇa) had been discovered upto this time and this is just what we can expect. The silver purch-marked coins discovered near Patna, the old capital of the Maurya Empire are based upon the Kārṣāpaṇa of 32 ratis.[67] So we are not justified in accepting any standard except 32 ratis for the silver Kārṣāpaṇas or Dharaṇas, many of which perhaps date from the Pre-Mauryan period.

THE TABLE OF WEIGHTS FOR THE BIMETALLIC SYSTEM

Silver	*Weight*	*Copper*
1 Kārṣāpaṇa	= 32 ratis = 56 grs.	
½ =Ardha-Kdrṣapana	= 16 ,, = 28 ,,	
¼ = 1 Pada-Kārṣāpaṇa	= 8 ,, = 14 ,,	= 1 Chatur-Māṣaka. Tri-Māṣaka.

1/8 Kārṣāpaṇa	= 4 ,, = 7 ,,	= 1 Dvi-Māṣaka.
* 1/16 Kārṣāpaṇa (in value only)	= 2 ,, = 3.5 ,,	= One Māṣaka,
*1/32 Kārṣāpaṇa (in value)	= 1 ,, = 1.75 ,,	= Half Māṣaka.
* 1/128 Kārṣāpaṇa (in value)	= .5 ,, = .82 ,,	= One Kakanika.
* 1/128 Kārṣāpaṇa (in value)	= .25 ,, = .41 ,,	= Half Kakanika.

The Table given above was the one in use at the time of Kauṭilya, most probably in Magadha, the scene of his activities. We have to take certain things in our consideration in this connection. The coin denominations based upon such minute measures of weight with an elaborate division of multiples and sub-multiples can only be needed by a state which is as highly developed economically as the Magadhan Empire of the Mauryas. But any province which had not progressed to this stage would be satisfied with a lesser number of measures of weight and corresponding coin-denominations. Moreover there is no certainty that a particular measure of weight corresponding to a particular coin denomination would remain the same throughout the ages, or would even be of the same weight all over the country in a particular period of time. Even if the denominations would remain constant, the measures might vary, This may explain the variations in the weight of Maṣa, Kakani etc. The statement may be corroborated with reference to certain measures of weight like the Maund and the Seer "There are many varieties of mans in India, the variation being as much as 19 lbs in Travancore to 163 1/4 lbs, in Ahmadnagar. The Madras mān weighs 25 lbs., the Bombay mān 28 Ibs."[68] A seer at present in Mymensingh (East Bengal) equals 60, 80, 82, 84 5/8 or 85 Tolas in weight and in every transaction, a reference must be made to the particular weight of the seer and an opportunity is given to the seller to deceive the buyer.

We shall now refer to the extant coins and try to identify them with the coin- denominations detailed above. The extant coins have much depreciated in weight, due to long wear but an additional cause for the variation of weights from the standard measurement is due to the inveterate habit of chipping the coins, and extracting the metal, however small it might be, for private gain, by those through whose hands the coins passed while in circulation. This was the practice of the dishonest people throughout the ages before the introduction of the milled edge to the coins. Even the coins of such a recent period as that of the Later Moguls suffered so severely in their hands that many of them are found much depreciated in weight for this reason only. Another point to be considered is that the variation is greater in the case of copper than silver coins. This is not only due to the nature of the two metals concerned[69] but also to the greater velocity of circulation of copper as compared with the silver coins. We can never expect any coin which had been in circulation for any length of time to be absolutely of the standard weight as it came out of the hands of the moneyers. We have got to be satisfied with approximations only and the closer it is, the better for us and the surer the ground we stand upon.

The silver Kārṣāpaṇas, Half-Kārṣāpaṇas and a Quarter-Kārṣāpaṇa are figured in Plate No. I of Cunningham's "Coins of Ancient India" and many such specimens are found in Smith's Catalogue. Ancient Ajodhya,[70] Avanti, Kosam etc., had only copper coins and these coins were based upon the copper Kārṣāpaṇa of 80 ratis and its sub-multiples. The Mālavas[71] availed of all the sub-multiples of the copper Kārṣāpaṇa ; the smallest weighs only 1.7 grains and this is surely a Half-Kakanika, as we have a number of other coins weighing 2.5, 2.6 grains etc. The higher denomination may be identified with the coins weighing from 3.4 to 5.4 grains and the next higher denomination would range up to 9 grains and so on for other denominations. In Taxila,[72] Magadha etc., bimetallism prevailed, but as the provenance of all the punch-marked coins is not known with certainty, it is not possible to identify all the states that found it necessary with economic progress to adopt bimetallism in the place of the monometallism of copper.

FOOTNOTES

1. Macdonald, G.—The Evolution of Coinage, p. 4.
2. "But though it is true that copper (and much less bronze) and iron were not totally unknown in the Neolithic Age and were used for some time side by side with polished stones, the same can scarcely be said of the precious metals and shining beads for which as for coloured stones, a fascination was never wanting from almost the earliest dawn of humanity * * *" Panchanan Mitra—"Pre-historic India," p. 177, In Pre-historic times at Mohenjo-daro and Harappa "ornaments were * * * * freely worn by all classes alike; necklaces and finger rings by both men and women; earrings, bangles, girdles and anklets by the latter only,"—Sir John Marshall's statement to the Press about the discoveries at Mahenjo-daro and Harappa.
3. "And it is practically certain that the precious metals, also, have come into use as money only because they were first used as ornaments. Thus among savage tribes gold and silver are used almost exclusively for display."—D. A. Barkar—"The Theory of Money," p. 13.
4. "They (the Niṣka, Suvarṇa etc.) are also the names of the weights according to which metals are weighed."—D. R. Bhandarkar- -"Ancient Indian Numismatics," p, 61.
5. Bhandarkar, D. R—A. I. N., pp. 68, 71.
6. "Students, of Indian numismatics know full well that very few gold coins have survived of the pre-Kuṣāṇa period and that none of these were struck by any royal dynasties native to India." —D. R. Bhandarkar—"Ancient Indian Numismatics, p. 91.

   "No gold coins of a Hindu dynasty have been discovered of a period anterior to the Guptas."—*Ibid*, p. 95.
7. Bhandarkar, D. R.—A. I. N., p. 59.
8. *Ibid*—p. 56-The reference is to "round" Śatamānas.

9. In the Brāhmaṇa period-"The Niṣka, originally a gold ornament, was also at this time a unit of value; and the cow as a unit was probably in course of supersession."—Prof. A. B. Keith in the Cambridge History of India, Vol. I, p. 137- In the Sūtra period- "Some measure of values may perhaps be obtained from the statement that the fee to the priest who performs the marriage-ceremony is a cow * * *"-Prof. E- W. Hopkins in the Cambridge History of India, Vol. I, p. 234.
10. "Barter was also permitted in special commodities by the law books ascribed to Gautama and Vasishtha, and was prescribed in certain cases for the Sangha, to whom the use of money was forbidden. Moreover, as a standard of value, it is possible that rice was still used when the Jātaka-book was compiled"—Mrs. C. A. F. Rhys Davids in the Cambridge History of India, Vol. I, p. 217.
11. Bhandarkar, D. R.—A. I. N., p. 189.
12. Ibid, 191.
13. "India, in fact, produced little or no silver, while gold was abundant."—Cunningham—"Ancient Indian Coins", p. 5.
"The relative cheapness of gold would act like a lodestone. Silver coins from the west would flow into the country freely, and would remain in active circulation."—"The Ancient Persian Coins in India"—in the Cambridge History of India, Vol. I, (Dr. G. Macdonald), p. 343.
14. Bhandarkar, D. R.—A. I. N-, p. 190—"I informed, you, that in some places such as Vidisa, there was nothing but copper currency only."
15. The Cambridge History of India, Vol. I, p. 217,
16. "In Ancient India silver and copper coinages were often independent of each other and circulated in different districts."— E. J. Rapson-Catalogue of Indian Coins—Andhras etc., p. clxxix.
16. D. R. Bhandarkar—A. I. N., p. 212.
"Ancient Indian Weights from Mann and Yājñavalkya.

Table No. 1.

Estimated Weights in grs. Troy.

		Silver		
3.5	2 .Ratis	= 1 Māṣaka.		
56.0	32 Ratis	= 16 Māṣaka	= 1 Dharaṇa or Purāṇa.	
560.0	320 Ratis	= 160 Māṣaka	= 10 Dharaṇa or Parāṇa	= 1 Śatamāna.
		Gold		
8.75	5 Ratis	= 1 Maṣa.		
140.0	80 ś	= 16 Maṣa	= 1 Suvarṇa.	
560.0	320 ,,	= 64 Maṣa	= 4 Suvarṇa	= 1 Pala or Niṣka.
5600.0	3200 ś	= 640 Maṣa	= 40 Suvarṇa	= 10 Pala or Niṣka = I Dharaṇa.
		Copper		
140.0	80 Rati	= 1Kārṣāpaṇa		

17. XIII. 2, 3, 2.
18. III. 2, 6, 3; II. 3; II, 5 (Bhandarkar, p. 58). "According to Manu and Yājñavalkya, Śatamāna was a silver coin only, whereas, in the Brāhmaṇa period, it was also a gold coin."— Bhandarkar—A. I. N., p. 180.
19. Cambridge History of India, Vol. I, p. 137.
20. Bhandarkar, D. R.—A. I. N., p. 60.

21. Cunningham, A.—C. A. I., p. 1.
22. M Sir A. Elliot—Coins of Southern India, p. 48.
23. *Ibid.*, p. 47.
24. Sir A. Elliot—Coins of Southern India, p, 48.
25. Bhandarkar, D. R.—A. I. N., p. 212.
26. Sir A. Elliot—Coins of Southern India, p. 53.
27. Bhandarkar, D. R.—A. I. N., p. 93—94.
28. Cambridge History of India, Vol. I, p. 343.
29. Alexander "broke down the wall of separation between west and east, and opened up four distinct lines of communication, three by land and one by sea. The land routes which he proved to be practicable were those through Kabul, the Mulla Pass in Balochistan and Gedrosia. Nearchos demonstrated that the sea voyage round the coast of Makrān offered few difficulties to sailors, once the necessary local information had been gained, which he lacked.—V. Smith—"The Oxford History of India," p. 66.

    ". . . . but it was not until Alexander's expedition, that the Indian trade, which was now so important to Alexandria, became a part of Greek commerce."—G. Banerjee—"India as known to the Ancient World," p. 20.
30. Smith, V.—"The Oxford History of India," p. 87.
31. Cunningham, A.—C. A. I., p. 50.

    "Without doubt commercial transactions with India during the time of the Romans, and for some time afterwards, were principally carried on in ready money, which is more than once mentioned as an article of importation .... How, indeed, could the case have been otherwise, when a country, which produced in superabundance every possible article, whether required for the necessaries of life or the refinements of luxury, would of course export a great deal, while it imported little or nothing in return; so that the commercial balance would always be in its favour. Hence it followed, that from the moment she possessed a foreign commerce, India would enrich herself with the precious metals by a necessary consequence from the very nature of things, and not by any fortuitous concourse of circumstances."—The Historians' History of the World, Vol. II, p. 520 (New Edition).

32. "The subject," he says (VI. 26) "is one well-worthy of our notice, seeing that in no year does India drain us of less than 550,000,000 sesterces ($22,000,000) giving back her own wares, which are sold among us at fully hundred times their first cost" —Pliny quoted in Periphis, (Schoff), p, 219.
33. Bhandarkar, D. R.—A. I. N., p. 59.
34. "The earliest gold coins of Northern India are one or two small pieces which were probably struck at Taxila."—R. B. White-head—The Pre-Mohammedan Coinage of Northwestern India, p. 44.

    These coins, however, are double-die struck and consequently must be much later than the punch-marked coins.

    "What became of this great influx of gold? My explanation is that in North India it was received by the Indo-Scythian Kushan princes, Wema Kadphises, Kaniṣka, Huvishka and Vasudeva, whose gold coinage is now found in such large quantities. Their gold coins are of the same weight as those of the early Caesars. In South India the gold coin circulated just as it came, which satisfactorily accounts for the frequent finds of Roman gold coins at the present day."—A Cunningham—C. A. 1., p. 50.
35. Allan, J.—Catalogue of Coins of Gupta Dynasties, p. cxxxiii.
36. "The Roman aureus and denarius were current throughout Western India, and strongly influenced the Kuṣāṇa and Kṣatrapa Coinages."—The Periplus of the Erythraean Sea edited by W, H. Schoff, pp. 192 and 219. See Rapson—Indian Coins, p. 4.

37. "It was on these two seminal units, the Māṇjāḍi and Kalanju, that the normal metrical system of the South appears to have been founded, smaller and more delicate weights not being required in the rude transactions of earlier times."—Sir A. Elliot —C. S. I., p. 48,
38. Sir W. Elliot—C. S. I., p. 53.
39. *Ibid*, p. 49.
40. Sir A. Cunningham—C. A. I., p, 51.
41. *Ibid*, p. 44.
42. *Ibid*, p.45.
43. Sir W. Elliot—C. S. I., p. 49.
44. Bhandarkar, D. R.—A. I. N., p. 212.
45. Smith, V.—Catalogue of Coins, p. 134.
46. Sir A, Cunningham—C. A. I., p. 45. .
47. Bhandarkar, D. R.—A. I. N., p. 77.
48. *Ibid*.
49. *Ibid*.
50. *Ibid*, p. 142.
51. Rapson, E. J.—Catalogue of Indian Coins—the Andhras etc., p. clxxix, footnote 1.
52. *Ibid*, (Footnote No. 2).
53. Allan, J.—Gupta Coins, p. cxxxiii.
54. Sir W. Elliot—C. S. I., p. 59.
55. *Ibid*.
56. *Ibid*.
57. Manu's Table of Weights—Bhandarkar, D. R.—A. I. N.,p. 212
58. In the Jātaka period "the nikkha was valued now at five, now at four Suvannas."—Mrs. Rhys Davids in the Cambridge History of India, Vol. I, p. 218.
59. Sir A. Cunningham—C. A. I., p. 45.
60. Bhandarkar, D. R.—A. I. N., p. 212.
61. *Ibid*, p. 71.
62. *Ibid*, p. 112.
63. *Ibid*.
64. *Ibid*—C. A. I., p. 46.
65. Bhandarkar, D. R.—A. I. N., p. 112.
66. *Ibid*, p. 93.
67. Walsh, E. H. C.—Journal of the Bihar and Orissa Research Society, Vol. V, Part I, pp, 17-72.
    * No such silver coins in circulation.
68. Sewell, R.— A Forgotten Empire (Vi jyanagar) , p. 402.
69. "Copper is a more perishable metal than silver."—Bhandar-kar, D. R.—p. 96.
70. Bhandarkar, D. R.—A. I. N., p. 190.
71. Smith, V.—Catalogue of Coins, pp. 170-178.
72. Sir A Cunningham—C. A. I., pp. 60-66.

CHAPTER V

THE METROLOGY OF THE COINS

The excavations in the Indus Valley enable us to have definite information about a period which is perhaps earlier than the Vedas and which belongs to the Copper Age of approximately 5000 years ago.[1] In the Vedas, we have the word "Ayas" which has the same basic root as Latin "aes" and Gothic "Aiz" and has been interpretated on the Latin and Gothic analogy to mean copper ; but side by side we have a reference to black 'ayas' in the Vedas,[2] and there are numerous references to iron weapons. Thus the old word which originally signified copper came to be applied to the newer metal, iron. The Indus Valley people of the Pre-Vedic Age were familiar with gold, silver, copper, tin and lead. So the new metal which was requisitioned by the Aryans and which revolutionised the cultural history was iron. At Mahenjo-daro and Harappā "the ornaments of the rich were of gold and silver or copper plated with gold,"[3] while the poor had to be satisfied with shell or terracotta ornaments. The girdles of gilded copper attracted attention and also "some of the small objects *e.g.*, ear-rings, and "netting" needles of pure gold, the surface of which is polished to a degree that would do credit to a present day jeweller."[4] They used copper for implements and weapons etc., and many copper daggers, knives, axes, domestic utensils and even personal ornaments have been unearthed from these sites. But the total absence of iron leaves no doubt about the fact that we have here to deal with a pre-historic culture of the Chalcolithic Age.[5]

For ceremonial purposes among the Hindus the metals are ranked in order of purity ; gold takes the first place and is followed by copper, silver, brass and iron.[6] It may embody a genuine tradition about the chronological sequence in the use of the different metals in this country. It can be safely asserted that the attention of the primitive men of the Palaeolithic Age was attracted by the bright yellow colour of gold as is testified by the Skt. word *Hiraṇya* ; Zend, *Zaranya* ; Pers, Zar ;[7] all having a reference to the yellow colour of the metal ; and the word Suvarṇa also refers to the colour—*Su* + *varṇa* or beautiful colour.[8] In India, this metal was easily available in the form of dust or nuggets in the beds of rivers.[9] The Indus was specially rich in gold and the other rivers which were noted for gold-bearing were the Hiraṇya bāha, the Erannoboas of Pliny[10] (the modern Son) and Suvarṇarekhā etc. Even now gold from alluvial deposits can be recovered from some of the river-beds in Assam, the United Provinces, the Punjab and Kashmir.[11] The washing of the auriferous sands in the river-beds is a means of livelihood to the poor people of the locality, though the old primitive process is uneconomical as compared with quartz mining. Men in a low state of civilisation "are passionately fond of ornaments."[12] and gold was specially fitted by its inherent qualities to serve the purposes of personal decoration, and the opinion has been hazarded that its first employment in arts began most probably in India, or at least in the East.[13] Among the Indus Valley people "ornaments were freely worn by all classes alike ; necklaces and finger-rings by both men and women ; earrings, bangles, girdles and anklets by the latter only,"[14] Thus "in history gold appears first as a valuable commodity"[15] specially sought for personal decoration and industrial purposes. It was treasured as a commodity, but its employment as a medium of exchange was much later when society had passed through the stage of Barter. "Rare and highly esteemed, portable, durable, readily divisible, homogeneous, and easily worked, it soon came into use independently among many nations, at early stages of civilisation, as a medium of exchange, to facilitate the process of barter."[16] Gradually other standards of value like grain, oxen, ornaments etc. came to be at best partially supplanted by metals which changed hands by weight.[17] To keep the metal in the natural state in which it was gathered from the sands of the river-beds, was surely inconvenient. Megasthenes notes that the gold dust of India was "sold to the merchants in its natural state, because it did not require to be purified"[18] and Cunningham is of opinion "that the Indian gold dust was usually kept in its natural state, in small -packets of fixed weight."[19] But there is no doubt that the metal was melted for industrial purposes as is evident from the discovery of ornaments etc., in the old Indus Valley towns. Moreover to melt the metal and to weigh it out according to a standard into small pieces of ingots would be convenient for exchange purposes, and the weight of the pieces might be testified to by certain symbols as we find in the silver ingots with 3 circular dots on the obverse in V. Smith's Catalogue.[20] It would not also be unreasonable to infer that the next step was to melt the metal in bars and to cut off pieces from them of required weight and to stamp symbols on them, which would be analogous in shape and manipulation with the 3 bent bars of silver described by V. Smith.[21] That pieces of ingots were in use has been conclusively proved by Prof, Bhandarkar who refers to the story of Janaka, the king of Videha who "collected a thousand kine, and we are told that to every single horn of each cow were tied ten pādas and it was proclaimed that they should be taken away by him alone who is best cognisant with *brahman*."[22] As pointed out by him, it would be absurd "to assume that Janaka on the spur of the moment had 2000 pieces of gold hammered out, each conforming to that weight."[23] We may also accept the view that the Śatamānas referred to in the Śatapatha Brāhmaṇa were round in shape.[23a] A spherule of gold "quite plain and smooth, save for a single very minute punch-mark too small to be identified"[24] a little flattened and weighing 52 grains is reproduced in Elliot's Coins of Southern India. The Śatamānas at least some of them, must have approximated in shape to this globule of gold. It can therefore be definitely asserted that gold changed hands as a commodity and also as a medium of exchange as ingots of irregular shape, sometimes globular either melted out in separate pieces or cut off from a bar, each piece conforming to a standard weight system. Small dots or circles might have been impressed on these pieces as marks of weight or purity, but we are not in a position to claim for them the honour of being the authorised mediums of exchange—the coins, for the business transactions as not. a single piece of gold coin analogous to the punch-marked coins of silver and copper in shape and weight and with the peculiar symbols has been discovered in India that can be referred to the early period. There is nothing improbable in it. For ordinary purposes of exchange silver, copper or lead were requisitioned but gold was merely a theoretical standard of value and we would not be justified in the present state of our knowledge in asserting the existence of gold coinage. The final step in the progress was perhaps retarded by the high value of the metal in spite of its comparative abundance in the country. Niṣka, Śatamāna etc. are therefore not to be deemed coins exactly in the modern sense of the word, though they perhaps served one of the most important functions of coinage as mediums of exchange on occasions. On the other hand there is no doubt that gold would have come into use for coinage at a later period and the last advance forward would have been made but for the fact that it was too valuable in the economic condition of the time. A few golden darics have been discovered in this country[25] but no gold coin of indigenous manufacture contemporaneous to the punch-marked coins of silver and copper have been found[26] and this should surely embolden us to conclude that in spite of the comparative abundance of the metal, it was not exactly suited to the economic condition of the time and India had not progressed to the stage of gold coins before the Kuṣāṇas. We know however that India was famous in ancient times for her trade in gold,[27] and that the Western countries were eager to participate in it. This surely proves the paucity of the yellow metal in the West ; and whatever doubt we might have about the identification of the Biblical Ophir or Sophir of the Septuagint with Sauvira[28] has been set at rest by the new discoveries which have conclusively established the existence of a very early culture "which extended from the Adriatic to Japan but was focussed primarily in the great river valleys of the South ; of the Nile, the Euphrates, the Tigris, the Karun, the Helmund and the Indus"[29] and a cultural connection existed between the civilised races of antiquity. Ophir was famous for its gold and the "gold of Ophir became proverbial in Hebrew, and most of the articles of commerce mentioned in the Jewish annals have names which may be traced to Indian originals."[30] This reputation of being a pre-eminently gold-producing country remained unimpaired and long afterwards when Darius annexed the Indus Valley and organised it into a Satrapy, the twentieth of the Persian Empire, the Great King according to Herodotus levied the enormous annual tribute of 360 talents of gold[31] (= 20736 lbs. = 107272) from the new province in the natural state of gold dust. But a time came when a great change took place in this trade and India imported huge quantities of precious metals from the West, specially from Rome.[32] This was due to the fact that Indian luxuries were very much coveted in the West and the trade was so much in favour of this country that huge quantities of gold and silver coins had to be sent to India in payment, and this economic drain was much lamented by Pliny. Roman coins in large numbers have been discovered in India and the Periplus refers to the profitable trade in foreign coins of gold and silver at Barygaza (modern Broach) in the Bombay Presidency.[33] These foreign gold coins were supplemented by standard issues of gold, the Kuṣāṇa gold coins in Northern India, and perhaps the Kaḷanju of gold in the South which was based upon the traditional Indian system of weight.

Copper is found in ores throughout the country. It is no longer extensively produced in India but "was formerly smelted in considerable quantities in South India, Rajputana, and at various parts of outer Himalaya, where a killas-like rock persists along the whole range and is known to be copper-bearing in Kullu, Garhwal, Nepal, Sikkim and Bhutan."[34] It came into use after the Neolithic period but surely much later than gold which exercised a fascination over mankind from "the earliest dawn of humanity."[35] "Copper Age antiquities have been forthcoming from Rajpur, Mathura, Mainpuri, Niarai, Bithur, Allahabad, Behar, Hazaribagh, Karachi and Beluchistan, while the most important discovery of instruments of copper in the old world has come from Gungeria in the Balaghat district of the Central Provinces."[36] It was freely used by the Indus Valley people in pre-historic times for ornaments, weapons, utensils etc.[37] The metal gradually began to serve as a medium of exchange, at first by weight and when later on coinage was introduced in the country, its service was requisitioned for the purpose. On the evolution of coinage in the proper sense of the word, the Kārṣāpaṇa of copper became the medium of exchange and it came to be so intimately identified with coinage that it was used as a general term for coins and signified coins of copper, silver or even of gold of a particular weight.[58] In this connection we must remember that copper was not cheap as in modern times and was well-fitted for the purpose as pointed out by Prof. Bhandarkar and side by side with this metallic money there were cowry shells and other tokens in circulation. Some of the states like Eran[39] and others were all along satisfied merely with copper and this conservatism was perhaps due to low economic development or force of habit. But silver began gradually to assert its position and we find a number of states like Taxila,[40] Magadha[41] etc., having both the metals in circulation.

The assertion that India produced no silver cannot be accepted,[42] though we must admit that the quantity produced in it was small indeed. Small quantities have been found though "associated with lead, in Kulu and Manbhum, and at Deaogurh in the Santhal Pargana."[43] In Gungeria 400 flat axes of various lengths all in copper and 102 objects in silver were discovered in 1870 and these must date from the Copper Age.[44] Silver ornaments and utensils have been found in the excavations at Mahenjo-daro and Harappā, But it is noticeable that silver is not so abundant as gold and this would explain the higher ratio for silver in India,[46] and this fact is reflected in the statement of Jeremiah who "points to the East as the source of gold, and to the West as that of silver, when he speaks of "*silver beaten into plates* brought from Tarshish, and gold from Uphaz (or Ophir)."[46] So the importation of silver was in fact a regular feature in the ancient commerce of India. The relative cheapness of gold would facilitate the flow of silver coins to this country, where they would remain in active circulation.[47] That this was exactly what happened is evident from the presence of *sigloi* or shekels, the silver coinage of the Persian Empire,[48] and from the reference in the Periplus to the importation of silver and gold plate to Barbaricum at the mouth of the Indus river,[49] gold and silver coins to Barygaza[50] and "coins in great quantity" to Muziris[51] Nelcynda and Bacare in the Chera and Pāṇḍya kingdoms.

The Andhras had a "special partiality for lead"[52] and the smaller leaden coins were "exceedingly rude" and Smith opines that the Andhra coinage, "as a whole, is devoid of all beauty or artistic merit, and is interesting, primarily, as a document of dynastic history, and secondarily, on account of its peculiar materials" lead and potm.[53] Lead is very scarce in

India though the metal was obtainable in small quantities in ancient times in the form of ores ; at present lead mining is "practically in a dormant condition."[54] The supply of the metal had to be supplemented in ancient times too. According to the periplus which dates from the first century A.D., lead was imported to Barygaza (modern Broach) in the kingdom of Nambanus[55] (Nahapāna, the Saka Satrap) and to the ports of Southern India, namely, Muziris (Cranganore), Nelcynda near the modern Kottayam and Bacare, modern Porakad.[56] Though Pliny's statement that—"India has neither brass or lead but exchanges precious stones and pearls for them"[57] may not be strictly accurate, yet it points to the prevailing condition of trade in his days ; this importation of lead was mainly necessitated by the employment of the metal for the purposes of coinage[58] and as pointed out by Rapson in the Andhra Empire "the coinages of lead predominated."[59] "They have been found exclusively in Andhradeśa, the home of the race, in the Anantapur and Cuddapah districts, in the region of the Coromandel coast, in the Chitaldrug District and in the Karwar District."[60] Lead currency was associated also with Potm in the Kolhapur district and it preceded the coins of potin and copper in certain parts of Malwa. Lead is referred to in the Jātaka Literature as "Sisa-Kahapana or lead Kārṣāpaṇas."[61] It was also used in Northern India. Strato,[62] the Indo-Greek king, Azes,[63] and Ranjubula[64] the Indo-Parthian Satrap of Mathura issued lead coins in the North about the beginning of the Christian Era.[65]

Nickel was first discovered by Cunningham in the coins of the Indo-Greek kings, Euthydemos, Agathokles and Pantaleon ;[66] and he is of opinion that it was employed by the Oxydracae (the Kṣudrakas) and the Malli (the Mālavas), the Indian tribes that were contemporary with Alexander the Great, for their coinage ; and he arrives at this conclusion from the statement of Quintus Curtius that Alexander "received a present of 100 talents of 'white iron' *(ferri candidi)*"[67] from these two Indian tribes. This "white iron" might refer to tin or nickel but as tin is very soft for the purposes of coinage and was well-known to the Greeks, Prof. Bhandarkar would make it refer to nickel.[68] But we have as yet no known specimen of nickel coin issued by a purely Indian prince or tribe. *Ferrum candidum* is identified by Schoff with fine steel for swords and mirrors for which India was famous.[68a] *Ferrum indicum* was a dutiable article under Marcus Aurelius and Commodus.[68b] Marco Polo refers iron and *ondanique* in the markets of Kerman, and Yule derives it from "hundwaniy" *i.e.*, Hindustani or Indian steel. I would rather prefer the interpretation of Schoff and regard the 'talent' as a measure of weight.

Coins of mixed metals can be traced to an early period ; it is difficult to determine whether this was to a conscious attempt at depreciation, though we not be justified in putting the likelihood out of consideration, at least at certain periods. Some amount of alloy was surely necessary to impart the requisite hardness to the metals but sometimes the difficulty in separating the metals led to the introduction of alloys. The use of Potin, Billon or Brass may be on occasions the result of conscious attempt at depreciation promoted by avarice or due to financial stress.

Potin was a "curious" alloy of copper and was so dubbed by Rapson who followed M.

Babelon. It was "composed of yellow and red copper, lead, tin and some dross."[69] In appearance it approximated to bronze or lead according to the varying proportions of copper and lead. Another mixed metal is Billon and as pointed out by Prof. Bhandarkar "it is to silver what potin is to bronze"[70]— "it is silver with a great, proportion of alloy. "[71] Brass is an alloy of copper and zinc usually in the proportion of 2 to I, or 4 to 3 and a cheap alloy of copper and tin is called Kansā or bell-metal.[72] The proportion of the metals used in the coins of the different periods in the various parts of the country, would be a valuable asset to the historians but at present the available data are insufficient to come to any definite conclusions.

The Andhras favoured potin coinage, and coins in potin are found in Kolhapur and Malwa in association with other metals and "exclusively in the Chanda District of the Central Provinces." Coins in brass or pale bronze were discovered at Ajodhya, Kosam, Avanti and other places while a plated coin is described by Smith in his Catalogue (p. 138, No. 41).

When coins gradually came into use monometallism must have been the rule and the smaller transactions were carried on with the help of cowries or other tokens. The complicated relations between two metals, circulating side by side would have been too complex for the time and also unnecessary ; and this may be the reason that in ancient India we find a preference for monometallism either of copper or silver. Rapson infers "directly from the statements of the law-books, and more generally from the study of the coins, that in Ancient India silver and copper coinages were often independent of each other and circulated in different districts. A copper currency was not necessarily regarded as merely auxiliary to the silver currency ; but a copper standard prevailed in some districts just as a silver standard prevailed in others."[73] When we remember that coinage in ancient India was essentially local in character,[74] we have no reasons to be surprised that different metals were used independently, without being linked up together, in the different provinces of the same Empire *e.g.*, of the Andhras, the Guptas and others. Silver was high in price and scarce, and its supply mainly depended upon foreign importation, while copper was available all over the country and its relatively high value in those days would point to it as the basic metal for the purposes of coinage. The states which were very conservative or economically backward retained the copper currency throughout, for example among the Mālavas and in Eraṇ ; but gradually silver on account of its intrinsic qualities for the purpose and the higher economic development of the society came into use and the advantages of monometallism restricted the employment of one metal at a time in a definite locality ; the earlier metal, namely copper either fell out of use or when allowed to circulate conjointly became a subsidiary coinage serving as mere tokens. This process would be exemplified by the change in the meaning of the word Kārṣāpaṇa which was preeminently a copper coin but gradually came "to mean the standard coin whether of silver or copper"[75] and we find from Nārada that Kārṣāpaṇa was a silver coin in the South. A similar change from one metal to the other can be met with in the case of *libra or litra* and *dinar*. Libra was a "copper unit" and was of silver when first minted," while at present it is "so closely associated with gold."[76] The Roman Denarius now connected with copper was at first minted with silver and among the Arabs attained "to the dignity of gold."[77]

This preference for one metal only in a particular locality was surely not universal. In Taxila and among the Kuṇindas and others we have silver and copper circulating side by side and lead and potin circulating in the same way, in the Kolhapur district under the Andhras. And whatever doubt we might have about the advance towards bimetallism is set at rest by Kauṭilya. He definitely lays down that there were two kinds of coins of silver and copper, circulating in his time in the Magadhan Empire ;[78] and it is evident from the coin denominations given by him that silver and copper were linked in a certain definite ratio.

The difficulties of bimetallism are well-known ; the ratio between the two metals must vary and any attempt at fixing an artificial ratio would be almost impossible, owing to the ease with which the old hand-made coins could be manipulated by private forgers. This may explain to some extent at least, the variation in weight from the standard of many extant coins. If the weight of the silver coin were kept constant, a fall in its price would make the copper coins lighter, or a rise in sliver would necessitate an increase in the weight of copper coins. Similar would be the case with copper coin too, if the weight is kept constant ; a rise in its value would make the silver coins lighter and a fall in copper would necessitate an increase in the weight of silver coins. Gardner's statement[79] that the ratio of the metals was regulated by the will of the kings in Asia may be applicable to Persia only, where the Great king tried to maintain the mint-standard of 1 : 13.3 between gold and silver.[80] The attempts of the Greek cities to adjust the silver coinage to the gold ratio,[81] when the proportional value of the two metals changed, was the only natural counterpart of what we find in India with a wide range of variations in the weight of coins—the two metals employed being silver and copper. But in India it depended upon the predilection of the particular state, whether silver or copper would occupy the privileged position, leading to the change in the weight of the other in case of a change in the relative value of the metals.

The introduction of gold coinage by the Kuṣāṇas led to a greater complexity which was partially obviated by linking up gold to copper and dropping silver altogether in the Empire directly under the Kuṣāṇ rule,[82] though silver was retained by the Satrap Nahapāna and his successors in their dominions. Wema Kadphises issued gold and copper coins only and Kaniṣka, Huviṣka and Vasudeva followed in his footsteps. But already the people were habituated to silver and the attempt to shut it out could not be wholly successful. The ultimate result was the victory of gold which now came to be linked up with silver ; and copper fell practically into disuse or was retained only as a token currency. This, change can be exemplified with reference to the coinage of the Guptas. At first gold was tentatively introduced and the gold coins were denominated the dinaras and were based upon the Kuṣana standard weight.[83] The name 'dinara' may be ultimately traced to the Latin *denarius (aureus)*"[84] and the "standard itself to the Roman *solidus.*"[85] Under Skandagupta the traditional weight standard of 80 ratis was put into operation and the gold coins were now fittingly called 'Suvarṇa.' The copper coins degenerated into tokens only as is apparent from the poor condition of the Gupta coinage in copper,[86] in which naturally much attention was not bestowed by the coin-makers under the changed conditions, when the importance of copper coins had dwindled away. "The silver coins of the Guptas show considerable variation in weight"[87] and this is perhaps due to the variation in the relative price of the two metals, gold and silver. The acceptance of gold we cannot expect to be universal, and parts of the country might have stuck to the principle of bimetallism of silver and copper. ToraMāna and Mihir-gula in later times fell off from gold[88] and restricted the Huna coins to the older system that had prevailed in the country before the introduction of gold by the foreign rulers—the Kuṣāṇas.

The relative value of the metals cannot remain constant for any length of time. The variations have been so great that it is impossible to visualise the currency problems in the different periods, unless we have at least tentative ratio for the metals used for coinage, at a particular period of Indian History. It would be necessary for purposes of comparison to know the relative value prevailing at present. The price of a tollah of gold (English Bar) is Rs. 21-12-6 pies[90] and of silver bar per 100 tollahs is Rs. 60-3 as.; this will give an approximate ratio of 1 : 36 between gold and silver. The price of copper ingot has varied from Rs. 58-4 as. to Rs. 62-4 as. per cwt., this giving a mean of Rs. 60. So the approximate ratio, taking gold as the standard is 1: 36 : 1236 between gold, silver and copper respectively. Pig lead is Rs. 19 per cwt., that is, less than one-third the price of copper.

In the West, for about 1000 years silver was in use for trade purposes before the advent of the yellow metal.[91] Gradually gold asserted its pre-eminence. In Solomon's days his drinking vessels were of gold for silver "was nothing accounted of "(1 Kings, X, 21) and he "made silver to be in Jerusalem as stones"[92] (I Kings. X. 27). This progress downward went on for centuries and we find the ratio of gold and silver at the time of Darius the Great to be I : 13 1/3 ;[93] in Athens under Pericles the ratio was 1 : 14[94] and later on 1 : 12 1/2[95] or 12[96]; at the time of Philip and Alexander the ratio was 1 : 10.[97] In Rome under Julius Caesar 47 B.C., it was 1 : 8.9[98] and at time of Augustus the first Emperor in the first century A.D., the ratio was 1 : 9.3.[99]

In India we have no definite knowledge of the relative value of gold and silver before the time of Darius but it can be reasonably presumed that on account of its paucity, as India had mainly to depend upon foreign countries for its supply, silver had greater appreciation At the time of the Persian Emperor Darius the ratio in the Indian Satrapy was 1 : 8[100] while in Persia it was 1 : 13.3. We would naturally expect the importation of silver bullion and coins in large amount from the West to India in exchange for her gold, of which she had an ample supply. This will explain the paucity of the golden darics in India which would be exported as soon as possible for silver. But the silver sigloi or shekels "are frequently offered for sale by Indian dealers, and it is a reasonable inference that they are fairly often disinterred from the soil of India itself."[101] and "that is precisely what might be expected from the working of the economic law."[102]

We have sufficient data in the first quarter of the 2nd century A.D., to estimate the relative value of the precious metals and we find that silver had gone down in price and that it approximated to the ratio which prevailed contemporaneously in the Roman Empire. In the Nasik inscription of Ṛṣabhadatta of the year 42, month Vaiśākha,[103] there is a reference to a large gift to the gods and Brāhmaṇas amounting to 70,000 Kārṣāpaṇas equal to 2000 Suvarṇas The year 42 must be referred to the Saka Era,[104] so it is equivalent to 120 A.D., the last year of Kaniṣka or the first year of Huviṣka as Emperor.[105] Thirty-five Kārṣāpaṇas are equated to one Suvarṇa. If we can definitely determine the weight of the two coins referred to, it will be easy to fix the ratio beween gold and silver, under the Kuṣāṇas in the first quarter of the and century A.D. Prof. Bhandarkar takes the standard weight of the Sanskrit classical works for the Kārṣāpaṇa and the Suvarṇa *i.e.*, 32 ratis or 58.5 grains and 80 ratis or 146.4 grains respectively[105a] and works out the ratio of gold and silver as 1 : 14. But this estimate does not tally with that of Rapson who takes the ratio approximately as 1 : 10 ; his view seems to be better authenticated. Rapson takes the weight of Kārṣāpaṇa as 36 grains and in this he is justified, for Ṛṣabhadatta was the son-in-law of Nahapāna, the Saka Satrap of Western India whose silver "coins were apparently imitated, as regards size weight and fabric, from the hemi-drachms of the Graeco-Indian kings"[106] and we would naturally expect that the Kārṣāpaṇas in Ṛṣabhadatta's inscription referred to the silver coins of his time and issued by his father-in-law Nahapāna ; and from the extant coins we are justified in taking the weight as equal to the maximum of 36 grains The Survarṇa based upon the standard weight of 80 ratis was issued in later times under Skandagupta (ace. 455 A.D.) but the gold coin of the earlier monarchs of the Gupta dynasty and even some of the issues of Skanda-gupta[106a] were based upon the traditional Kuṣāṇa standard[107] which must be referred to the Roman aureus; and these gold coins are mentioned in the inscriptions sometimes as Suvarṇa and sometimes as Dinara.[108] Any doubt would be set at rest by the fact that the gold coins of Kumaragupta which are all referable to the Kuṣāṇa standard are mentioned as Suvarṇas in the inscriptions.[109] So we are justified in taking the Suvarṇa as equivalent to 124 grains in weight, specially when we remember that the Western Kṣatrapas were subordinate to the Kuṣāṇas whose gold coins the standard weight of 124 grains and that there was absolutely no gold coin in this period for 3 centuries more, that can be based upon the aditional Indian standard Suvarṇa of 80 ratis or 146.4 grains. weight of the Kārṣāpaṇas and whose gold coins had the standard weight of 124 grains and that there was absolutely no gold coin in this period or for 3 centuries more, that can be based upon the traditional Indian standard Suvarṇa of 80 ratis or 146.4 grains. If we take the weight of the Kārṣāpaṇas and the Suvarṇas mentioned in the Nasik inscription of Ṛṣabhadatta as 36 and 124 grains (the maximum) respectively, the ratio of gold to silver is 1 : 10. If we however refer to the extant gold coins of Kaniṣka, we find that the Dinaras weigh 122 grains and the silver coins of Nahapāna average 32 grains. The ratio in that case is a little higher than 1 : 9. But we must also take into account, in this connection, the percentage of alloy used, of which we have no definite information. However this conclusion is borne out by the fact that in the West, the relative value was approximately the same ; under Augustus in the 1st century A.D., the ratio was 1 : 9.3[111] or 1 : 11.9.[112] There is no reason to suppose that there was a very great difference in ratio between the East and the West which had. now intimate commercial connection. Otherwise, there would have been no importation of silver coins side by side with the gold . ones as referred to in the Periplus,[112a] for it would have been more profitable to bring gold and take out silver from the country. The economic condition reflected in the Periplus is of the time of the Western Kṣatrapas, as there is a reference to a king Nambanus in Western India who is obviously Nahapāna the Saka king. Viṣṇugupta who flourished in about 500 A.D., writes thus: — *i.e.*, Twenty-eight Ropakas are equal to one Dīnār a and a Ropaka is 1/70th of a Suvarṇa. It is evident that the Ropaka and the Dīnār had gone out of use altogether, or the name Dīnāra had come to be applied to the contemporary gold coin which was entirely different from the Kuṣāṇa and early Gupta coins in weight, being only 32 ratis ; otherwise there would have been no necessity for determining the value of a Ropaka a silver coin, in such a round-about way by equating it to 1/70 of gold Suvarṇa, thus making a Dīnāra equal to 32 ratis. So the equation of 28 Ropakas to 1 Dīnāra was the tradition which had come down to his time and he was driven to identify the Dīnāra with the gold coin of 32 ratis, the Kalanju.[114] Now if we take the Ropakas and the Dīnāras to be the silver and the gold coins of the later Kuṣāṇa period or the early Gupta period of 36 and 124 grains respectively, the ratio between gold and silver is found to be 1 : 8 1/2. We would be justified therefore in taking the ratio as 1:8 1/2to early centuries A.D. and I would rather prefer 1 : 9 in India.

The fluctuations in the relative value of gold and silver was rather great, as India had mainly to depend for silver on foreign supply, but once practically the same ratio had been established in the East and the West, we would expect it to remain more constant. We can naturally expect that the ratio between gold and copper would remain constant for a longer period and would not exhibit the same fluctuation as that between gold and silver, as both copper and gold were procurable in this country. Prof. Bhandarkar points out that Brihaspati and Katyayana Dharma-Sastras[115] (6th cent. A.D.) establish the rate of exchange between the copper Kārṣāpaṇa and the gold Dīnāra as 48 : 1 and if we accept the copper Kārṣāpaṇa and the gold Dīnāra as of 146.4 and 124 grains respectively, the ratio between copper and gold would be 1: 56.7. If the ratio between gold and silver had not much varied from that in the 2nd cent. A.D. as we have every reason to expect, we might take the relative value of silver and copper as 1 : 5.7 approximately, on the supposition that the ratio of gold to silver was 1:10. But we should bear in mind that the value of the different metals and their relative values were always liable to variation, and that, though the ratios arrived at might not be exactly correct, yet these would enable us to enunciate certain principles as regards the currency problems of Ancient India. It is evident that in "early times copper had comparatively much greater value than it possesses at present."[116] It is however not exactly "twenty times as much as now,"[117] as has been remarked by Prof. Bhandarkar. He himself points out later on that a Kārṣāpaṇa which weighed a double pice is equivalent to 20 modern pice,[118] thus indicating that it was ten times its present value. But in this connection the value of copper can only be estimated separately with reference to gold and silver, whichever might be taken to be the standard metal. If we take gold, then copper was about 22 times more valuable ; but if we compare copper with silver as the standard metal, then it was only 6 times more valuable. It may be reasonably expected that in earlier times when silver was more valuable, the ratio was in favour of silver, but with the cheapening of copper the same process would be continued and it silver remains constant in value, more and more copper would be demanded to equate it with silver.

The next topic of discussion would be to determine the standard coin in the different periods of ancient Indian History. In the earliest period under review the copper Kārṣapaṇa of 80 ratis was undoubtedly the I standard coin ; and this is attested to by a number of extant punch-marked copper coins. But we have definite Information from Kauṭilya's Arthaśāstra that in the 4th century B.C.. it had been supplanted by silver, at least in the Magadhan Empire. There is a reference to Paṇa Half, Quarter and One-eighth Paṇa as silver coins ; and Māṣaka, Half-Māṣaka and Kakani as copper coins.[119] Evidently the silver Kārṣāpaṇa of 32 ratis was the standard coin of the Maurya Empire and the copper coins were linked up with silver in a definite proportion for smaller payments. Though it is not possible to decide for want of necessary data, whether the quantity of copper in these coins approximated to the value of the metal, yet we have every reason to expect that it was so. It was pointed out previously that some of the states did not accept the silver standard. Sometimes they were satisfied with the traditional standard of 80 ratis *e.g.*, Eraṇ ; but in other cases, it is evident that an attempt was made to increase the amount of metal in the copper coin to equate it in value to the silver Kārṣāpaṇa of 32 ratis or one of its sub-multiples, which was the prevailing currency of the mighty Empire of the Mauryas and perhaps of the Suñgas and their successors in Northern India. Had we exact information about the relative value of silver and copper in the different periods over the various parts of the country, it would have been an easy task to estimate the quantity of copper that might be needed to make the particular coin of copper equal in value to the standafd Dharaṇa. A few references to extant coins would be sufficient to establish this general proposition that monometallism of copper, even when adhered to, was modified by an attempt to establish an equality with the silver coin in value by increasing the weight of the copper coin, while copper continued to be the only metal for purposes of currency. It is perhaps a fully satisfactory theory which can explain the issue of "massive copper coins" in later times, *i.e.*, at least after the Mauryas. The variation which is generally slight in the reigns of the different kings of the same dynasty must be due to the fluctuation in the price of copper. As copper becomes cheaper in value as. compared with silver, the coins also would tend to become heavier. So it is reasonable to attribute the lighter coins of the massive type to an earlier period generally ; and this is attested to by the fact that the big single die-struck coins which were earlier than the double die-struck coins were lighter as compared with the double die-struck ones.[121] The coins of the so-called Mitra Dynasty of Panchala and Kosala are ascribed by V. Smith to first century B.C., to first century A.D.[122] We know that in the early mediaeval period the ratio of silver to copper was 1 : 5.7 (approximately). Now we may expect that in the coins of this dynasty an attempt would be made to equalise the standard issues of copper to silver, as monometallism of copper was throughout adhered to. As a matter of fact these copper coins are of a massive type, one weighs 285.2 grains viz., a coin of Bhadraghosha.[123] The standard weight for silver Dharaṇa was 58 grs. (maximum) but the extant coins average about 50 grains, the heaviest being 55.6 grs in Smith's Catalogue and if we take into conderation the fact that copper coins suffered more from wear we find that these massive copper coins are about 5 1/2 times the weight of the silver Dharaṇas. As the aproximate ratio of the two metals was 1 : 5.7 later on, very reasonable inference may be made, that these coins of copper were increased in weight to tally with the silver standard coins in value, which circulated in certain other parts of the country, in order to facilitate commercial transactions. These big coins of copper suffered much in the course of ages, as their worn and defaced condition clearly testifies. But it is possible to identify the 3/4, 1/2 and 1/4 pieces. The coin of Sūryamitra[124] weighing 221.5 grs. or of Phalgunimitra[125] of 225.7 grs. are the three-fourth pieces ; and the coins weighing 123 grs. of Satyamitra[126] and Sanghamitra[127] are perhaps the half pieces. We must however take into consideration the fact that variation in the weight of these copper coins is inevitable, if the silver standard be kept constant and the price of copper fluctuate relative to that of silver. The big Taxilian cast coin of 306 grs.[128] may be referred to this period or a later one, and is surely equal in value to one silver Dharaṇa of 58 grs. in the ratio of 1 : 5.7 between silver and copper, after making the necessary allowance for the decrease of weight brought about by active circulation. Cunningham identified it as a Two-paṇa piece but the One-paṇa pieces cannot average more than 146.4 grs. (the maximum for a paṇa) and the Two-paṇa piece cannot in any case, even without taking the wear into consideration, weigh more than 292.8 grs. The difference in weight would be very much greater if we take the original weight of the coin into consideration and is a strong argument against its identification with the copper coin of the traditional standard. The suggestion made here that the copper coins were increased in weight to equate them in value with the current silver coins which were circulating in the neighbouring states, though the probability of circulating side by side in the same state cannot be put out of account altogether, at least in some cases, may be well-exemplified by a reference to some of the coins of Taxila, though in the case of these coins the silver ones were based not upon the traditional Indian standard but upon the Greek standard of Drachma. In 1884, 143 square copper coins were found at Shahdheri (ancient Taxila) and Cunningham classifies 135 of them as follows.[129]—

"84 Indian Coins of One face only, average weight,		140.8 grs.
27 ,, ,,	Two faces ,, ,,	183.3 ,,
9 Coins of Pantaleon	,, ,,	180.5 ,,
	24 Greek (*i.e.* Indo-Greek)	
15 Coins of Agathokles		

It is evident that the 84 single-die coins are referable to the ancient Indian standard. But the 27 double-die coins and those of Pantaleon and Agathokles, 24 in number, must be of a different standard. Cunningham classifies them as belonging to the heavier standard of 100 ratis or 180 grains. A suspicion about this indenti-fication is sure to arise. The extant coins of the traditional standard of 80 ratis weigh 140.8 grains only. So the 100 rati pieces ought to be 176 grains but the 27 Indian double-die coins weigh 183.3 grains, a little more than the maximum for the standard weight of 100 ratis or 176 grains. This makes no allowance for depreciation in weight by use. So we are bound to explain the weight of these coins by reference to some other standard. One thing however is apparent that the 24 coins of Greek kings and the 27 Indian coins are exactly of the same class. We know that the silver coins of the Indo-

Greek kings are based upon the standard weight of a drachma[130] and the silver coin of Agathokles weighs 64 grains ;[131] and that is also the average weight of the extant silver coins of Nahapāa,[132] though the standard for a *hemi-drachma* is 36 grs. Now if we apply the ratio of 1 : 5.7 between silver and copper we find that the copper double-die coins of 183 grains are approximately equal in value to the hemi-drachma silver coins. If there be any doubt about the adoption of the silver standard of a hemi-drachma by an Indian state, it will be set at rest by a reference to the silver coins of the Kunindas (150 B.C.—100 A.D. ?).[133] The eight silver coins in Smith's Catalogue average 32.6 grs. In a copper coin of Yaudheyas the legend as given by Smith is[134]—"*devasya drama Bra[hma]ṇa.*" He notes—"the word drama seems quite clear but I cannot explain it." The word evidently refers to the Greek standard Drachma which later on came to be known in India as "drama." The proper arrangement of the legend would be—"Brahmanya devasya drama"—the drama of Brahmanya Deva (2nd cent, A.D.). Now the weight of this copper coin is 109 grains *i.e.* a little more than 3 times a silver 'drama' in weight. So two of these coins would be equivalent in value to a silver *hemi-drachm* of 32 grains ; it is there-fore evidently a *quarter drachma* in value. There was actually a sub-division of the 'drama' known as pàda the quarter, and the same word appears in later times *e.g. Śrimad Adivardhadrammasya pāda.*[135]

So long we have discussed the variation in weight of the copper coins, consequent on the attempt to make them equate in value to the silver standard coin with a fixed weight, by reference to the fluctuation in the ratio of the two metals. But if the weight of the copper coin be kept constant, variation would be needed in the weight of the silver coins as the ratio swings to and fro. The rise in the value of copper would increase the weight of the silver coin and a fall would lessen its weight. Prof. Bhandarkar was puzzled by the variations in weight of the silver coins of the Peshawar hoard.[136] These punch-marked coins weigh from 42.09 to 56.73 grains and Prof. Bhandarkar arranged them into eight groups each differing in weight from the other by half a Masha, from 15 1/2 Masha (56.73 grains) to II 1/2 Masha (42.00 grains).[137] But he himself points out that since "the ordinary human hand cannot unaided detect a difference of even 15 grains," detect a difference of half a Masha *i.e.*, of 1.75 grs. would be absolutely impossible. This gradual deterioration in weight he wanted to explain away by referring to the debasement of the coinage but a conscious attempt at depreciation would rather have led to an increased addition of alloy, instead of lessening the weight, which could not go on undetected for any length of time. The other suggestion made by him is that a sudden rise in the price of silver made it imperatively necessary to change the weight just as under Aurangzeb the copper dams were reduced in weight owing to the rise in the price of the metal. But here we have to differentiate the two classes of coins. The copper *dams* were token coins but if the punch-marked coins of the Peshawar hoard be the standard coins, it would be unreasonable to expect a diminution in their weight brought about by a rise in the price of silver, rather a greater amount of alloy would be used. We would however expect that the weight in any case, of the standard coin of the realm would remain constant. Prof. Bhandarkar himself is not satisfied with his own explanation—"No solution that is absolutely convincing has yet suggested itself."[139] If the heavier coins under discussion be of an earlier date, then the diminution in weight might be due to a great extent if not wholly, to the gradual rise in the price of copper keeping the copper coins, the standard coin of the province, constant ; or a fall in the price would increase the weight of the silver coins ; the lighter coins are then to be ascribed to an earlier date and I would rather prefer the second suggestion. But it is also within the bounds of probability that a percentage in the diminution in weight for some of these coins might be due to clipping and wear, though this cannot be a sufficient explanation of the nature of the fall or rise in weight which was *slow and gradual*. Another reason for the uncertainty in the estimation of the relative value of the two metals is the paucity of our information about the amount of alloy introduced in the coins of the different periods, or under the different kings. But if we take all these into consideration—the variation in the alloy, debasement of coinage due to selfishness or dishonesty, and the fluctuations in the price of silver and copper, and keep one class of coins either of silver or copper constant in weight, we can have a working hypothesis to explain the variation in the coin weights in the different periods of history in the various provinces of the country. Another possible arrangement is not to show any partiality either to silver or copper, but to have coins of the two metals of exactly the same weight, circulating side by side. The number of copper coins to be offered in exchange of a silver coin might be definitely fixed by the state, making these were token coins, or might be left to be determined by the market price of the metals. This arrangement we find as a matter of fact in the bimetallic currency of Alexander the Great of Macedon.[139a] A similar arrangement is found in India too. The Ādi-varāha coins (silver) of Mihir Bhoja, the king of Kanauj (840-890 A.D.),[140] weigh about 60 grains and his copper coins also are of the same weight. The coin No. 6 (silver) in Smith's Catalogue weighs 61.4 grains, while No. 9 (copper) weighs. 61 grains.

Evidently the two classes were based upon the same weight standard, and a similar arrangement we find in the Gadhaiyā currency of Rajputana and Gujrat from about 750-1 1100[141] A.D. In ancient times this simple arrangement might have been accepted by some of the states but the lack of detailed information about the provenance of the coins makes it impossible for us to come to any definite conclusion.

The Kuṣāṇas used coins in gold and copper only. A single piece of silver of the Kadphesis group[142] is in the British Museum, and Whitehead regards it in the nature of a proof-piece. So it may be presumed that gold was the standard coin, at least within the Kuṣāṇa Empire. In the territory under the direct control of the Emperor, gold was linked up with copper, while in the territory under the Western Satraps it was linked up with silver. In an inscription at Nasik,[143] we find that Ṛṣabhadatta, son-in-law of Nahapna made an investment of 1000 Kārṣāpaṇas with a guild of weavers at Govardhana, "and the annual interest from this source viz., 90 Kārṣāpaṇas provides the monks with Kusaṇa-mula."[144] Prof. Rapson opines "that the meaning of the term 'is doubtful." Prof. Bhandarkar has suggested that "Kuṣāṇa in particular denotes the silver coinage of Nahapāna and was socalled, because he issued it for his Kuṣāṇa overlord."[145] We may agree with Prof. Bhandarkar only so far, that the word Kuṣāṇa refers to a particular kind of coin but we cannot accept his view that it was of silver and that it stood in the ratio of 8 : 9 with, Kārṣāpaṇa. The difference of only 1/8th *i.e.*, 5 grains (the standard weight of Nahapāna's silver coins is 36 grains) would make it impossible to detect the difference between the coins in circulation side by side— the so-called silver Kuṣāṇas and the Kārṣāpaṇas. It is also improbable that the capital sum invested is referred to in one kind of coins and the interest in another kind of the same metal *e.g.*, silver. There must be some other reason for this reference. As we find that the inscription is dated in the year 42 of the Śaka era, the date is 120 A D . and this was either the last year of Kaniṣka or the first year of Huvishka.[146] We also know that Nahapāna Satrap under the Kuṣāṇas, and that if his son-in-law referred to any coin, it must have been of Nahapāna his father-in-law or of the Kuṣāṇa Emperor, his overlord. The gold coins of Kaniṣka have the legend—"*Shaonano-shao Kaneshki Koshano*"[147] but the copper coins omit the word "Koshano." So it may be inferred that the gold coins of Kaniṣka are referred to in the inscription in the word "Kusana-mūla" — the value of Kuṣāṇa, the gold coin of Kaniṣka ; because gold was the standard coin of the Empire. Moreover, that the reference is to the gold standard is apparent when we find that Ṛṣabhadatta mentions a large sum of 75000 Kārṣāpaṇas[148] "which had been given to gods and Brāhmaṇas" but immediately hastens to add that these were equal to 2000 Suvarṇas, It was needless to equate the 75000 Kārṣāpaṇas of silver to 2000 Suvarṇas unless the Suvarṇas were the standard coins of the Kuṣāṇa Empire. The identification of the Suvarṇas, the gold coins, with the Kuṣāṇas, which were also of gold offers no difficulty as we know that the Suvarṇas of the Indian standard of 80 ratis were only issued long- afterwards by Skandhagupta[149] for the first time and the words Suvarṇa and Dīnāra were applied before his time to the gold coins of the Kuṣāṇas, or of the Guptas based upon the Kuṣāṇa standard. So we are justified in inferring that both the words Kuṣāṇa and the Suvarṇa in the same inscription refer to the gold coins of Kaniṣka and "*Kusaṇa-mula*" made a pointed reference to the legends of the gold coins of the Kuṣāṇa Emperor ; and we have an analogous case in Kedāra[150] which was used as a synonym for a coin, because the name occurs on the obverse of the coins of the Kidāra Kuṣāṇas. The gold coin of 124 grains was the standard coin of the Kuṣāṇa Empire but it was most probably confined to the territories of the Kuṣāṇas and their subordinate rulers. In other parts of India, copper alone or linked with silver served the purposes of currency. The Kuṣāṇas were imitated by the Guptas in the issue of their gold coins, the Dīnaras and the Suvarṇas. In the provinces under the direct control of the Kuṣāṇa Emperors, copper was linked up with gold; and this arrangement led to the augmentation in weight of the copper coins. The heaviest specimen in Smith's Catalogue is No. 64 of Kaniṣka which weighs 266 grains.[151] We must make some allowance for depreciation in weight on account of wear and tear and we can reasonably take the original weight of this coin to be approximately 280 grains *i.e.*, about 2 1/4 times the weight of the gold Dīnāra of 124 grains. If we apply the ratio of gold and copper which prevailed in the 6th century A.D.—1 : 56.7, we find that about 25 of these massive copper coins would be equal in value to a gold Dīnāra ; but we can reasonably infer that the price of copper was higher in terms of gold in the 1st century A.D., and if the ratio be 1 : 45 a gold Dīnāra would be equal in value to 20 of these massive copper coins. Are these copper coins the Viṁśopakas[151a] (that were 1/20th of the standard coin of the country) which have not yet been identified?

Silver or gold superimposed on copper made the copper coins mere tokens, but we have to take into consideration the ease with which coins could be manipulated in those early days. It would have been very difficult to lessen the weight of the metals used and bring them down below the market value, at least an attempt had to be made to keep the ratio of the two metals unimpaired ; and the chief device by which the value of the token coins was brought down below the weight of the metal in these coins was the common practice of debasing the coins with baser alloy. In addition to metallic tokens there were many other things that were employed for the purposes of currency, and some of these were as old as the time when Barter was the ordinary means of exchange. Cowry shells were in use from time immemorial and though they are now rapidly disappearing, yet they are found employed as currency in certain parts of the country, specially in the villages These shells are imported from East Africa, Maldive land Laccadive Islands[152] and are used for minor transactions and are linked up with copper. We have a reference to cowry shells (Sippikāni) in the Jātakas in the sense of "doits or mites"[153] and already they had been supplanted by metallic coins. The cowry remained the medium of exchange when the coins were found too valuable for the purpose. But what was the relationship between the cowry and the standard coin is very difficult to determine There can be no doubt that the number of cowries in lieu of a particular coin differed in various parts of the country. At present in Bengal 20 cowry shells are given in exchange for a pice, a copper coin. So 1280 (20 x 64) cowries are equated to a rupee, the silver standard coin. According to Cunningham, in ancient times 80 cowries were equal in value for exchange purposes to a copper Kārṣāpaṇa of 80 ratis and 16 panas of 80 cowries each he equates to a silver Kārṣāpaṇa or Dharaṇa of 32 ratis.[154] The question however to be decided is whether the Kārṣāpaṇa here referred to, is the silver or the copper coin of this denomination. If we accept the Kārṣāpaṇa to be of sliver, then it establishes a ratio of 1 : 40 between silver and copper. But we have seen, that in the early part of the Medieval Period, the ratio was 1 : 5.7 and it was higher perhaps in earlier times. So it would not be reasonable to equate a silver Kārṣāpaṇa to 16 paṇas of cowries ; rather it is the copper Kārṣāpaṇa Kahapāna of the Jātakas or the Kahan of the modern vernacular that is referred to. It gains support from the fact that in the rules for Prayaschitta or expiation,[155] it is expressly laid down that certain gifts are to be made in cows, failing cows in cowries and if cowries cannot be procured in copper, and last of all in the standard coin of either silver or gold. This order of preference seems to link up cowries with copper. The lightest coins of copper from Ujjain, Eraṇ and Mālawā "are actually less than 4 grains in weight,"[156] and according to Cunningham these were worth only 2 cowry shells.[157] This will highly restrict the use of cowry for small purchases and as we have found that copper preceded silver for purposes of coinage, it would not be unreasonable to equate the 16 paṇas of cowries to the copper Kārṣāpaṇa. The result of this equation will be as follows : -

1	Kārṣāpaṇa (copper) of	80 ratis	= 1280 cowries.
½	,, Ardha-Kārṣāpaṇa	40 ,,	= 640 ,,
¼	,, = 1 Kakani	20 ,,	= 320 ,,
1/8	,, = ½ Kakani	10 ,,	= 160 ,,
1/16	,, = ¼ Kakani	5 ,,	= 80 cowries or 20 gandas.

The weight of the one fourth Kakani is equal to the light coins of Ujjain, Eran etc. (4 grains) after making the allowance for wear and tear.

Though cowry-shells were in general use, yet we find various other things mentioned as mediums of exchange. In Pāṇini,[158] we have a reference to some of these things *e.g.*, vasana or "pieces of cloth of definite value,"[159] *go-pucchal*[160] or "bovine-tail" (the meaning suggested by Prof. Bhandarkar but I would rather prefer the *chamara*) and certain measures of capacity Kaṁsa Sūrpa and Khārī. These were nothing but reminiscences of the old practice of Barter, which does not fail to influence even the most highly developed society. Buddhaghosha[161] who flourished in the 5th century A.D. in his commentary on the Vinaya-Piṭaka, refers to three varieties of Māṣaka. One is metallic — copper, iron or some other metal ; "another variety is that made of Sara wood, the outside of the bamboo, or palmyra leaf, each of which has been turned into the Māṣaka coin by a rūpa or figure being cut into it. The third variety consists of lac or gum on which a rupa or figure has been caused to rise up and which has thus become a Māṣaka."[162] He also refers to other mediums of exchange which were current in his days in the different parts of the country. They were "of bone or skin or the fruits or seeds of trees." These non-metallic substances were requisitioned to help the people in minor exchange transactions and served as mere tokens. This practice was necessitated by the paucity of the metals which were consequently too valuable for small business purposes.

FOOTNOTES

1. Marshall, Sir John—Statement to the Press on the recent Archaeological Discoveries in India.
2. Mitra, Panchanan—Prehistoric India, p. 193, footnote 1.
3. Marshall, Sir John—Statement to the Press on the Archaeological Discoveries in India.
4. *Ibid*. 5 *Ibid*.
6. Watt, Sir George—The Commercial Products of India, p. 403.
7. Skeat, W. W.—The Etymological Dictionary of the English Language, p. 244.
8. Cunningham, Sir A.—Coins of Ancient India, p. 22.
9. Watt, Sir George—The Commercial Products of India, p. 566.
10. Cunningham, Sir A.—Ancient Geography of India, p. 520 (Calcutta, 1924). Cunningham however thinks that the Sona river is "called the Hiraṇyabaha, or the golden, on account of its bad yellow sands."
11. Watt, Sir George—The Commercial Products of India, p. 566.
12. Lord Avebury—The Origin of Civilisation, p. 54.
13. Palgrave, Sir R. H. Inglis—The Dictionary of Political Economy, Vol. II, p. 219.
14. H. Marshall, Sir John—Statement to the Press on Archaeological Discoveries in Mahenjo-daro and Harappā.
15. Palgrave, Sir R. H. Inglis—The Dictionary of Political Economy, Vol. II, p. 220.
16. *Ibid*.
17. Palgrave, Sir R. H. Inglis—The Dictionary of Political Economy, Vol. II., p. 220.

18. Cunningham, Sir. A.—The Coins of Ancient India, p. 5,
19. *Ibid.*
20. Smith, V.—The Catalogue of Coins in the Indian Museum, Calcutta, p. 136.
21. *Ibid.*
22. Bhandarkar, D. R.—Ancient Indian Numismatics, p. 59.
23. *Ibid*, p. 59, footnote No, 2. 23a *Ibid*, pp. 56 & 57.
24. Elliot, Sir Walter—Coins of Southern India, (The Inter. Numismata Orientalia), p. 53, (Plate I, No. 2).
25. Rapson, E. J.—Indian Coins p. 3, (Plate I, No. 5).
26. "The earliest coins of Northern India are one or two small pieces which were probably struck at Taxila and bear the peculiar symbols which Sir Alexander Cunningham called the Taxila mark,"—Whitehead, R. B.—The Pre-Mohammedan Coinage of North-western India, p. 44. One of these coins is figured in Plate II, No. 18 in Cunningham's Coins of Ancient India. But it is a die-struck coin and therefore of a much later date.
27. Cunningham, Sir A.—Coins of Ancient India, p. 5.
28. Cunningham, Sir A.—Ancient Geography of India, p. 570. (Calcutta, 1924).
29. Marshall, Sir John—Statement to the Press about the Archaeological Discoveries in the Indus Valley.
30. Rawlinson, H. G.—Intercourse between India and the Western World, p. II. Schoff, W. H.--The Periplus of the Erythraean Sea, p. 175.
31. Rawlinson, H. G.—Intercourse between India and the Western World, p. 18, (footnote 1).
32. Schoff, W. H.—The Periplus of the Erythraean Sea, pp. 43, 44, & 219.
33. *Ibid*, pp. 42, 219, 220 & 287.
34. Watt, Sir G.—The Commercial Products of India, p. 401.
35. Mitra, P.—Pre-historic India, p. 177.
36. *Ibid*, p. 189.
37. Marshall, Sir John—Statement to the Press about the Archaeological Discoveries of the Indus Valley.
38. Rapson, E. J.—Catalogue of the Coins of the Andhras etc., CLXXIX. Bhandarkar, D. R.—Ancient Indian Numismatics, p. 81.
39. Bhandarkar, D. R.—Ancient Indian Numismatics, p. 88. 40 Cunningham, Sir Alexander—Coins of Ancient India, p. 54.
41. Kauṭilya—Arthaśāstra, p. 98, (English Translation).
42. "India, in fact, produced little or no silver, while gold was abundant."—Cunningham, Sir Alexander—Coins of Ancient India, P. 5.
43. Elliot, Sir Walter—Coins of Southern India, p. 51 (footnote No I).
44. Mitra, P.—Pre-historic India, p. 189.
45. Cunningham, Sir Alexander—Coins of Ancient India, p. 5.
46. *Ibid*, p. 6.
47. Cambridge History of India, Vol. I, p. 343.
48. *Ibid.*
49. Schoff, W. H.—The Periplus of the Erythraean Sea, p. 38.
50. *Ibid.*, pp. 42 aud 287.
51. *Ibid.*, pp. 44 and 287.
52. Smith, V. A.—The Catalogue of Coins in the Indian Museum, p. 208.
53. *Ibid.*, p. 209.
54. Watt, Sir George—The Commercial Products of India, p. 707.

55. Schoff, W. H.—The Periplus of the Erythraean Sea, pp. 175 and 198.
56. *Ibid.*, pp. 205, 208 and 211.
57. *Ibid.*, quoted from Pliny xxxiv. 17, p. 221.
58. Elliot, Sir Walter—The Coins of Southern India, p. 22. Schoff, W. H.—The Periplus of the Erythraean Sea, p. 190.
59. Rapson, E. J.—A Catalogue of the Indian Coins,—Andhras etc., p. clxxxii.
60. *Ibid.*
61. Bhandarkar, D. R.—Ancient Indian Numismatics, p. 142.
62. *Ibid.*, p. 143.
63. *Ibid*,
64. *Ibid.*
65. *Ibid.*
66. *Ibid.*
67. *Ibid.*, p. 144.
68. *Ibid.*
68a. Schoff, W. H.—The Periplos of the Erythraean Sea, p. 70.
68b. *Ibid*, p. 70.
69. Bhandarkar, D. R.— Ancient Indian Numismatics, p. 145.
70. *Ibid.*
71. The Encyclopedia Britannica (Ninth Edition), Vol. 17, p. 630.
72. Watt, Sir George—The Commercial Products of India, p. 402. 73 Rapson, E. J.—The Catalogue of the Indian Coins (the Andhras etc.), p. clxxix.
74. *Ibid.*, p. xi.
75. *Ibid.*, p. clxxx.
76. Macdonald, G.—The Evolution of Coinage, p. 38.
77. *Ibid.*
78. Bhandarkar, D. R.—Ancient Indian Numismatics, p. 112.
79. Gardner, P.—The Earliest Coins of Greece Proper, p. 16. 80 *Ibid.*, p. 12. 81 *Ibid.*, p. 16.
82. Whitehead, R. B.—The Catalogue of Coins in the Punjab Museum, p. 174.
83. Rapson, E. J.—Indian Coins, p. 25.
84. Allan, J.—Catalogue of the Coins of the Gupta Dynasties, etc., p. cxxxii. .85 *Ibid.*
86. *Ibid.*, p. cxxxiv.
87. *Ibid.*
88. Rapson, E. J.—Indian Coins, p. 29.
89. *Ibid.*
90. Calcutta Market Report, October 8, 1928.
91. The Historians' History of the World, Vol. II, p. 339.
92. *Ibid.*, p. 342.
93. The Cambridge History of India, Vol. I, p. 343.
94. Gardner, P.- The Earliest Coins of Greece Proper, p. 12.
95. Palgrave, R. H. I.—Dictionary of Political Economy, Vol. II, p. 221.
96. Macdonald, ,G.-The Evolution of Coinage, p. 42.
97. *Ibid*, p. 43.
98. Schoff, W. H.—The Periplus, p. 219.
99. *Ibid.*
100. Cunningham, Sir A.—Coins of Ancient India, p. 5.
101. The Cambridge History of India, Vol. I, p. 343.

102. *Ibid.*
103. Rapson, E. J.—The Catalogue of Coins (The Andhras etc.), p. lviii.
104. The Cambridge History of India, Vol. I, p. 583. 105 See The Ara Inscription of year 41 of Kaniṣka. Mr R. D. Banerjee's Theory holds the ground.
105a. Bhandarkar, D. R.—Ancient Indian Numismatics, p. 192.
106. Rapson, E. J.—The Catalogue of Coins (The Andhras etc.), p. cviii.
106a. Allan, J.—Catalogue of the Coins of the Gupta Dynasties, pp. cxxxiv and 117.
107. Rapson, E. J.—Indian Coins, pp. 17 and 25.
108. Allan, J.—Catalogue of the Coins of the Gupta Dynasties, p. cxxxiv.
109. *Ibid.*
110. The 9 coins of Nahapāna in Rapson's Catalogue weigh 287.3 grains, *i.e.*, average approximately 32 grains.
111. Schoff, W. H.—The Periplns of the Erythraean Sea, p. 219.
112. Encyclopaedia Britannica, Vol. 17, p. 653 (Ninth Edition). 112a Schoff, W. H.—The Periplus of the Erythraean Sea, paras 49 and 56.
113. "Vishnngupta, the author of Panchatantra flourished in the 5th Cent. A.D. and he was a man of the South. For the book is "introduced with the story of king Amarasakti of Mahilaropya, a city of the South who wishes to discover a scholar capable of training his three stupid and idle sons."—Arthur A. Macdonald— "A History of the Sanskrit Literature," pp. 369 and 370.
See MS:
114. Elliot, Sir Walter—Coins of Southern India, pp. 47-52 and 146.
115. Bhandarkar, D. R.—Ancient Indian Numismatics, p. 189.
116. *Ibid.*
117. *Ibid*, p. 190.
118. *Ibid*, p. 191.
119. Kauṭilya—Arthaśāāstra, p. 98. (English Translation, 1915).
120. Smith, V. A,—The Catalogue of Coins in the Indian Museum, pp. 156-159.
121. Cf. The Coins of Taxila—Smith's Catalogue—Single-die coins, p. 156 and Double-die coins, p. 158.
122. Smith, V. A.—The Catalogue of Coins in the Indian Museum, pp. 184-189.
123. *Ibid*, p. 187.
124. *Ibid*, p. 188.
125. *Ibid.*
126. Cunningham, Sir A.—Coins of Ancient India, p. 93.
127. *Ibid*, p. 94.
128. *Ibid*, p. 62.
129. *Ibid*, p. 65.
130. Brown, C. J.—The Coins of India, p. 25. Whitehead, R. B.—Catalogue of Coins in the Punjab Museum, p. 5.
131. Whitehead, R. B.—Catalogue of Coins in the Punjab Museum, Vol. I, p. 17.
132. Rapson, E. J.—Catalogue of Coins (The Andhras etc.), pp. 65-67.
133. Smith, V. A.—Catalogue of Coins in the Indian Museum, pp.- 167-170.
134. *Ibid*, p. 182 (Coin No. 18b).
135. Bhandarkar, D. R.—Ancient Indian Numismatics, p. 210.
136. *Ibid*, p. 123.

137. *Ibid*, p. 115.
138. *Ibid*, p. 116.
139. *Ibid*, p. 115.
139a. The Encyclopaedia Britannica, Vol. 17, (Ninth Edition), p. 641. Macdonald, G.—The Evolution of Coinage, p. 43.
140. Smith, V. A.—Catalogue of Coins in the Indian Museum, p. 241.
141. *Ibid*, pp. 240-241.
142. "There was, moreover, at this time a world shortage of silver; not only do we find the Pahlava kings striking didrachms in debased silver, but the silver denarius itself, was during the early empire, being reduced in weight and fineness. This accounts for the disappearance of silver and the important place of gold in the Kuṣāṇa coinage,"—Brown, C. J.—The Coins of India, p. 34.
Whitehead, R. B.—Catalogue of the Coins in the Punjab Museum, Vol. I, p. 174.
143. Rapson, E. J.—Catalogue of Coins (The Andhras etc.), p. lviii.
144. Kusaṇa-mūla—"M. Senart translates, 'money for outside life'; but it would seem probable that reference is here made to the custom of 'Kathina,' *i.e.* the privilege of wearing extra robes, which was granted to the monks during the rainy season."— Rapson, E. J.—–Catalogue of the Coins (The. Andhras etc.), p. Iviii.
145. Bhandarkar, D. R.—Ancient Indian Numismatics, p. 200.
146. Kaniṣka's reign is of 41 years, if the Ara inscription be dated in his last year.
147. Smith, V. A. — Catalogue of Coins in the Indian Museum. P. 69.
148. Rapson, E. J.—Catalogue of Coins (The Andhras etc.), p. lviii.
149. Allan, J.—Catalogue of Coins of the Gupta Dynasties, p. cxxxiii.
150. Bhandarkar. D. R.—Ancient Indian Numismatics, p. 205. 151 Smith, V. A.-Catalogue of Coins in the Indian Museum.
I51a. Bhandarkar, D. R.—Ancient Indian Numisinatics, pp. 187 and 209.
152. Watt, Sir G.-—The Commercial Products of India, p. 989.
153. Cambridge History of India, Vol. I, p. 218.
153a. "The use of the cowrie shell as a medium of exchange has long been known in Bengal; but that they were well-known in Dravidadesam is proved by their Tamil name Kavadi (cowrie?)." "In 1740 a rupee in Bengal exchanged for 2,400 cowries; in 1840 for 6,500."—Elliot, Sir Walter —The Coins of Southern India, p. 59, footnote 2.
154. Cunningham, Sir A.—Coins of Ancient India, pp. 46 and 47.
155. See MS:
156. Cunningham, Sir A. — Coins of Ancient India, p. 46. 157 *Ibid*.
158. Bhandarkar, D. R. — Ancient Indian Numismatics, pp. 169 and 170.
159. Pāṇini, V. I. 27. (Bhandarkar— A.I.N.).
160. Ibid
161. Bhandarkar, D. R.— Ancient Indian Numismatics, p. 140.
162. Ibid.

CHAPTER VI

THE MODE OF FABRICATION

In the Vedic period, gold was sometimes kept in the natural state, as it was convenient to weigh out the gold dust like any other commodity.[1] This practice has even come down to our times and as pointed out by Trail "gold dust separated into Phetāṅgs (covered money ?), each tied-up in a bit of cloth" was current in Bhotea Mahals of Kumaon "at eight rupees the Phetang."[2] But each such transaction would necessitate an appeal to the balance, as there is no knowing that the contents had not been tampered with. So it is not strange that the metal was kept in lumps as referred to in the phrase "dasa Hiraṇya piṇḍān"[3]—"ten lumps of gold." As pointed out by Thomas "the near juxtaposition of the term *Hiraṇya* piṇḍān with the preceding *Kosaiyih* seemingly points to refined or wrought metal, in contrast to the *native* gold enclosed in the latter. It is probable that the former consisted of buttons of cast metal, which originally took the form of rough balls or imperfect pyramids, . . ."[4] There is no doubt that other metals also at this stage were kept in lumps of definite weight and served two purposes as weights and mediums of exchange. But when coinage was evolved the metals that were requisitioned for the purpose went through a process that gave the peculiar shape to the Indian pieces. In the West, in Asia Minor and Greece the earliest coins were small ingots of metal "bean-shaped or oval" impressed with a punch—"with an official mark as a guarantee of just weight, thus rendering an appeal to the scales on every fresh transaction no longer a matter of necessity."[5] In the same category we may place the solid ingots of silver similar to the three pieces in Smith's catalogue which have only "three circular dots in" one face,[6] and it has been surmised that this represents the earliest form.[7] The next stage in the order of evolution is perhaps represented by "the heavy bent bars of silver with devices stamped out with a punch on one side."[8] But there is no reason to suppose that it was the earlier, on the ground that the earlier and the cruder system of manufacture was replaced by the later system ; rather we find on occasions that when a better system comes in vogue, the older system is given the preference *e.g.*, among the Indo-Sassanians.[9] It is doubtful whether the 3 solid ingots and the heavy bent bars in Smith's Catalogue actually served as coins before the advent of the punch-marked coins for it is not always safe to infer an early age by a mere reference to a ruder system of manufacture. However in the punch-marked pieces of India, "we see money in the very infancy of the numismatic art.[10] From a close examination of the extant pieces, it is possible to find out the system of manufacture that was in vogue. "Silver was first beaten out into a sheet somewhat thinner than a quarter-dollar. Strips about half an inch in width were then cut off and each strip was divided into pieces of the same weight, approximately 56 grains, and a final adjustment of the weight was made by cutting small bits off one or more corners of the heavier blanks. The marks of the chisel still remain on the edges of the thicker pieces, which were broken off when the cut did not go clean through the strip of metal."[11] The copper coins were "cut out of a thicker bar"[12] and "some of the copper pieces may have been made from cast blanks."[13] These coins were known as punch-marked, as the devices were impressed on the face of the coins by separate punches "applied irregularly at various points on the surface. Naturally the impressions so effected often interfere with one another, and in cases where they are numerous the result is a confused jumble of symbols. Ordinarily, no difficulty is experienced in distinguishing the obverse from the reverse, the former being occupied by the larger symbols, commonly numerous, and the latter being some times blank, more often marked by a single minute device and not infrequently marked by two or three comparatively inconspicuous devices. The cases in which both sides are crowded with symbols are rather rare."[14] Prof. Bhandarkar points out that "in a few cases punches were applied to the surface of the hammered sheet before it was cut into strips."[15] The principal symbols which perhaps referred to the authorisation of the state or the *provenance* "were punched on before other marks,"[16] and Walsh surmises from an examination of "the surface of the coins that all the obverse marks were punched on the metal when heated, and so, probably, at one time."[17] The punches which were hammered into the blanks must have been of hard metal, perhaps iron and were in relief. The impression was sunk into the surface and this rather increased the period of circulation by protecting the devices from being nibbed off. Cunningham computes that the average loss of a punch-marked coin "was not more than one grain and a half in a century."[18] In shape these coins were irregular, generally oblong and this was necessitated by the peculiar mode of fabrication. As pointed out by Smith[19] "the cutting of circular blanks from a metal sheet" is "a more troublesome process than snipping strips into short lengths, the circular coins are presumably a later invention than the rectangular ones." So these coins are generally rectangular and gradually approximated to a roughly square shape which was imitated by the Greek kings Pantaleon and Agathokles (C 190 B.C.)[20] and it is correct to state that the square coins exercised a fascination "upon Indian moneyers of all periods."[21] Even so late as the 18th century Rajesvara (1751-1769 A.D.) the king of Assam issued square coins. The roughly circular coins are seen in the bas-relief (B.C. 150) from the railing of the Great Stūpa at Bharhut but there is no doubt that the vast majority are rectangular ; or rather it is evident that practically no attention was bestowed upon the shape of the coins at the time of manufacture. The punch-marked coinage has been characterised "in respect of form" "the simplest of all"[22] but there can be no doubt that the angular corners were an "obvious inconvenience" and gradually the circular pieces supplanted them.

We also find, casting the coins extensively in use. Sometimes the blanks of copper were cast in the mould and later on devices were punched on them. But the coins with the devices which were not surely as sharp-cut and clear, were manufactured by pouring molten metal into the moulds. "A cavity was formed by joining two moulds together" and this appears to be a "very ancient practice in India."[23] A few are blank on the reverse and therefore must have been the product of one mould.[24] The moulds were perhaps of burnt clay or of hard metal like bronze, stone or iron. Each piece had to be cast separately but a number of them might be manufactured by a single casting. In that case the moulds were connected by "narrow channels for the passage of the heated metal from one form to another."[25] After the metal had cooled, the pieces were separated by breaking off the joints and not only the projections were not always obliterated but two coins joined together in this way were found by Cunningham and are depicted in his book (Plate I, Nos. 24 and 25) .[26] Some of the states Kauśāmbi, Ajodhyā, Mathurā etc. issued cast coins as late as the 3rd century A.D., even though the system of die-striking had come into use in the North-West.[27] The devices were in intaglio in the moulds and were in, relief on the coins and thus it obviated the necessity of punching the devices separately. Later on the full type supplanted the smaller symbols. The reason for the preference of this system of casting the coins seems to be due to the introduction of much alloy in the metal which consequently could not stand the blows from hammer. The cast coins were all of copper and in this term Smith included its various alloys.

The latest development in the technic of manufacture of coins was to strike them from dies. But before it was finally reached various intermediate experiments had to be gone through, and the double die-struck coins emerged as the final product of the experience of perhaps centuries. The method that was employed in Europe with the mechanical means then available had been detailed by Macdonald. "A lump of metal that had previously been adjusted to the proper weight, was heated, and, while till hot, placed upon an anvil and held firmly in position by a punch, the upper end of which was struck sharply several times with a hammer. If on or in the anvil there had previously been laid or embedded a 'die' — that is, a piece of cold hard metal with a device of some sort cut upon it in intaglio — the effect of the striking was to produce upon the heated metal a corresponding impression in relief, and so to provide the coin with a type upon its lower side. If there were a device in intaglio on the lower end of the punch, then the coin received a type upon its upper side as well."[28] In India the first stage of progress is markedfy grouping the symbols in a distinct type and by impressing them from a die which however covered only about two-thirds of the piece, the lower face remaining blank. "The next advance may be traced in the adaptation of the anvil to the first crude idea of a reverse, in a sunk-die or catch of small dimensions cut into the anvil itself ; which invention may be followed in its various stages of elaboration, from the rough intaglio, which served to fix the planchet, upto the complete superficial reverse of later examples."[29] Thus in the third stage the obverse die covers the whole face "but the reverse die is smaller than the blank" and the last stage was reached when both the faces of the coin, the obverse and the reverse were fully covered by devices and were struck by two dies. A variation in the third stage is marked by "a parallel series, of independent growth, essayed to effect the fixation of the metal to be impressed, by giving a cup-like form to the reverse die, which was gradually advanced from its unadorned convexity to all the honours of a device equal in spread and finish to the leading obverse."[30]

The first step is exemplified by some of the coins of Eraṇ where a "definite type" was evolved which was struck from a die but was merely a collection of symbols that were previously punched on the coins separately. Prof. Rapson thinks that "this is usually the case in those parts of India which were least affected by foreign influence."[31] For the next development we may refer to some of the coins illustrated in Plate II of Cunningham's book.[32] Prof. Rapson is of opinion that "the art of striking from a die" was first adopted in Taxila in this country,[33] and the earliest specimens had the impress of the die only on one side and the reverse was blank but the method of striking was "peculiarly Indian."[33a] The metal was impressed with the die in a semi-molten condition and the result was that "the impress of the die was left enclosed in a deep incuse square."[33b] The variations of this system are found in the coins of Pañcāla Tripurī, Kauśāmbī and Mathurā.[34] The double-die coins of Taxila are illustrated by Cunningham in Plate III and these coins whether round or square "show not only greater symmetry of shape, but an advance in the art of die-cutting."[35] The guild tokens in Plate III (Cunningham) are looked upon as "some of the earliest of this type" and the finest specimens have been found in the Gandhāra region. The cup-shaped coins are found among the Western Chalukyas and the Kadambas[36] and the cuplike reverse was favoured by the Indo-Scythians and the Sassanians, though there can be no doubt that they were fully cognizant of the "more advanced methods of coining."[37]

The dies were surely of hard metal, perhaps of iron, bronze or steel like the ancient dies of the West, of later Greek and Roman times ;[38] these naturally entailed much labour and the method of working must have been analogous to that of the gem engraver. The lower die was generally embedded in the anvil and the device when struck stood out in relief, but the upper die did not cover the whole face and the impression was in incuse. This is found clearly in the local Taxilian coins with "Elephant and Lion type' (Plate III, Cunningham). The lower device is denominated the obverse and it is generally embellished with elaboration, and the other side is called the reverse ; but when one side of the coin is blank the other is always designated the obverse whether it is the upper or the lower side. It is generally found that the reverse die had a shorter life than the obverse one,[39] because it could not so well stand the shock of the hammer. Another thing to be marked in this connection is that the obverse and the reverse types are not parallel to each other but they lie "at any angles to one another. The precision in the adjustment of the dies was secured in the West by having the two dies connected by a hinge but it is evident that no such contrivance was in use in India.[40] The blanks were sometimes cast in moulds (cf. the coins of Mathura),[41] and then struck with dies but the general practice was to take a hammered sheet and to strip off pieces which were then adjusted to the standard weight. The blanks were next put in the fire and then placed on the dies in a semi-molten condition to take the impressions which were hammered into them.

The Arthaśāstra refers to some of the officials connected with the manufacture of coins. The *lakṣṇādhyakṣah* or the Superintendent of Mint was later known as rūpyadhyakṣah and he carried on the manufacture of coins, The standard silver coin (rūpyarūpa) wa's the Paṇa, and its subdivisions were the half, the quarter and the one-eighth. The copper coins (tamrarupa) were the Māshaka, half a Māshaka, kākaṇi[42] Evidently Māshaka was 1/16th of a Paṇa and the weight of the copper coins must vary with reference to the variation in the ratio of the two metals. Another officer, (rupadarsaka) the Examiner of Coins regulated the currency in its two-fold functions of vyavaharika, *i.e.* as a means for exchange purposes and kosapravesya, that is, as legal tender. The silver coins were received in the treasury and the tamra-rūpa, the copper coins were the *vyavahārika* or token coins. It was the duty of this officer to collect the rupika of 8 per cent., the *vyāji* of 5 per cent., the *pārīkṣika* or testing charge of 1/8th Paṇa per cent, and the fine of 25 paṇas imposed on offenders other than the manufacturer, the seller, the purchaser and the examiner. The *rūpika* was paid by the manufacturer and Prof. Bhandarkar takes this to be the tax paid by a private individual who brought a quantity of bullion to the mint for being coined on his own account and infers that "there was a system of free coinage" and rūpika was the premium which he had to pay.[43] Kauṭilya lays down that "the State Goldsmith shall employ artisans to manufacture gold and silver coins (rūpyasuvarṇa) from the bullion of citizens and country people."[44] We however know that the corporations or the Naigamas had the right of coinage and it may be presumed[45] "that the royal prerogative of coining money was less understood and less jealously guarded." Prof. Bhandarkar also opines that there was a "regular sale and purchase of coins going on"[46] and *vyāji* was the 5 per cent, paid by both the parties "on their profit to the state"; pārīkṣika was the tax on the profit of pārīkṣitṛ "to whom the people brought, for appraising, coins coming from all quarters in the course of commerce." Prof. Bhandarkar's interpretation requires a little modification. We have strong reasons to hold that coins were manufactured on behalf of private individuals and corporations under the control of the state[47] and rupika was the tax which was paid by the manufacturers in general and was not merely confined to the manufacture of coins ; as the word was derived from rūpa or coin, most probably it refers to the fact that this tax was paid in coins as distinguished from vyāji which was paid in kind. Vyāji is evidently the portion which had to be paid by the buyers and the sellers to the state, analogous to the modern practice of *māthat* or *tolā* which is levied in kind by the Zaminders on the sellers and the buyers in their *hāts* or bazars. But a regular sale and purchase of coins seems to be a superfluous economic transaction ; I would rather think that it refers to the practice which even now prevails of paying the battā or premium for small change, and the phrase— buyers and sellers" does not refer to those who were engaged in the sale and purchase of coins but rather to the general body of merchants. Moreover, it also appears that the pārīkṣika was the fee which was levied by the *rūpadarśaka* for appraising the coins ; and that a different class of men is not referred to is evident from the fact that the duty of the *rūpadarśaka* was to regulate currency as a medium of exchange which must include the principal duty of appraising the coins. So the correct interpretation of the passage seems to be that the *rūpika* was collected by that officer from the private individuals on whose behalf the State Goldsmith manufactured the coins, and he helped the merchants in general by supplying them with small change and appraising the coins. He also levied the vyāji, the state's share as well as the pārīkṣika and these threefold functions with that of levying fines on offenders were included in his duty of regulating the currency in general. The *rūpadarśaka* must have a large number of subordinates under him whose duty was to identify the coins and to find out whether they were genuine or counterfeit. These duties were performed "by observing the coins, by handling them by sounding, smelling and even licking them,"[48] and one of these subordinate officers must have been the Hairaṇyika or the Sauvarṇika[50] of Kauṭilya.

A certain amount of alloy was needed in the manufacture of coins. As found by Cunningham who examined 113 silver Kārṣāpaṇas the percentage of alloy varied from 13.8 to 24.3. But Kauṭilya lays down that silver coins should be manufactured by the *Lakṣaṇa dhyakṣa* with 5/16 ths, *i.e.*, 31.25 p.c. of alloy and the copper coin with 1/4th (pādajīvam), *i.e.*, 25 p.c. of alloy Why the percentage of alloy is so high in the Arthaśāstra has not been satisfactorily explained. Prof. Bhandarkar suggests that this was due to the increase of the price of silver, This however does not carry conviction, for there is no reason to infer that silver became scarce all on a sudden under the Mauryas, and no actual specimen of a coin with this high percentage of alloy has yet been identified and referred to the Maurya period. The different articles which were used as alloys in silver coins were *tāmra, tikṣṇa, trapu*, sīsa and añjana.[51] Tāmra or copper to be used to the extent of 1/4 of the weight and any one of the four others to the extent of 1/16th; the total amount of alloy therefore was 5/16ths or 31.25 p.c. Tīkṣṇa has been identified by Shamasastry with copper sulphate.[52] But it was a hard metal as is evident from the fact that one of the four different ways of deception practised was the ullekhana,[53] the scratching of the compact pieces of metals by tīkṣṇa. It is therefore practically sure that it is iron or as the commentator puts it lohaviśeshah.[54] *Trapu* is tin, sīsa lead, añjana a special kind of material of the black pigment, such as antimony. The alloy for copper is not expressly mentioned by Kauṭilya but the commentator takes it to be "made up of four parts of silver, eleven parts of copper and one part of tīkṣṇa or any other metal." This however gives the alloy 31.25 p.c., exactly the same as for the silver coins and differs from the percentage allowed in the Arthaśāstra *i.e.*, pādajīvam or one-fourth for the copper coins.

The easiest method of debasing the coinage is to increase the amount of alloy. This may be needed by the economic exigencies of the time (as in the reign of Skandagupta)[55] or from the selfish greed of the ruling prince. But when the debasement is the work of the state a strong suspicion would naturally arise that the times were troublous, for no prince would be foolish enough to do injury to the trade and commerce of the territory under his control, unless driven to desperation. The manufacturers of counterfeit coins however would be sure to introduce as much alloy as possible. This was their main source of profit and incidentally, they were also saved from the payment of the rūpika. So it was the state as well as the individual citizens that suffered in their hands. The punishment, therefore, according to Kauṭilya is banishment, not only for those who manufacture counterfeit coins but "also those who deal in such coins or try to lower their quality by mixing them with alloys."[56] It is also laid down that the counterfeit coins should be cut to pieces by the Sannidhatā the Chamberlain and any one offering him a piece of counterfeit coin should "be punished with the first amercement."[57] The articles that were generally used in the manufacture of counterfeit coins are enumerated by Kauṭilya. These were the "various kinds of metals, alkalis, charcoal bellows, pincers, crucibles, stove and hammers" and the other accessory instruments, the punches etc., needed for the purpose.[58]

Another method of deception was to plate the coins ; the copper blank was covered with silver and then "received the impress of the punches."[59] It has been pointed out by Theobold that this practice is found among the Grseco-Bactrians of the Punjab, the Hindu kings of Kabul and various Muhammadan dynasties. "The plating is extremely well executed and of the most durable character, covering the edge of the coin as licell as its surface"[60] It was however done very easily by merely dipping "the bright copper blank" in melted silver. To detect these plated coins was very difficult; so we find that the shroffs generally struck the coins with a sharp metal and many of the Pathan coins are found covered with shroff marks. Another method of plating the coins was detected by Mr. Walsh in a hoard of punch-marked coins found at Patna in 1917. He found that some of the coins were "debased by the addition of molten copper to the original silver coin, presumably to make up for weight. That this was subsequently added is shown by the fact that it remains over the punch arks."[61] This verdigris (copper acetate)[62] deposit came up to 13 p.c. of the coins. Kauṭilya refers to two methods, scratching (ullekhana) and rubbing that were resorted to for bringing about the diminution in weight of the gold and silver articles. There can be no doubt that the coins were treated likewise, and this would explain to some extent the variation in weight of the coins from the fixed standard. The compact pieces were scratched by tīkṣṇa which was evidently a hard metal, perhaps iron, and this was called ullekhana or scratching and "when, by a piece of cloth painted with the powder of sulphuret of arsenic (haritāla), red arsenic (Mānaśśila), or vermilion or with the powder of *Kuruvinda* (black salt?), gold or silver articles were rubbed, that act was termed rubbing, *parimarddanam.*"[63]

When we discuss the chronology of the introduction of the different systems adopted for the manufacture of coins, we are confronted with a difficulty which is due to two factors—the innate aversion to change and the vastness of the country with its innumerable divisions into states. The conservatism of the people led them to shun the later but the better method as long as possible, and this is to be found in other spheres also. In architecture, the transition from wood to stone "which was effected for Northern India under Asoka in the third century B.C. was delayed for nearly a thousand years in the Far South"[64] and V. Smith points out this as an "illustration of the immense length of the course of Indian history and of the extreme slowness with which changes have been effected so as ultimately to cover the whole country." In matters numismatic, we find that progress in the technic of manufacture was equally slow and when we consider that the different states were in various stages of culture and separated from each other by long distances and impassable mountains and rivers, we find it absolutely impossible to make any general statement as regards the gradual progress from the punch-marked to the double-die system. It does not always follow that the knowledge of a better system led to the ousting of the earlier and ruder system of manufacture ; the case of the Indo-Scythians is to the point.[65] When we come to the undoubtedly foreign influence which was exercised over the purely indigenous system, we find it impossible to generalise.

There is no doubt that when a state was left to itself, it had to pass through different stages, but if at any point it came into contact with a more developed system it might skip over the intermediate stages. So to determine what were the successive stages in the evolution of technic of manufacture of coins and how much we are indebted to foreign influence we have to concentrate our attempts to a particular state ; and no statement can be found broad enough to include all the states in India in the course of centuries. It is only with reference to a definite state, if we had ample data, that we might succeed in determining how it progressed to the latest system of manufacture and what was its indebtedness to a foreign source. The only result of the discussion whether the die system was indigenous or introduced by foreigners, would be to make it impossible to come to any definite conclusion, which might be applicable to the whole country and the disputants of the rival theories might be correct in their assertions, though but partially, and their conclusions would be applicable only to the particular parts of the country on whose monetary system they relied upon.

The punch-marked coins were in use in Northern India from the earliest time to the beginning of the Christian era at least, though these might have remained in circulation till the time of the Kuṣāṇas. In Southern India, the circulation of punch-marked coins was continued for 300 years more. The use of cast coins also prevailed in some parts of the country from a very early time. The casting of metals for the manufacture of ornaments was as long in use as the Indus culture. So this practice must have been very old and indigenous in origin ; and we may safely accept the assertion of Brown that sonic of the copper cast coins were as old as the 5th century B.C. This practice was continued even when striking from dies had come into use in some parts of the country.

The question whether the credit for the invention of the system of striking coins from dies belongs to the Indians or was introduced by the foreigners in this country is a subject of controversy among the Numismatists. James Prinsep is the advocate of the foreign origin for the system of dies.

Vincent Smith differentiates between the single-die and the double-die systems and maintains that "the final adoption of the 'double-die' system was undoubtedly due to Greek and Roman example.[66] Thomas enunciates the different stages[67] in the evolution of the mechanical processes leading up to the double-die system and points out that "these mechanical epochs must be taken to represent a large measure of time when initiated among a people so ever unwilling to move out of old grooves." According to him "all these advances, it is clear, must have been effected before the advent of the Greeks ; for had the Indians waited till the Macedonians came to teach them, they would have spared themselves all these manifest efforts of invention, and humbly have essayed to copy the perfect coins of Alexander now ready to their hands, and would probably have succeeded in achieving about as curious an imitation of Greek art as the modern fabricators of Rawal Pindi reproduce from Bactrian originals, to tempt unwary collectors of Indian antiquities."[68] Prof. Bhandarkar supports Thomas, and Smith comes in for strong criticism in his hands and he tries to expose the absurdity of Smith's position by pointing out "that the Indians were capable of introducing improvement into and thus developing the technic manufacture of coins before the advent of the Greeks, but their last step, although it was the natural culmination of their gradual advance in the indigenous numismatic art, they could effect only when the Macedonians came to teach them."[69] It appears that the conclusions of these scholars are off the mark and vitiated as these are based on false perspective of thc cultural and political condition of ancient India, the respective backgrounds being entirely different. That in some parts of the country the progress was gradual and uninterrupted by foreign influence must be conceded. We may refer to the coinage of Eraṇ and here we can trace "the development of the Punch-mark system into the type system. In the place of a number of symbols punched on to the coin from time to time, there appears at a later period a definite type, made up of a collection of these symbols struck from a die."[71] Prof. Rapson is of opinion that similar development is usually found "in those parts of India which were least affected by foreign influence." The die-system is found in the North-Western part of the country, in the Punjab and the Gandhara" region and Prof. Rapson thinks, that it was in Taxila that the art of striking from die was adopted "at an earlier period than elsewhere in India.[71] Whether we accept the claim made on behalf of Taxila or not, her coinage exemplifies how the indigenous process was supplanted by the foreign system. "The earliest specimens are struck only on one side, and by a method peculiarly Indian, according to which the metal was stamped while in a semi-molten state, with the result that the impress of the die was left enclosed in a deep incuse square."[72] At first the symbols were struck with a die on one side of the coin but later on inscriptions also came to be struck on them *e.g.*, the Vatasvaka and the Kadasa coins. These inscribed coins cannot be assigned to a period later than the 3rd century B.C., so the coins that preceded them must belong to an earlier period, the 4th or the 5th century B.C. As we have the imitation in India of the types of the Grecian coins which were not minted after the Persian Invasion of Greece, it would not be unreasonable to infer that these Indian imitations are as old as the 5th century B.C.[72a] The fact that the die system was first introduced as early as the 5th century B.C., in the North Western region of India which had intimate connections with the West and was likely to be influenced first by the foreign system would lead us to infer that the die system, at least in this region, was introduced from abroad. In the third century B.C., the Maurya Empire included this part of the country but the coinage of Magadha followed the punch-marked system. So it is evident that even in the different provinces of the same empire, no attempt was made to introduce uniformity in the system of manufacture of coins, Moreover, when we consider that the die system moved from the Western part of the country to the Eastern, and later on to the South the Deccan, we have to cover a period of at least 800 years ; and foreign influence in the earlier stage, specially in Gandhara and the Punjab region, must be accepted.

FOOTNOTES

1. Thomas, E.—Ancient Indian Weights, p. 33.
2. *Ibid.*, footnote 3.
3. Ṛgveda Saṁhitā—referred to by Thomas—"Ancient Indian Weights,'' p. 33.
4. Thomas, E.—Ancient Indian Weights, p. 34.
5. Head, B. V.—Coins of the Ancients, p. 1.
6. Smith, V. A.—Catalogue of the Coins in the Indian Museum, p. 136.

7. Brown, C. J.—The Coins of India, p. 14.
8. *Ibid.*
9. "The Indo-Scythians and Sassanians, though in full possession of all the more advanced methods of coining, still continued to use this shape."—E. Thomas—"Ancient Indian Weights, p. 55, footnote I.
10. Whitehead, R. B.—The Pre-Mohammedan Coinage, of Northwestern India, p. 42.
11. *Ibid.*,40.
12. Walsh, E. H. C.—Indian Punch-marked Coins, J. R. A, S. (Centenary Supplement), p. 175.
13. Smith, V. A.—Catalogue of the Coins in the Indian Museum, p. 134.
14. *Ibid.*, p. 131.
15. Bhandarkar, D. R. Ancient Indian Numismatics, p. 150.
16. Walsh, E. H. C.—Indian Punch-marked Coins, J. R. A. S. (Cent. Sup.), P. 187.
17. *Ibid.*
18. Cunningham, A.—Coins of Ancient India, p. 55.
19. Smith, V. A.—Catalogue of the Coins in the Museum, p. 134.
20. Rapson, E. J.—Indian Coins, p. 14.
21. Brown—The Coins of India, p. 16.
22. Macdonald, G.—Evolution of Coinage, p. 57.
23. Brown, C. J.—Coins of India, p. 18.
24. Smith, V, A.—Catalogue of the Coins in the Indian Museum, p. 198.
25. Macdonald, G.—The Evolution of Coinage, p. 60.
26. Cunningham, A.—Ancient Indian Coins, p. 54.
27. Brown C. J.—Coins of India, p. 19.
28. Macdonald, G.—Evolution of Coinage, p. 62.
29. Thomas, E.—Ancient Indian Weights, p. 54.
30. *Ibid.*, p. 55.
31. Rapson, E. J.—Indian Coins, p. II.
32. Cunningham, A.—Coins of Ancient India, pp. 60-62.
33. Rapson, E. J.—Indian Coins, p. 14. 33a *Ibid.* 33b *Ibid.*
34. *Ibid.*
35. Brown, C. J.—The Coins of India, p. 19.
36. Rapson, E. J.—Indian . Coins, pp. 37 and 38. Elliot, W.— Coins of Southern India, pp. 66 and 67.
37. Thomas, E.—Ancient Indian Weights, p. 55. Footnote I.
38. Macdonald, G.—The Evolution of Coinage, p. 64.
39. *Ibid.*, p. 63.
40. *Ibid.*, p. 65.
41. Smith, V. A.—Catalogue of the Coins in the Indian Museum; pp. 193, 194.
42. Kauṭilya's Arthaśāstra translated by R. Shamasastry (1915), p. 98.
43. Bhandarkar, D. R.—Ancient Indian Numismatics, p. 152. 44 Kauilya's Arthaśāstra (trans. Shamasastry), p. 106. 45 Thomas, E.—Ancient Indian Weights, p. 57, footnote 4. Thomas points out a passage in Ferishtah "that in A.D. 1357-1374 goldsmiths and dealers in bullion were authorized, by perspective right, to fabricate money at will on their own account, without being subjected to any check or control on the part of the ruling power This supposition is farther confirmed by recently prevailing custom. 'There are mints at almost all the principal towns in Central India ..... The right of coining is vested in no particular body or individuals; any banker or merchant sufficiently conversant in the business has merely to make application to Government, presenting at the same time a trifling acknowledgment, engaging to produce coin of the regulated standard, and pay the proper fees on its

being assayed and permitted to pass current!—Sir J. Malcolm, Central India 1832, ii. p. 80."
46. Bhandarkar, D. R.—Ancient Indian Numismatics, p. 158.
47. Kauṭilya's Arthaśāstra, (trans. by Shamasastry), p. 107.
48. Bhandarkar, D. R.— Ancient Indian Numismatics, p. 160. 49. *Ibid.*, P. 160.
50. Kauṭilya's Arthaśāstra (Shamasastry) p. 106. (Sanskrit Edition, p. 89).
51. Kauṭilya's Arthaśāstra (trans. by Shamasastry), p. 98.
52. *Ibid.*, p. 105, footnote 2.
53. *Ibid.*, p. 110.
54. *Ibid.*, p 105, footnote 1.
55. Smith, V. A..—Early History of India, p. 328.
55. Bhandarkar, D. R.—Ancient Indian Numismatics, p. 161
57. Kauṭilya's Arthaśāstra (trans. by Shamasastry), p. 64.
58. *Ibid.*, p. 266.
59. Bhandarkar, D. R.—Ancient Indian Numismatics, p. 164.
60. *Ibid.*
61. Walsh, E. H. C.—J. B. O. R. S., 1919, pp. 16 and 17.
62. Watt, G.—The Commercial Products of India, p. 403.
63. Kauilya's Arthaśāstra (trans. by Shamasastry), p. III.
64. Smith, V. A.—Oxford History of India, p. 210.
65. Thomas, E.—Ancient Indian Weights, p. 55, footnote I.
66. Smith V. A.—The Imperial Gazetteer of India, II, p. 137.
67. Thomas, E.—Ancient Indian Weights, p. 55.
68. *Ibid.*
69. Bhandarkar, D. R.—Ancient Indian Numismatics, p. 152.
70. Rapson, E. J.—Indian Coins, p. 11.
71. *Ibid.*, p. 14. 75 *Ibid.*
72a. See Chapter VIII—The Rakṣasa Type Coins of Taxila.

CHAPTER VII

THE STATE IN RELATION TO COINAGE

The question whether the initiative in the institution of coinage was taken by the merchants, who were most concerned in the furtherance of their commercial interests, or the State which was responsible for the whole body of the people, including the merchants, is a subject of controversy among scholars, The commercial class surely felt the need for a satisfactory medium of exchange of a metallic nature of a definite weight and purity for their daily transactions, and there is nothing to be surprised at, if they in their own interest in the first instance and ultimately in the interest of the whole people, took upon themselves the responsibility of issuing coins to serve as a circulating, medium. When the advantage of the institution became apparent and its national importance recognised, the states stepped into the place of the private bankers, either directly, or through certain other corporate bodies, the resultant effect being beneficial to all the parties concerned,—the State, the commercial class and the people at large. This theory had a strong advocate in M. Babelon.[1] That the private coins were "the precursors of regular state-issues"[2] can be definitely proved by reference to a coin in Plate I, No. 7 in Head's "*Coins of the Ancients*".[3] It is a coin in Electrum and is "the earliest inscribed coin known."[4] It was found at Helicarnassus and was perhaps struck at Ephesus. It is a short inscription—"I am the sign of Phanes",—(retrograde in archaic letters) and "stag feeding" on the observe. This right of private issue is found even in later times. On occassions the State as a special favour bestowed this right on private individuals. A Syrian prince Antiochus Sidetes wanted to secure the support of Simon Maccabaeus and addressed him thus,—"I give thee leave also to coin money for thy own country with thine own stamp."[5] In Gaul, the Marovingian period was an "epoch of private coinage",[6] when many private individuals usurped the authority of the State. This state of affairs was, however, brought to an end by Pepin and Charlemagne. In the medieval period of Europe, the principle that the issuing of coins was an attribute of sovereignty was surely recognised, but the feudal barons usurped the right. By 1500 A.C. centralisation had set in througout Europe and except in Germany coinage was fully under the control of the State.[7] In India also the private issue must have preceded the State issues, and for the introduction of coins we are most probably indebted to the private bankers. Vincent Smith held the view that all punch marked coins were specimens of private issues. According to him "it is clear that the punch-marked coinage was a private coinage issued by guilds and silversmiths with the permission of the ruling powers"[8] and "the numerous obverse punches seem to have been impressed by the different moneyers through whose hands the pieces passed, and the reverse marks may be regarded as the signs of approval by the controlling authority."[9] But the hoards of punch-marked coins which have been studied by scholars like Spooner,[10] Bhandarkar[11] and Walsh[12] have revealed a different state of things and it is practically certain that the coins examined or the majority of them are state issues. But thousands of these coins have been unearthed and there, is nothing to be surprised at the escape of the private issues from the notice of the scholars, specially as we know that punch-marked coins had no inscriptions, many of them being marked with symbols which have not yet all been identified and properly interpreted. Another-point to be marked is that when the State entered into the field, the private issues might have been called back and given the new impress. So Vincent Smith's propositions require a thorough modification. The coins that he wrote about were surely State issues but there is something to be said about the view that the initiative came from private bankers whose symbols have up to this time escaped recognition.

When the State brought the coinage under its control, it sometimes acted through the experts, the private bankers, who were specially fitted for the work and were in a position to help the State with their expert knowledge. The State surely found it to its advantage to delegate its authority on occasions and though it would be a bit presumptuous to claim this evolutionary stage to be of universal application, yet from the, position occupied by the merchants and the bankers in the social organisation in India and the corporate nature of their organisations,[1] we are inclined to attribute to India what we find actually in existence in Athens. The Greeks had an arrangement called Liturgy according to which the State entrusted certain of its functions to wealthy private individuals who had to discharge onerous duties even at personal expense.[14] From an examination of the Athenian coins Macdonald comes to the conclusion "that two wealthy citizens had to supervise the issue of silver for a year, and to meet the cost of mintage out of their own resources, the State supplying the raw material."[15] It surely conferred distinction on them, and their names were handed down to posterity. This may be very well applicable to the Indian conditions, but by the time of the Mauryas we have a definite record that the issuing of coins was a function of the State under its direct control, though private individuals and different corporate bodies were allowed to have coins issued through the royal mint.[16] The practice of allowing merchants and other citizens, the privilege of coining money in the royal mint was current up to the recent times.[17] Any banker or merchant had only to apply for permission to the government and to offer an undertaking to pay the proper fees and to keep to the regulated standard.[18] It would therefore be not unreasonable to infer that a similar custom prevailed in earlier times, though from the nature of the case definite proof cannot be supplied. But as regards corporate associations we have clear records. These organised associations enjoying a privileged position were the Naigamas, the Pauras and the Janapadas, In the Punjab at Taxila a number of coins were discovered of a peculiar type, having the word Negamā on the reverse and on the obverse such proper names as Tālimata, Dujaka. Dojaka, Atakatakā.[19]

In the Pura or the capital of a State there was, as pointed out by Jayaswal, the Association of the City Merchants called the Naigama and it was intimately connected with Paura association.[20] The Naigama is thus interpreted by him to be the Guild of the City Merchants and not "a general term for Guild Merchangs" as taken by Buhler who first recognised the importance of these coins.[21] The Naigama was a corporate body with its own Assembly Hall and Office and was connected with the Śraṇīs or the guilds of the city."[22] Jayaswal takes the Negama coins "as coins struck at the capital by the State for the association of the City Merchants"[23] and Dojaka, Tālimata and Atakataka as the names of the capital towns." He also points out the true nature of these organised bodies. The Naigama of the capital was according to him "the mother of the Paura Association" but it was mainly concerned with the economic interests of the people, and the connection between the two bodies, the Naigama and the Paura was so intimate that they were sometimes referred to as identical. The Paura during the period 600 B.C. to 600 A.D. signified the organised body of the citizens of the capital which had number of constitutional powers in addition to its functions as a municipal corporation, *e.g.*, the Paura or the Capital Assembly exercised the economic function of minting coins in the royal mint as referred to in the Arthaśāstra[25] and it had a sister body, the Janapada.[26] "The term Janapada, which literally and originally meant the 'seat of the nation' and which had been secondarily employed as denoting the nation itself, lost its old significance, and came to mean what we call to-day *country* without reference to the racial elements inhabiting it."[27] It was a constitutional body for the whole kingdom with the exclusion of the capital. They also, like the Paura, "got gold coins minted by the royal mint-master as laid down in the Arthaśāstra.[28] The Janapada, however, as an organised political unit is referred to in a number of coins, *e.g.*, Rājanya Janapada and Mahārāja Janapada. Rājanya is the proper name of a political tribe and similar is the case with the Māhārāja Janapada. [29]

The earlier coins were not, however, inscribed but had only symbols punched on them. So a definite information like what we have been enabled to obtain for later times is lacking and the careful study of the symbols is the only resource left to us. Smith's view that the punch-marked coins "are not assignable to any particular State or locality"[30] has been proved erroneous. Asa matter of fact the symbols if properly interpreted do point out the identity of the State or the locality, and in this connection the provenance of the coins is of extreme importance in our inquiry. But up to this time its importance has not been properly recognised and definite information on this subject as regards the past discoveries is partially lacking. Mr. Walsh has conclusively proved that the Indian punch-marked coins were not 'a purely private issue.'[31] Nor were the marks on them "impressed by the different moneyers through whose hands the pieces passed,"[32] but a public coinage issued under the authority of the State. This theory which is well attested controverts the views not only of Smith but also of Rapson who remarks, — "the symbols punched on to the coin on the obverse are supposed to be the private marks of the moneychangers, while those on the reverse, which are invariably fewer in number and of a somewhat different character, may possibly denote the locality in which these coins were issued."[33] Mr. Walsh closely studied the two finds of punch-marked coins, one from Patna, 107 in number, and the other from Gorho-Ghat in the Bhagalpur District which included 58 coins. The result of his investigation was embodied in an article to the Centenary Supplement of the Journal of the Royal Asiatic Society. He found that some of the symbols occurred 'in certain constant and regular groups on the obverse,'[34] although other varying symbols were added to these constant groups. Naturally he agrees with the conclusion of Dr. Spooner that the symbols "were not the private marks of individual moneyers impressed haphazard from time to time,"[35] through whose hands the coins passed. The marks "on the obverse represent the issuing authority and constitute the coinage, while those on the *reverse* would appear to be the private marks of moneyers through whose hands the coins passed, or in some cases, to indicate the locality."[36] Two marks are found on all the Patna coins and these are the symbols representing the discus, the *cakra* and the *chatras* (umbrellas) bound together in the middle in the form of a circle. Two other marks are found associated with the majority of the coins while the fifth mark is of a more irregular character and varies more frequently. The 58 Gorho-Ghat coins are of three distinct types and appear to belong to three different areas and governments (Walsh. JRAS., 1924, Centenary Supplement, page 181). The conclusion of Mr. Walsh tallies with that of Dr. Spooner who examined the 61 punch-marked coins found at Peshwar,[37] and Dr. Bhandarkar[38] also comes to the same conclusion from the examination of the 83 punch-marked coins found at Besnagar. This is supported by the Arthalśāstra which brings before us the condition of things in the Maurya Age when coinage was a royal prerogative,[39] though sometimes the royal mint could be utilised by corporate bodies like the Naigamas and Janapadas. The result of this investigation is thus summarised:-"It may be suggested, to account for a constant group of marks, that one mark may represent the state, one the reigning king, one the place where the coin was struck and perhaps one a religious mark recognising the presiding deity ; also the master of the mint may have had his mark, which would fix his responsibility for the coin, and the additional varying marks may have been those of the *Saṅghas*, village, communities, in which the coin was current, affixed at the time the *rupiya* or the local tax on it was levied on its admission to circulation in that jurisdiction. And the various and unsystematic punches on the reverse would appear to have been the marks of private shroffs and moneyers through whose hands the coin passed in the course of circulation."[40] Thus we find that the marks on the reverse are of an entirely different nature. They are less deeply punched, and when they correspond to the marks on the obverse, are of a much smaller size. The reverse marks may very well be the marks of the merchants through whose hands the coins passed. But there are certain exceptions ; for example, the coins of Taxila, Eraṇ, Benares, Ujjain etc. have their peculiar mint-marks on the reverse. But on the whole, the opinion of Rapson may be accepted that the reverse marks are "the official stamp of the local authority and indicate that the coins had been tested and sanctioned within that area."[41] The smaller reverse marks which are similar to the marks on the obverse are perhaps "the official marks of the testing authority"[42] and these are smaller in size in order to distinguish them from the original mint marks. The suggestion of Cunningham that some of the marks on the reverse stand for the names of the moneyers concerned seems to be plausible. He would make the symbol of the Sun to stand "for Sūrya Dās, a 'Snake' for Nāga Sen ; and an Elephant for Gaj Siṇh. Bir Deo might have had a 'soldier,' Gopal a Bull, and Khajur Varma a 'Palm' tree (Khajur)." Some of these symbols "may be the emblems of their castes or clans."[43] There is absolutely no doubt that even if the punch-marked coinage owed its origin to private enterprise, yet at a very early time, even long before the Maurya period, the coinage had definitely come under State control. The different communities that participated in the privilege of the State mint cannot always be identified when we have to rely only on the symbols punched on the coins. But later on inscriptions were put on them and the symbols were either discarded and replaced by types, or were retained as a matter of minor importance as we find on the Eran coins. It is thus possible for us to assign those coins definitely to the different political communities of antiquity, and also from palaeographical and other considerations to come to an approximate conclusion as regards their date of issue. Those coins with the legends testify to the existence of many monarchical and republican States before the Christian era, and the inscriptions which were a new feature in the coins of these States might have been imitated by the Indians from the Persian and the Greek coins, specially from those of the Indo-Greek kings. Thus the chronology of those States that have left their coins behind can only be determined with reference "to the style of the coins and the script of the legends."[44] Many free tribes and autonomous republican States issued their coins. The nature of their constitutions has been elaborately discussed by Jayaswal[45] and he has succeeded in clearing up many obscure points. These non-mona archical States were technically called Gaṇas and Jangadas. Gaṇa signified number and Gaṇarājya is, therefore, interpreted as the rule by number, the rule by many. "Gaṇa thus was the assembly or parliament, so called because of the 'number' or 'numbering' of the members present. Gaṇarājya, consequently, denoted government by *assembly* or *parliament*. The secondary meaning of Gaṇa came to be 'parliament' or 'senate,' and as republics were governed by them, gana came to mean a republic itself."[46] The Janapada emphasised the tribal character of the constitution as a political community. Jayaswal would take it to be a political unit and sometimes a city state.[47] Prominent among the Gaṇas were the Audumbaras, the. Yaudheyas, the Mālavas and others ; and among the Janapādas, the Rājanya and the Mahārāja.

FOOTNOTES

1. M. Babelon, Origines de la Monnaie.
2. G. Macdonald, Evolution of Coinage, p. 7.
3. Barclay V. Head, A guide to the Principal Gold and Silver Coins of the Ancient, p. 4.
4. *Ibid.*
5. G. Macdonald, Evolution of Coinage, p. 13.
6. *Ibid.*, p. 29
7. *Ibid.*, p. 35.
8. V. A. Smith, Catalogue of the Coins in the Indian Museum, p. 133.
9. *Ibid.*, p. 133.

10. Archaeological Survey of India, Annual Report, 1905-6, p. 153.
11. *Ibid*,, 1913-14, p. 220; D. R. Bhandarkar, Carmichael Lectures, 1921, p. 98f.
12. Centenary Supplement to the Journal of the Royal Asiatic Society, October, 1924, p. 175.
13. Radhakumud Mookerjee, Local Government in Ancient India, Chapter III (Organisation).
14. G. Macdonald, Evolution of Coinage, p. 18.
15. *Ibid.*, p. 19.
16. D. R Bhandarkar, Carmichael Lectures, 1021, p. 158.
17. *Ibid.*, p. 153. K. P. Jayaswal, Hindu Polity, Part II, p. 76, f. I.
18. E. Thomas, Ancient Indian Weights p. 57, foot-note 4.
19. In Cunningham's Coins of Ancient India, Plate III, pp. 63-65, there are four coins from Taxila with the following legends :

No. 8	T(?)alima(ta)	(N)eg(m)
No. 9	Dujaka	Negamā
No. 10	Dojaka	Negamā
No. 11	A(taka?) takā	Negam(ā)"

"The legends in the coins are in beautifully formed Asokan characters both Gamlharian (Kharosthi) and Indian. Over the word Negamā there is a single stroke or bar as if to designate one negama On the opposite side there is a 'steelyard' very clearly represented." Quoted by Dr. R. Mookerjee in his Local Government in Ancient India, pp. 114f. Rapson, Indian Coins, p. 3. JRAS., 1900, p. 99.

20. K. P. Jayaswal, Hindu Polity, Part II, p. 76.
21. E. J. Rapson, Indian Coins, p. 3.
22. K. P. Jayaswal, Hindu Polity, Part II, p. 78.
23. *Ibid.*, p. 78.
24. Hindu Polity, Part II, p. 79—Rapson "regards the names as those of the rulers of the guilds," while Bhandarkar regards them as those of the towns. He things that these were self governing political bodies and not merely industrial guilds. Dr. Mookerjee supports Jayaswal and regards these coins as "mercantile guild-tokens."—Rapson, JRAS., 1900, p. 99; Mookerjee, Local Government in Ancient India, pp. 114f.; Bhandarkar, Carmichael Lectures, 1918, pp. 175-179; *Ibid.*, 1921, p. 6.
25. Arthaśāstra, p. 107, (II. 14; 32).
26. K. P. Jayaswal, Hindu Polity, Part II, p. 79.
27. *Ibid.*, p. 61.
28. *Ibid.*, p. 79.
29. *Ibid.*, Part I, pp. 158f.
30. V. A. Smith, Catalogue of Coin's in the Indian Museum, p. 131.
31. Cent, Sup.to JRAS., p. 176.
32. V. A. Smith, Catalogue of Coins, p. 133.
33. E. J. Rapson, Ancient India, p. 151.
34. E. H. C. Walsh, Cent. Sup. to JRAS., 1924, p. 176.
35. Archaeological Survey of India, 1905-1906, p. 153.
36. E. H. C. Walsh, Cent. Sup. to JRAS., 1924, p. 177.

37. Quoted by Walsh, Cent. Sup., JRAS., 1924, p. 179. 38 D. R. Bhandarkar, Carmichael Lectures, 1921, p. 98.
39. *Ibid.*, p. 156.
40. E. H. C. Walsh, Cent. Sup., JRAS., 1924, P.184.
41. Rapson, JRAS., 1895, p. 874 referred to by Walsh.
42. E. H. C. Walsh, Cent. Sup. JRAS., 1924, p. 189.
43. A. Cunningham, Coins of Ancient India, p. 58. E. H. C. Walsh, Cent. Sup., JRAS., 1924, p. 189.
44. V. A. Smith, Catalog of Coins, p. 144.
45. K. P. Jayaswal, Hindu Polity, Part I, Chapter XVIII.
46. K. P. Jayaswal, Hindu. Polity, Part I, p. 27.
47. *Ibid.*, pp. 134, 135.

CHAPTER VIII

THE COINS WITH SYMBOLS

The earliest coins of India are designated the punch-marked coins by the Numismatists. This is merely a descriptive appellation from the system of manufacture peculiar to these coins. "The devices on the coins are impressed, not by means of a die covering the face (*flan*) of the coin, but by separate punches applied irregularly at various points on the surface. Naturally the impressions so effected often interfere with one. another, and in cases where they are numerous the result is a confused jumble of symbols."[1] The obverse is "occupied by the larger symbols, commonly numerous"[2] while the reverse is sometimes blank or is marked by a fewer and smaller devices which are "comparatively inconspicuous." It is rather an exception to have both the sides equally crowded with symbols—on the obverse "the average number of symbols is about five, whereas on the reverse the average does not exceed two."[3] These coins are found all over India and thousands of these pieces have been unearthed in this vast country. The silver coins are more numerous and the copper ones "are comparatively few."[4] Prof. Bhandarkar opines that this is due to the fact that "copper is a more perishable metal than silver"[5] and that these coins "are more apt to be melted down into domestic utensils."[6] His other argument to explain the paucity of copper coins is that in the ancient period "the standard issue was generally silver Kārṣāpaṇa."[7] But this statement is open to objection as we have found in a previous chapter. Silver came into use for purposes of coinage later than copper and Prof. Bhandarkar's statement would seem to be applicable only to certain parts of the country and that perhaps a century or two, before Kauṭilya. The earlier issues of copper were put out of use when silver became the metal for standard coins, though even then certain parts of the country *e.g.*, Besnagar, retained copper only for exchange purposes when silver had come into use in other parts. The devices on the copper coins as evident from the extant specimens became defaced in a comparatively short period and this might have necessitated their demonetization ; and another reason might have been the use of cowry-shells, a certain number of which always, perhaps from a very early time came to be equated to copper coins. This practice which was very extensive would naturally limit the issue of copper for coinage. These are reasons enough to explain the paucity of the copper coins that have come down to us.[8]

That these coins are indigenous has now been generally accepted. The arguments in support have been ably and clearly summarised by Prof. Rapson.[9] The shape, the weight, the symbols, the fabrication and the denominations would prove without the least shadow of doubt that these coins are particularly the products of India and have been evolved in this country by successive stages. The ancient coins outside India as pointed out by Cunningham, with the exception of Corinth (and also of China) are thick round knobs or buttons of metal, which must have been cast for the particular purpose,"[10] while in India the oldest coins "are all flat thin pieces, which have been cut from beaten plates."[11] The weight is based upon the units referred to in the Vedic Literature and corresponds to the weight of the seeds indigenous to this country. The symbols except those that seem to be the common property of all races on the earth were pre-dominantly Indian in character, and the denominations in spite of the attempts to explain them otherwise[12] are purely Indian or rather Aryan in base.

The number of these coins which have been and are being unearthed in all parts of the country would clearly point to a long circulation of centuries for these issues. It was from the 2nd century B.C. that foreign coins in large numbers came to circulate in Northern India, It may be conceded that the Persian Darics of gold and the sigloi of silver might have been introduced in the Punjab uinder Darius the son of Hystaspes and that the Athenian and Macedonian coins influenced the currency of India to some extent. But there is no doubt that the coinage of India was for centuries influenced by the foreigners. Northern India was subjected to a series of invasions by the Persians, the Greeks, the Parthians, the Sakas and others ; and naturally the indigenous coins were gradually modified by coming into contact with the foreign issues. The punch-marked coins were put out of circulation in the North three or four centuries before they went out of use in the South,[13] where coinage was left free "to develop by slow stages on strictly Indian lines."[14] How long they continued to circulate in Northern India is difficult to determine accurately,[15] for we have reasons for presuming that even when the coins of foreign type were circulating in the country, the punch-marked coins were used side by side with them. Three punch-marked coins were found by Cunningham "in the deposit at the foot of the Vajrāsana, or throne of Buddha, in the temple of Mahabodhi at Buddha Gaya."[16] This deposit was made in the reign of Huvishka (120—140 A.D.).[17] So it is evident that punch-marked coins were in circulation in the middle of the second century A.D. These 3 coins were extremely worn and must have been in circulation for a long time ; Cunningham thinks for about 600 years. Gradually however punch-marked coins were replaced by coins with types and all the different stages in the manufacture of coins are exemplified in the coinage of Eraṇ in which we have an illustration, as Prof. Rapson says, "of the development of the punch-mark system into the die-system."[18]

In Sanskrit Literature, the punch-marked coins have various denominations and these were continued even when the system of manufacture was changed and the cast and die-struck coins came into use. Kārṣāpaṇa was mainly applied to copper coins but later on it became the generic expression for, coins whether of copper or silver. But as detailed before the units for copper and the precious metals varied and the Kārṣāpaṇas of silver were of 32 ratis based on the Māna unit and the Kārṣāpaṇas of copper were of 80 ratis. The word Kārṣāpaṇa is derived "from Karsha, the weight, and āpaṇa, "custom or use" ; that is, the current Kārsha."[19] According to Manu a Karsha is equal in weight to 80 ratis.[20] In the South the word was changed to Kāsu and it had "the general significance of money, wealth, and likewise of coin."[21] Similar was the case in Northern India too and Karsh-apana, the copper coin became the general expression for coins. The silver Kārṣāpaṇa was also known as dharaṇa and Cunningham derives this word from dhṛi"—to hold, "probably meaning a handful of 16 copper paṇas."[22] That it was a handful of some sub-multiples, either of cowry or metal may be accepted ; we find a similar case in a Greek drachm which signifies a handful of six bars or spits of bronze.[23] In Southern India it was known as Sālāka[24] which was applied to a domino or "the oblong die used at the game of pachisi." Cunningham inferred that the name was given. "partly on account of the marks upon them."[25] But as pointed out by him the name commonly used was purāṇa or "old." The explanation suggested to him that the punch-marked coins came to be known as purāṇa "after the Greek occupation of the Punjab."[26] He opines that the Kaārṣāpaṇa was called purāṇa by the Indians "when they came in contact with the Greek money of Alexander's successors. The round Greek drachms and hemi-drachms were the new silver money and the square native Kārṣāpaṇas were the old money or the purāṇas."[27] There is a similar explanation of the word, if we refer to the method of manufacture of the coins of the different periods.[28] The punch-marked coins came to be gradually supplanted, at first only partially, by cast and die-struck coins and as the earliest cast coins can be ascribed to the 5th century B.C.[29] at the latest, it is but reasonable to infer that the coins manufactured in the old way by punching as distinguished from cast and the die-struck coins were denominated the Purāṇas, "the old," as compared with the newer coins cast in mould or die-struck. This would explain the use of the word throughout Northern India.

The sub-multiples of the standard Kārṣāpaṇa are Half, One-fourth and One-eighth (Maṇu and Kauṭilya) and Cunningham had in his possession "specimens of the paṇa, and its multiples and divisions, varying from 1 ¾ down to 1/16, or from 250 grains down to 9 grains." [30] Coins smaller than these circulated among the Mālavas ; the smallest being 1.7 grains only, though we must make allowance for clipping and wear.[31] The small size of these coins is a peculiarity of the coinage of the Mālavas and this particular coin "may claim the honour of being one of the smallest coins in the world."[32] A specimen from Ephesus in the British Museum weighs only one grain and is the smallest coin known.

The standard weights of the old law books do not however conform to the actual specimens of coins that have come down to us.[33] It has been rightly pointed out that "the various systems of weight used in India combine uniformity of scale with immense variations in the weight of unite."[34] The other reasons for discrepancy have been noted in the Chapter on the Metrology of Coins. An attempt may however be made to identify the extant specimens with the standard coins referred to in the literature. V. Smith in his catalogue has divided the silver coins into four sections according to their shape.[35] First of all, he takes the 3 silver ingots and thinks that these "ingots merely marked with 3 dots, must be very ancient" ;[36] these "range in weight from 21.5 to 26.7 grains" and he fails "to connect these figures with the standards commonly used."[37] But a reference to the weight of these ingots will clearly show that these are half-dharaṇas. Two of these weigh 26.7 grains each ; consequently a One-Dharaṇa piece would approximate 53.4 grains and we have in his catalogue coins Nos. 14, 17, 19, 21, 30 etc., weighing respectively 54, 54.9, 53, 54.8 and 53.5 grains, while the standard weight should be 56 to 58 grains,—this small discrepancy might be due to wear and tear. Smith's opinion was surely based on the rude shape of the pieces, leading him to infer that these belonged to an early stage in the evolution of the manufacture of coins. But it has to be taken into account that with the introduction of a better system of manufacture, the coins of a ruder shape do not always go out of use. Even at the present time the Dhabuas,[38] irregular shaped ingots of copper are used in certain parts of the country as the sub-multiples of the Rupee, the standard coin of the land, and the price of these pieces varies according to the season. So when we have the indisputable evidence of weight there is surely no justification in ascribing them to a very early date. The half-dharaṇas might have circulated side by side with the punch-marked coins, at least in some parts of the country.

Next he takes up the three "heavy bent bars of silver (Nos. 4—6) marked with simple symbols on the concave side and blank on the convex side,"[39] and from their "extremely archaic appearance,"[40] he ascribes them to 500 or 600 B. C. But a reference to the weight of these bars makes us doubtful whether these are coins or mere measures of weight, perhaps for metals. The heaviest No. 6 weighs 174.1 grains which is exactly 3 times the weight of a Dharaṇa of 58 grains and approximates 100 ratis as pointed out by Smith.[41] His suggestion would lead us to refer these pieces to the coins of the Greek kings and the double-die Indian coins which were of 100 ratis.[42] This will bring down these pieces to the 2nd or the 1st Century B. C., but if we attach any importance to the "extremely archaic appearance," then we have got to accept them as Three-Dharaṇa pieces ; though I would rather be disposed to identify them with measures of weight as no such Three-Dharaṇa punch-marked coins of the usual shape have yet been discovered.

The Third class of Dharaṇas are shaped as rectangular dominoes of various shapes, oblong, nearly square and even triangular. This irregular shape is to be ascribed to the peculiar system of manufacture of the punch-marked coins. The weight varies in Smith's Catalogue from 35.7 grains (No. 55) to 55.6 grains (No. 31). The variation in the weight of the coins may be due to various causes as discussed previously—the use of different units in the different localities, the practice of clipping, perhaps a deliberate attempt in debasing the coinage by a particular prince or state and the usual wear and tear. But some of the coins very nearly approximate the standard weight of the Dharaṇas *e.g.* No. 14, 17, 21, 31, 52 ; and as these are all above 54 grains in weight, there cannot be any doubt as regards their identification. There are no specimens of Half or Quarter Dharaṇas in Smith's Catalogue but Cunningham gives 3 specimens of Half-Dharaṇas and one of a Quarter Dharaṇa. (Plate I, fig. 19).

In the Fourth class, Smith places all roughly circular or oval coins and sub-divides the coins of silver (C and D classes) *i.e.* the punch-marked coins of the ordinary shapes into different sections with reference to the reverse, whether completely blank or with one, two, or three or more marks. The copper coins are divided into three classes—(A) approximately square ; (B) distinctly oblong; and (C) circular. The weight system of these coins is based on the Kārṣāpaṇa of 80 ratis. In Smith's Catalogue we can recognise the ¾, ½ and ¼ pieces, but there are no specimens of a full Kārṣāpaṇa. Cunning-ham's No. 20 (Plate I) is perhaps a Paṇa though rather heavy. In Smith's Catalogue, we can identify certain specimens without any misgivings *e.g.* Nos. 92 and 100 are 3/4 Kārṣāpaṇas ; Nos. 80, 83, 105 etc. are 1/2 Paṇas ; Nos. 84, 85, 86 etc. are surely 1/4 Paṇas.

Smith's classification of these coins is based upon their shape and the condition of the reverse and he offers a suggestion about the chronological position of these coins. He opines that "the circular coins are presumably a later invention than the rectangular ones"[43] and this suggestion is based upon the difficulty of manufacturing the circular pieces as compared with those of irregular shape. But no such inference can be generally accepted as we find that he himself modified his views latter on. We know that coins of various shapes circular or other wise were in circulation contemporaneously. This will be evident from a careful examination of the basrelief in the railing of the Great Stūpa at Bharhut, depicting the sale of Jetavana to Anāthapiṇḍika who had to cover up the ground to be bought with coin pieces.[44] And later on when the shape of the coin came to be standardised, much depended upon the predilection of the particular locality *e.g.* in Taxila rectangular and square coins were preferred and similar was the case with Eraṇ too. This is borne out by the general conclusion that the Indian coin-types were "essentially local in character."[45] But there can be no doubt that the peculiar system of manufacture of the punch-marked coins rather favoured the irregular shape ; to make them perfectly square or circular necessitated greater attention and labour. Another suggestion that among the "punch-marked coins the earliest place must be assigned to those with blank reverse, at least to those of thin, fabric,"[46] cannot be accepted without qualification. Though the coins with blank reverse are likely to have preceded others, yet the thin pieces can very well be presumed to be of a later date. Moreover the theory of the Numismatists that "the punch-marked coinage was a private coinage issued by guilds and silversmiths with the permission of the ruling powers," that the obverse punches, were "impressed by the different moneyers, through whose hands the pieces passed" and that the reverse marks were "the signs of approval by controlling authority"[47] has to be practically given up in the light of later researches. It has now been definitely proved that the punch-marked coins are "a public coinage issued by authority"[48] and consequently these are assignable to a particular state or locality,[49] if we only had the key to the interpretation of the different symbols and their combinations employed in the coins. We surely must accept the opinion of Smith that these coins have no legends and "cannot be precisely dated"[50] but we must demur against the statement that they are 'ugly.' The silver coins in spite of their irregular shape cannot be called "ugly," though these might be 'rude,' and the ugliness of the copper coins must be to a great extent ascribed to the corroding influence of climate. But Smith has fully recognised the importance of these coins to the historians of India. They are the "authoritative records of the symbolism—religious, mythological and astronomical—current throughout India for many centuries."[51]

FOOTNOTES

1. Smith, V. A.—Catalogue of Coins in the Indian Museum, Vol. I, p. 131.
2. *Ibid.*
3. *Ibid*:
4. Bhandarkar, D. R.—Ancient Indian Numismatics, p. 96.
5. *Ibid.*
6. *Ibid.*

   ". . . . their proverbial absorption by all classes for the construction of domestic utensils."—E. Thomas—"The Ancient Indian Weights," p. 53. See also footnote No. 3 giving Tavernier,s account of the Persian practice—"Whence it came to pass that when a workman has need of copper, rather than lose time in going to buy it, he will melt down his cashbekes."
7. Bhandarkar, D. R.—Ancient Indian Numismatics, p. 96.
8. ". . . , the relative proportions of each, which reward modern collectors, would seem to indicate that of the joint currencies, the silver issues must have already constituted a predominant feature in the circulating media of the day; and this evidence is by no means unimportant, as showing that while the standard of value was essentially copper, the interchangeable rates of the two metals must have been conventionally recognised while these imperfect currencies were in the course of formation and reception into the commerce of the country."—E. Thomas —"Ancient Indian Weights," p. 53.
9. J. R. A. S. 1895, p. 869.
10. Cunningham, A.—Coins of Ancient India, p. 6.
11. *Ibid.*, p. 7.
12. Cf The etymological explanation of Niṣka in Max Muller's History of Ancient Sanskrit Literature.
13. Brown, C. J.—The Coins of india, p. 17.
14. *Ibid.*
15. Brown, C. J.—The Coins of India, p. 17.—". . . . may have remained current in some districts of the north as late as the second century B.C."

    Smith, V. A.—Catalogue of Coins, p. 135.

    "Mr. Loventhal was of opinion that in Southern India the use of punch-marked coins extended from the most remote times down to about 300 A.D. In Northern India, I doubt if they were much used after the Christian era."
16. Cunningham, A.—Coins of Ancient India, p. 55.
17. The Cambridge History of India, Vol. I, p. 585.—(The Date of Kaniṣka).
18. Rapson, E. J.—The Coins of India, p. 20.
19. Cunningham, A.—Coins of Ancient India, p. 45.
20. Laws of Manu—VIII, 136.
21. Elliot, W.—Coins of Southern India, p. 59.
22. Cunningham, A.—Coins of Ancient India, p. 47. Thomas, E.—Ancient Indian Weights, p. 12. Footnote 1.—Another interpretation is given—"*' "to hold, uphold, support," etc.—Wilson." Secondary meaning "to weigh in a balance," weight etc. "Hence the progression to a standard of fixed value."
23. Percy Gardner—The Earliest Coins of Greece Proper, p. 10.
24. Thomas, R.—Ancient Indian Weights, p. 36, footnote 1.— "Salaku (Telugu)," A dent or mark on a coin denoting its goodness"—Wilson, Glossary. The leading meaning of the Sanskrit Salaka is given as a dart, an arrow; one of its derivative meanings is "an oblong quadrangular piece of ivory or bone used in playing a particular game; a domino"—Wilson, Sanskrit Dictionary."
25. Cunningham, A.—Coins of Ancient India, p. 55.

26. *Ibid.*, p. 47.
27. *Ibid.*, p. 54.
28. *Ibid.*
29. Brown, C. J.—Coins of India, p. 18.
30. Cunningham, A.—Coins of Ancient India, p. 45.
31. Smith, V, A. Catalogue of Coins, p. 163.
32. *Ibid.*
33. . . . the simple weight-systems given in the law-books do not afford a satisfactory explantion of the weights of ancient Indian coins in general."—Rapson, E. J.—The Coins of the Andhra Dynasty, etc., p. clxxxi.
34. Rapson, E. J.—The Coins of the Andhra Dynasty, etc., p. clxxxi.—(Quoted).
35. Smith, V.—Catalogue of Coins, p. 136-140.
36. *Ibid.*, p. 133.
37. *Ibid.*, p. 134.
38. Bhandarkar, D. R.—Ancient Indian Numismatics, p. 70.
39. Smith, V.—Catalogue of Coins, p. 133.
40. *Ibid.*, p. 133.
41. *Ibid.*, p. 134.
42. Cunningham, A.—Coins of Ancient India, p. 65.
43. Smith, V. A.—Catalogue of Coins, p. 134.
44. Cunningham, A.—The Stūpa of Bharhut, p. 84, Plate lxii.
45. Rapson E. J.—Coins of the Andhra Dynasty etc., p. xi.
46. Smith V. A.—Catalogue of Coins, p. 133.
47. *Ibid.*
48. Centenary Supplement,], R. A. S.; October 1924, p. 175.
49. *Ibid.*, 177.
50. Smith, V. A.—Catalogue of Coins, p. 131.
51. *Ibid.*

CHAPTER IX

THE PROVENANCE AND COIN-TYPES

The assignment of the punch-marked coins to a particular province is possible, only when some of the symbols can be definitely identified as the special insignia of that state *e.g.*, the 'Taxila mark' is the exclusive characteristic of the punch-marked coins from Taxila and the 'Mālava' symbol is found only in the coins of the Mālava region. But it has not been possible to identify all these special insignias or emblems, of the different states. This will be possible only when we have definite information about the provenance of these coins. As regards the coins with Types, many of which have inscriptions, we stand on a firmer ground, but even in these cases our data are insufficient and the assignment to a particular state had not been always found possible. This is specially true of the cast coins without inscriptions. The coins which can be definitely assigned to a state or province are here grouped together according to their *provenance*. Many doubtful and unassigned specimens have to be excluded from the arrangement.

I. Almora (or Kedārabhūmi).

Three specimens of coins were found near Almora and these are "different in fabric from every other known Indian coinage."[1] The metal used was 'some alloy of silver' and the coins "are heavier than any other Indian coins."[2] Two of these coins bear the names of Sivadatta, and Sivapali(ta) in Br. letters which are taken to be by Prof. Rapson 'of a date between the 1st cent. B.C. and the and cent. A.D.' The *obv.* type has some similarity with that of a few coins of the Pañcālas, and the 'Stag' on the *rev.* has great resemblance to the 'Stag Type' coins of the Kuṇindas. Prof. Rapson attributes these coins to a branch of the Kuṇindas "whose territories 'extended further east along the southern slopes of the Himalayas as far as 'Nepal."[3]

Type—Legend *Sivadatta*.[4] *

Obv. : Two symbols between the posts ; the upper one is the triangular symbol, and the lower one may be a nandipada (?)

Rev. : The legend—*Sivadatasa* ; in the margin a stag and a tree within railing ; in the centre, an uncertain type, may be a symbol or a letter.[5]

II. Aparanta.

Cunningham wants to identify Aparanta with "Northern Sindh, with parts of Western Rajputana which would agree with the localities in which the coins are found."[1] The actual position of Aparānta is not doubtful ; it is assuredly to be identified with Northern Konkan.[2] So we must reject Cunningham's suggestion. Moreover the legend—Mahārājasa Apalātasa, seems to refer to the name of a king and not of a country. I have strong suspicion that Apalātasa has been misread for Apaladatasa, but the reproduction of these coins is so indistinct[3] that it is not possible to come to any definite conclusion in the matter. The similarity in appearance of these coins to those struck by the satraps of Mathura and other Hindu princes ruling nearby, led Prof. Rapson to assign them to "the latter part of the 1st cent. B.C. or the first part of the 1st cent. A.D."[4]

Type—Man and the Elephants Type.[5] *

Obv. : Man standing to f. with r. hand upraised ; Legend in Br.—Mahārājasa Apalātasa, "of Mahārāja Apalata (or Apaladata ?) ; to 1. a star (perhaps the countermark) ; to r. 'a three-pronged symbol', perhaps a *nandi-pàda*. (Cunningham takes it to be a *tri-ratna* symbol).

Rev. : Group of Three Elephants with riders ; the middle elephant facing to f., the others to r. and 1.

III. Arjunayanas, The.

As a people they do not appear in Pāṇini, Patañjali or the Mahābhārata.[1] A reference is found for the first time in the Gaṇapāṭha on Pāṇini (IV 1. 112.),[2] and in the Allahabad Inscription of Samudragupta (c. 380 A.D.), they "appear among the peoples on the frontiers of the Gupta Empire.[3] The Arjunayanas as a political community are supposed to have come into existence "about the Śuṅga times (200 B.C.),"[4] and the name is derived from Arjunayana the founder, "one of the family of Arjuna."[5] They issued coins as early as the first cent. B.C.[5a] but these are "extremely rare."[6] They were then settled in Rājputānā, perhaps in the 'region lying west of Agra and Mathura, equivalent, roughly speaking, to the Bharathpur and Alwar states J.R.A.S. 1897, p. 886)."[7] These coins, all in copper, bear the legends—'*Arjunāyanāna*,' 'coin of the Arjunāyanas' or 'Arjunayanana jaya', 'Victory of the Arjunayanas', in Brāhmī script".[8] The Ārjunāyana coins are closely related in style to the coins of the Northern Satraps, the Yaudheyas, the Audumbaras, the Rājanyas and others.[9] Cunningham hazards the suggestion that *Ajudhan* 'on the bank of the old Satlej river, may still preserve some trace of their name.'[10]

Type No. I. The Standing Figure and the Humped Bull[10a] Type (c. 100 B.C.). AE

Obv. : Humped Bull standing to 1.

Rev. : Standing Figure with r. hand raised as in the Northern Satrap coins ; the legend in Br. in the margin— Arjunāyanāna, and a symbol on 1. perhaps a flag or a spear.[11]

Type No. 2. The *Elephant and the Bull* Type.[12] AE Var. a. *Obv.* : A Tree in railing to r.:

on the l. an Elephant facing f. with head r. and trunk raised. The head of the elephant has resemblance to that on the *obv*. of a coin of the Indo-Parthian king Maues.[13]

Rev. : A 'curved object' rising from a railing ; and the Br. legend on the margin—'*Arjunayanana jaya*, (Arjunāyānānām jayah), 'Victory to the Arjunāyanas.' The 'curved object' seems to have some resemblance to the flagstaff with 2 symbols dangling from it in a coin of Dhanadeva.[14] There is an indistinct figure in front of it[15] which had not been marked by Smith. Perhaps it is a Bull as in **Type No.** I., though to r. The rev. side of this coin (Smith Pl. XX., 10.) has a great resemblance to the Yaudheya coin,[16] where a Bull standing r. faces a 'curved object' with a railing. Cunningham takes it to be a 'pillar with pendant garland', and on this analogy the indistinct figure of the Ārjunāyana coin may be a bull.

var. b. *camel* (?) *and the Bull Type*. AE.

obe. : A camel (?) to r. facing Tree within railing.

Rev. : Hum Ped Bull to I. Faciny sacrificial fast within railing; Br legend Arjunāyanāna *jaya*, (Victory to the Ārjunāyanas). It has striking resemblance to the Vaudheya coins. Its *rev.* type is the same as that of the Vaudheya coin in c. CAI, Pl. IV., 3; and it is struck in the same manner-slightly incuse.'it is struck in the manner-slightly incuse.'-JRAS, 1900., p. 107.

IV. Asvakas, The.

The coins with the legend *Vataśvaka* were found in the neighbourhood of Taxila and cunningham includes them among the Taxilian coins[1] The inscription is in Brāhmī characters and the coins are of the single-die variety. Prof. Rapson is of opinion that the date of these coins "is probably at least as early as 200 B.C."2 but they may be actually of an earlier date. Buhler explained the legend-Vaṭasvaka," as a tribal name, equivalent to Sanskrit Vaṭāśvakāh, meaning the Aśvaka tribes of the Vaṭa or fig-tree clan."[3] The meaning however seems to be far-fetched. The Asvakas have been correctly identified with the *Assakenoi* mentioned by Arrian. and they dwelt in the lwāt valley. They "Were the first Indian people to receive the burnt of the invasion"[4] of Alaxander the Great. The fighting was of exceptional ferocity and their chief town Massaga fell into the hands of the invader after a stout resistance. We have, however, no reference either in the writings of the Greeks or in Sanskrit literature of the *Vaṭa* (fig-tree) clan of the Asvakas. The word *Vaṭa* also means acowry shell, and we know that cowries were, and even at present are, used as mediums of exchange. So it might mean a "coin" and this will give a better meaning to the legend Vaṭasvaka, (Aṣvakānām Vatah = Vaṭāśvakah, acc. to Pāṇini—II, 2. 31.), "the coin of the Asvakas. " These coins as pointed out by Prof. Rapson are 'connected by identity of type with some of the single-die coins found in the neighbourhood of Taxila."[5] (Cf. C. CAI, Pl. II., figs. 9, 11 and 14). The symbols are the same but there is no legend; obviously these coins belong to the same tribe, and are of an earlier date. Two of these symbols are very prominent in coins Nos. 9 and 11; and I am disposed to classify them as varieties of the Asvaka coins. A tentative classification of the coins of the Asvaka tribe may be effected by dividing them into two Types of two varities each.

Type No. 1. Var. a.[5a] AE

There are two symbols—(a) the so-called pile of 'bales'[6] and above, (b) the so-called chaitya, (both are perhaps the different varieties of the Hill Symbol) ; to r. a robed human figure with an upraised arm in an attitude of worship with a *nandipada* below ; to 1. the Br. legend—Vatasvaka in characters of 3rd cent. B.C. Var. b.[8] These coins have only the two common Hill Symbols and the figure of the man is standing between with an upraised hand ; there is no legend, nor the *nandipada*.

Type No. 2. Var. a.[9] AE.

The two prominent Hill Symbols, a svastika above, and a zig-zag line (river?) below. *Var.* b.[10] This variety has the three symbols (the two Hill Symbols and the river Symbol) common with Var. a. but two peculiar symbols are introduced below them. V. Smith only notes that these symbols are "made of curved lines"[11] and Prof. Rapson takes them to be "wavy lines and uncertain designs" and suggests "vine branches (?)."[12]

V. Audumbaras, The.—

The name Audumbara, the *Odomboerae* of Ptolemy[1] is derived from the Udumbara fig tree (Ficus glomerata).[2] They are unknown to the early Pāṇinian literature but are mentioned in the Rajanya group in the Gaṇapāṭha ; and are also referred to in connection with the Punjab republics in the Sabhā-Parvan of the Mahā-Bhārata.[3] Varaha Mihira places them in the company of the Kapisthalas, 'while the Viṣṇu Purāṇa couples them with the Traigarttas and the Kulindas."[4] In the Bṛhat Saṁhitā, Udumbara is the name of 'the district of Nurpur (or rather Gurudaspur).'[5] The Audumbara coins are 'extremely rare' and are found in the Kaṅgarā and Hoshyarpur Districts of the Punjab.[6] Perhaps they dwelt in the country between Kaṅgrā and Ambālā;[7] and as Pliny locates them in Cutch, so it is evident that one branch of the people must have migrated to that region and their descendants are found there and form "the modern community of Gujrati Brahmins of the Audumbara caste."[8]

The Audumbara coins resemble those of the Ārjunāyanas and 'other classes of ancient coins,[9] and were struck "in the name of the community and the king."[10] These coins probably date from the first century B.C. and have legends in Kh. and Br. Jayaswal is of opinion that 'the Kharoṣṭhī script indicates that about 100 B.C. they came under the influence of the Satraps like their neighbours of the Punjab, and were finally absorbed."[11] There is a great similarity in style between the Audumbara coins and "the hemi-drachms of Greek prince Apollodotus and are found together with them."[12] Prof. Rapson also points out that 'a similarity in style is observable' between 'Viśvāmitra Type' and one of Azilises.[13]

Type No. I. The *Viśvāmitra* Type.[14]

Obv. : The standing figure of Viśvāmitra, the Ṛṣi with r. hand raised and the 1. resting on the waist ; the Kh. legend—Mahadevasa raño Dharaghoshasa Odumbarisa —across field,—Viśpamitra, 'Of His Exalted Majesty'[15] Dharaghosha of the Audumbaras', or of Dharaghosha, the worshipper of Mahadeva, *i.e.* Māhādeva, of the Audumbaras. Jayaswal takes 'Mahādeva' (or Māhādeva?) to mean 'His Exalted Majesty' but it appears that the word refers to their national god. Viśvāmitra was their patron saint.

Rev. ; The same legend in Br.; the Udumbara (fig tree) on the r. within a railing, and the trident battle-axe on 1. The tree was the 'lakṣaṇa and the trident, 'the figure of their standard.[16]

Type No. 2. The *Elephant and the Temple* Type. AE.

Var. a.[17] *Obv.* Elephant walking before the Udumbara tree surrounded by a railing and a zigzag line (snake or river?) beneath ; the Kh. legend incomplete— Odumbara . . ., placed under the wavy line.

Rev. : A pointed-roofed building of two or three stories, with pillars ; a pillar with *Svastika* on it to 1., and a shaft surmounted by a wheel (the so-called *Dharma-cakra* of Cunningham) with 'pendent garlands.' The building may be the temple, 'their mote-hall or some other public building,[18] and the 'shaft with the wheel' the figure of their standard.

Var. b.[19] *Obv*,:—There are two points of difference with the first variety—the position of the Kh. legend and the figure of the Elephant, In this variety, the legend is found on the r. of the Elephant and not under the zigzag line ; and while in Var. a., the whole body of the. Elephant is found, in this Var. b., the head, trunk and the forelegs are only seen. It is evident that the entire body must have been absent in the die, as the Kh. legend Odumbarisa is 'found to the right of the Elephant's forepart.'

Rev.: The temple is a three-storied one and slightly different from the first variety. There is a trident (trisula) with banners to r. and the Br. legend on top.

These coins have legends both in Br. and Kh. and the complete legends as given by Mr. Rakhaldas Banerjee are—[20]

Obv. : Kh.—Mahadevasa Raña Dharaghoṣasa Odumbarisa.

Rev. : Br.—Mahadevasa Rana Dharaghoṣasa Odumbarisa.

In the coins of two other kings Rudradāsa and Śivadāsa, their names spelt as Rudradasa and Śivadasa are introduced without any other change in the legends. The Br. and Kh. letters "belong to the first cent. B.C. and one peculiarity is that the long vowels a, u, ai. and au are avoided both in Br. and Kh."

Type No. 3.—The *Elephant and the Bull* Type.[21] AR

Obv. : Elephant with upraised trunk moving to 1.,[22] towards trident battle-axe ; Br. legend.

Rev. : Humped Bull to r., flower (lotus flower?) under head ; Kh. legend. The legends are—[23]

Obv. : Br.—bh (a) gavatomahādevasarājarājasa.

Rev. : Kh.—bhuguvusamahadevusarajaraña.

The legend on these coins had been interpreted to refer to a king named Mahādeva. But this cannot be taken to be certain. The word *bhagavata* is generally applicable to gods,[24] and the title 'rājarāja', the king of kings' is more applicable to a god than to the king of a small principality. Moreover '*Mahadevasa*' in the coins of Dharaghosha might refer to the national god, of whom Dharaghosha was the worshipper. So I would rather take this legend as applicable to god Mahādeva and the coin seems to be dedicated to him like the Catreśvara Type[25] of Kuṇninda coins. The legend therefore may be interpreted as follows—'In the name of the Almighty Mahādeva, the king of kings.'

Type No. 4. *Elephant and Man Type, AE.*

Var. a.[26] *Obv.*: Elephant with upraised trunk moving to 1., with[27] or without[28] a man on its back ; the legend either in Br. or Kh.

Rev.: Man standing to f. with spear in r. hand with or without zigzag line and the legend in Kh.

(a) (C. CAL, Pl. IV, 7.)

Br.— ñoajamitasa

Kh.—raña (or no) ajamitrasa.—'of king Ajamitra.'

(b) (C. CAL, Pl. IV, 9.)

Bh. : *r (.)- mahīm (.) ta

Kh. : ñamahimitrasa—'of King Mahīmitra.'[28a]

Jayaswal interprets the word Rajna or 'Rājanya' (Cunningham) as meaning a president, the executive head, or an elected ruler of a tribe.[29]

Var. b.[30] *Obv.*: Male Figure to f., with spear in r. hand ; the zigzag line (snake or river?) to r.

Rev.: Figure on Elephant to 1. ; Kh. legend— *Maharajasa Dhara* (?),—the reading is very uncertain.

Type No. 5, The *Elephant and Three Symbols*[31] AE.

Obv. : Elephant to 1 ; Kh. legend.

Rev. : The Three symbols—one is a *Tree*, the other Nandipada but the third cannot be recognised ; the snake (zigzag line) referred to by Cunningham seems to be a part of the Nandipada Symbol ; the legend in Br.—the same legend is found on both the sides—

Rev, : Br.—(ra) ñobhānumitra(sa).

Obv. : Kh.—ṛañabhana (or nu) mitrasa, 'of King Bhānumitra.'

Type No. 6.—The Sun and the Three Symbols.[32] AE.

Obv. : The Three Symbols as on the rev. of **Type No.** 5 ; Br. legend—Bhānumitrasa, 'Of Bhānumitra.'

Rev. : The rayed disc of the sun above a railing ; the figure of the sun refers to the name of the king Bhānu (the Sun). This coin is assuredly a Pañcāla coin and perhaps the **Type No.** 5 also should be assigned to that locality.

Cunningham included the coins of Rudravarman, Ajamitra, Mahīmitra, Bhanumitra, Virayasas and Vṛṣṇi among those of the Audumbaras. But Mr. R. D. Banerjee does not accept this view on the ground that we have not the name 'Odumbara' coupled with these names, while in the case of Dharaghosha, Śivadāsa and Rudradāsa "we invariably find that the name of the tribe is associated in the legend with that of the King. Consequently the attribution of coins which do not bear the name of the tribe to the Audumbaras, must be very doubtful."[33] But there is no reason that the same practice should be adhered to throughout the ages ; a change in the constitution of the Audumbaras might lead to the introduction of a new form of legends. So long as great importance was attached to the tribal character of the constitution, the name of the tribe was coupled in the coins with the names of their rulers ; but if later on with a change in the constitution and the augmentation of royal authority, the rulers gave only their own names and omitted that of the tribe, there is nothing improbable in it. We cannot, therefore, accept Mr. Banerjee's statement in full. Some of the coins *e.g.*, those of the Vṛṣṇis, Mahārāja Janapada, Vīrayaśas, and perhaps of Bhānumitra had been wrongly attributed by Cunningham to the Audumbaras. But the resemblance in style leads me to attribute the coins of Mahīmitra and Ajamitra to the Audumbaras ; and it is almost certain that they were the rulers of this tribe, of which the national god was Mahādeva or Śiva. It is also probable that the coins without the tribal name were of a later date than those of Dharaghoṣa, Rudradāsa and Śivadāsa who preceded them.

VI. Avanti.[1]—

The ancient name of Mālawā before the 7th or 8th cènt. A.D. was Avanti. Its capital was Ujjain or Ujjayinī. The coins included by Cunningham in Plate No. X. of his book "came not only from Ujjain itself, but from Eraṇ, Besnagar and other towns of Avanti.[2] Ujjain was the residence of Asoka in the 3rd cent. B.C. and is referred as *Ozene* in the Periplus and was according to Ptolemy, the capital of Tiastanes, the Saka Satrap Caṣṭana c. 150 A.D.[3]

The coins of Avanti have a peculiar symbol—"the cross and balls"—on the reverse. It was formerly designated the "Ujjain Sjymbol," but as it occurs also in the coins of Eraṇ, Besnagar and of the Andhras, the appropriate term as suggested by Prof. Rapson would be "Mālava Symbol." Smith divided these coins into two broad sections according to their shape—(a) rectangular ; and (b) circular. In Cunningham's opinion "the coins of Ujjain are nearly all round" and' even when the coins are rectangular "their impressions were made from round dies."[4] Though this statement cannot be accepted in its entirety, yet it proves that Ujjain had a preference for round coins, as Eraṇ had for rectangular ones. Another characteristic as pointed out by Smith is that the devices used on the punch—marked coins are combined in the dies of these coins from Ujjain, and the animals and symbols characteristic of the earlier series are repeated on the later.[5] It is therefore not unreasonable to infer that the 'Symbols Type' coins are older than the "Standing Man Type" and the coins with inscriptions. The coins with the legend "Ujeniye" are assigned to the 2nd cent. B.C. by Prof. Rapson on palaeographical grounds.[6]

Type No. 1.—*The Tree in railing Type.*[7] AE.

Obv.—The Tree in railing ; the other symbols that occur with it singly or in combination are : (a) river with fish ;[8] (b) tank with fish;[9] (c) tree;[10] (d) river," (e) 'Mālava Symbol.'[12]

Rev. 'Mālava Symbol' either with plain circles[13] or with inner circles in each orb,[14] and the 'Three Umbrellas' symbol.[15] The river with fish may represent the Sipra river on which Ujjain is situated.[16] The "*Three Umbrellas*" Symbol represents imperial power and may date from the Maurya period when Ujjain was included in the Magadhan Empire.

Type No. 2.—*The* Mālava *Symbol*' Type.[17] AE.

Obv.—The Mālava Symbol with plain circles, the 'Three Umbrellas' etc.

Rev.—The Mālava Symbol with plain circles.

Type No. 3.—The Hill Symbol—the so-called, *caitya.*[18] AE.

Obv.—The Three-arched Hill with crescent above and, a separate arch or small Hill in 1. field.

Rev.—'Mālava symbol' with plain circles.

Type No. 4.—The *Bull* Type.[19] AE.

Var.. a. : *Obv.*—The Bull standing r. with 'Tree in railing' in front ; the 'Three Umbrellas' and river (?) below.[20] The Bull is humped[21] or humped with long legs.[22] Sometimes the 'Tree in railing becomes the chief device,[23] The Bull may have a 'man' as the principal device in front with river below.[24]

Rev.—'Mālava Symbol' with plain circles,[25] plain circles in square incuse[26] and with circles in each orb.[27]

Var. b. Bull standing r. with inscription on the rev.[28]

Obv.—Bull standing r.

Rev.—'Tree in railing' ; 'Mālava Symbol' with plain circles to r.; below in early Br. characters.—*Runamāsa* or *Runamisa*, perhaps the name of a king.

Type No. 5.—*Rhinoceros* Type.[29] AE.

Obv.—Two-horned Rhinoceros standing r.; 'Mālava Symbol' above.

Rev.— 'Mālava Symbol.'

Type No. 6.—*Elephant* Type.[30] AE Var. a. *Obv.*—Tusked Elephant standing 1.; six-rayed wheel (Sun?) above.

Rev.—'Mālava Symbol' with inner circle to each orb.

Var. b.—Elephant and Inscription on rev.[31] AE. *Obv.*—Elephant to r.

Rev.—Legend—"*Ujeni* [ye]," 'Of Ujeni', the name of the city in its Prākṛt form ; not later than 150 B.C.; above, a 'hand.'

Type No. 7.—*Horse* Type.[32] AE.

Obv.—Horse, a wheel above, both in incuse.

Rev.—'Mālava Symbol.'

Type No. 8.—Lakṣmī Type.[33] AE.

Obv.—Lakṣmī seated on lotus with an Elephant on each side pouring water over her ; a tree in railing 1.

Rev.—'Mālava Symbol.' It has plain circles or *Svastikas, Nandipàdas*, etc. in the orbs. On one coin[34] Cunningham read three letters as *mu-bu-mi*. This reading gives no sense and seems to be doubtful.

Type No. 10.—The *Mahākāla* Type.[35] AE.

Obv.—The Three-headed standing figure of Mahākāla, the patron deity of Ujjain with a club in one hand and a water vessel in the other, the two emblems of Śiva or Mahākāla. The temple of this god even now stands at Ujjain but the original idol was destroyed by ṭhe Muhamedans in the 13th century ;[35] the present temple was built on the old site.

Rev.—'Mālava Symbol' with a circle in each orb.

Type No. II.—The *Standing Figure* Type.[37] AE.

The coins of this type are very common. A man with a standard appears on the obv. This standing figure may be a deity or a king or merely a standard-bearer with the special insignia of the state in the right hand.

Var, a.[38]: *Obv.*—A Man standing to front, wearing short-tailed coat and high tiara with 1. hand hanging down and r. hand grasping a standard. This figure occurs with other symbols, a number of them in combination. The principal ones are: (a) Tree in railing ; (b) Mālava Symbol' ; (c) *Nandipada* ;[39] (d) Tank with fish ;[40] (e) *Svastika* ;[41] (f) the '*Three Umbrellas*'

Symbol.[42] In one coin "the standard is surmounted by rayed sun,"[43] and in another we have the "mi (?) tasa" in Br. characters of about 200 B.C.[44] A Bull appears by the side of the standard in another coin.[45]

Rev. The 'Mālava Symbol' with (I) cross,[46] (2) *Svastika*,[47] (3) dot,[48] (4) or inner circle and dot[49] in each circle; or Two 'Mālava Symbols' with inner circle in each orb.[50] In one class of coins we have: (I) a humped Bull, and perhaps a *Nandipada* above,[51] (2) in another-forked *Svastika*,[52] or a frog.[53]

Var. b. Obv, : Man marching r. with right hand raised[54] and in one coin the figure is bearded.[55] There are others symbols, *e.g.* (I) river with fish or (2) 'Mālava Symbol.'

Rev. The 'Mālava Symbol'

VII. Ayodhya,—

The kingdom of Rāma, is the modern province of Oudh, the ancient Kośala. Its capital is situated on the Sarayū but the old town is overshadowed by the modern town of Faizabad, only a few miles distant. In the Buddhist Period the province of Ayodhya was divided into Uttara (Northern) Kośala and Dakṣina (Southern) Kośala. The river Sarayū divided the two provinces ; Śravastī on the Rapti was the capital of the former and Ayodhyā on the Sarayū of the latter.[1] It is the *Sāketa* of the Buddhists and *Sagada* of Ptolemy.

"The ancient history of Ayodhyā is lost,"[2] and the age of the coins discovered in the old site or at Faizabad nearby can be guessed only by "considering the style of the coins and the script of the legends."[3] The coins supply us with a list of about 10 kings, "of whom nothing is known but their names."[4] The earlier coins are cast in moulds, while the later ones are generally die-struck.

The oldest coins are included in the 'Symbols Type' and are likely to be anterior to 200 B.C. and the latest coins are assigned to the 2nd cent. A.D.[5]

Type No. I. The *Symbols* Type.[6] AE.

Var. a. *Obv.* :, A Symbol surrounded by a rayed circle. There is no reason to take it to be a peculiarly Buddhist Symbol as remarked by Cunningham ; it has some similarity with a symbol in a Taxilian coin.[7]

Rev. Blank.

Var. b.[8] The *Svastika* and *Nandipadas* Type. AE.

Obv. : The Svastika Symbol.

Rev. : Four Nandipadas arranged together in a circle. (The so-called four crescents with circle in the middle ace. to Cunningham).

Var. c.[9] The *Fish and the Steelyard* Type. AE.

Obv. : The Fish with a Svastika above.

Rev, : The Steelyard with a Nandipada above. Cunningham took the steelyard to be an 'axe' but Smith's identification seems to be the correct one.

Var. d.[10] *The Nandipada and Tree in Railing* Type AE.

Obv. : An elaborate Nandipada ; Legend below.— *Vijayamitasa.*

Rev. : Tree in railing; recumbent Bull 1. faintly visible above. The coin is suspected to be double-struck. Perhaps Vijayamitra got "the Nandipada and Tree in railing" coins struck in his name with the legend 'Vijayamitra' on the *obv*. and the recumbent Bull on the *rev*. So originally the coins must have been older than Vijayamitra of the "Cock and Bull" Type.

Type No. 2: The *Bull Type*. AE.

Var. a.[11] Bull standing 1.

Obv. : Bull standing 1. facing a peculiar post ; a symbol over the animal's hind quarter like a St. Andrew's Cross (Smith) .; legend above in early Br. characters of about 200 B.C.—*Visākha-devasa*.

Rev. : An elaborate Nandipada (the central boss with a circle of dots and outer rim with a triśūla) above[12] and Tree in railing on each side ; a zig-zag line (*i.e.*, a river symbol) below. The coin is cast in high relief. In the coins of Dhanadeva, there is no object in front of the Bull,[13] and the legend in early Br. letters— *Dhanadevasa*; on the rev. a Tree in railing r., river below ; a curved post rising from a railing 1. with a *Nandipada*, a Mālava Symbol and, perhaps a *Svastika* dangling from it.

In the coin of Kumudasena,[14] the Bull is standing 1. before the Tree in railing ; and a curved object rises behind it (a snake on end—Smith) ; below in clear, bold Br. characters—Rājñaḥ *Kumuda-senasa*, (coin) of Rājā Kumudasena ; all in square incuse. On the *rev.* an elaborate Nandipada in a 'double rectilinear frame.' These coins like those of Ajavarma are die-struck. The device in Ajavarma's[15] coins is the same as on the coins of Kumudasena, though the metal is brass ; the legend is—Ajavarwāna (or ?—varmaṇo), '(coin) of Ajavarma.' These die-struck coins must be much later than the cast coins of Visākhadeva, Dhanadeva and also of Sivadatta. The coin No. 40 (p. 151) in Smith's catalogue must be included in this Type. The only difference is that the legend—*Vijayamitasa* is on the *rev* and is placed below, an elaborate Nandipada. The coin of Sañghamitra[16] also belongs to this Type and the device on the *rev*. which is taken by Cunningham to be the "front view of a temple or shrine (?)" is nothing but an elaborate Nandipada and has great similarity with the *rev*. of the Kumudasena coins.

Var. b.—Bull moving r.[17] AE.

Obv. .-—Bull moving r. towards a post with a triangular head, rising from a railing ; above in early Br. characters—*Dhanadevasa*, 'Of Dhanadeva.'

Rev. A female figure r. in the centre ; a Tree in railing r, and 1. ; below a zigzag line, perhaps the river symbol, and above Svastika and two other symbols, very indistinct. It is similar in fabric and style to the coins of Visakhadeva. According to Smith the coins of these two kings "are of much the same date. Either prince may be regarded as the predecessor of the other."[18]

Type No. 3.—The Lakṣmī Type.[19] AE.

Obv. :—The goddess Lakṣmī standing to front. A small elephant on each side anointing her ; Br. legend— Visākhadevasa, 'of Visākhadeva.'

Rev. :— A Tree in railing on each side ; a symbol in the middle very indistinct, perhaps a Nandipada (?) ; river below and Svastika above.

Type No. 4.—The Elephant Type.[20] AE or pale bronze.

Obv.—The elephant is moving towards a post ; the legend in Br. gives the name of the king issuing it—

(1) Mūladevasa, 'of Mūladeva.'

(2) Vāyudevasa, 'of Vāyudeva,'

(3) Śivadatasa, 'of Śivadatta.'

Rev. An elaborate Nandipada (or wreath ?)[21] and a river symbol below in the coins of Mūladeva and Vāyudeva ; (a) a Tree in railing[22] and the (b) Mālava symbol in the coins of Sivadatta.[23] In Smith's catalogue we have an elephant standing r. but the attribution is uncertain, though it is tentatively assigned to Dhanadeva.[24]

Type No. 5.--The *Cock and Bull* Type. AE. (Of so-called Mitra Dynasty)

Obv.—Bull standing 1. before a post ;[25] Legend below in Br. characters.—Ayumitasa.[26]

Rev. —Palm tree in centre ; to 1. cock r., standing on curved line (?) facing the tree. The legends give the names of the different kings *e.g.*—

(1) *Ayū (or Ayu) mitasa*, 'of *Ayūmitra.*'

(2) *Satyamitasa*, 'of Satyamitra.'[27]

(3) *Devamitasa*, 'of Devamitra.'[28]

(4) *Vijayamitasa*,, 'of Vijayamitra.'[29]

On the rev. of these coins, the palm tree and the cock are invariably associated ; they only differ in their respective positions.

The kings whose coins have been discussed above may be arranged as follows (though no claim can be put forward as regards chronological sequence).—1. Visākhadeva ; 2. Dhanadeva ; 3. Mūladeva ; 4. Vāyudeva ; 5. Kumudasena ; 6. Ajavarma ; 7. Saṅghamitra ; 8.

Vijayamitra ; 9. Devamitra ; 10. Satyamitra ; 11. Ayūmitra. Perhaps they belonged to three different dynasties and ruled for a period of about 300 years. The kings from seven to eleven perhaps belonged to one dynasty and similar might have been the case with the two previous ones. The latest date is 150 A.D. according to V Smith.

VIII. Baran.—

Gunningham possessed 4 coins which he obtained at Bulandshahr, called Baran by the early Muhammedan writers. He derives the name from Raja Ahi-baran, "the cobra-complexioned'—a Tomar chief of unknown date.[1] The fort must be very-old ; it is called Uncānagar by the Hindus and *Bulandshahr* by the Muhammedans, meaning the 'lofty city.' But this identification is rejected by Buhler who points out that 'the old name of this place was *Varaṇa*, and the reading of the coin-legend is extremely doubtful."[2] The identification of Gomitra with his name-sake, the Hindu prince of *Mathurā* cannot also be accepted as "the types of his coins are different" and the Brāhmī letters are 'more ancient,' I am rather inclined to accept Cunningham's suggestion that these coins belong to 'Bāranāwa,' the Vāraṇāvata of the Mahābhārata to which the Pāṇḍavas retired on their expulsion from Hastināpur. Bāranāwa is situated only 16 miles to the north west of Mirat, at the junction of the Kṛṣna and the western Kāli Nadī, a distance of only 50 miles from Bulandshahr.[3]

The *Tree and the Symbols* Type.[4] AE.

Obv. : In middle a symbol, to r. a Tree within railing, to 1. nandipada ; Br. legend in two horizontal lines with a wavy line (river?) below.— *Gomitasa Bārānāyā*.

Rev. : A Tree within railing ; to r. an indistinct animal ; the whole within a square of dots.

IX. Eran.[1]—(or Erakina).

The ruins of ancient Eraṇ are situated on the river Bina in the Saugor District of the Central Provinces. It is 16 miles above the junction of the Bina with the Betwā or Vetravatī river, 50 miles to the N. E. of Bhilsa and 45 miles W. N-W. from Saugor. This ancient site has given us a large number of coins. These are usually square in form and have been divided into 4 classes.—(1) Punch-marked coins ; (2) Cast coins ; (3) Die-struck coins; (4) and inscribed coins.[2] The punch-marked coins of Eraṇ are reputed to be "the finest specimens of this class" and the punches are generally 'confined to one side' and are "placed clear of one another."[3] The 'earliest known example of an Indian inscribed coin' was perhaps discovered here.[4] Some of these coins are remarkably large and others very small.Cunningham points out that one Eraṇ coin weighs 192.5 grs. and if we make allowance for wear and tear, it must have been 210 grs. originally. He had in his possession 4 small coins averaging only 3.25 grs. At Besnagar(ancient Vidiśā) and Ujjain coins analogous to those of Eraṇ have been discovered in large numbers, and this clearly testifies to some sort of political relationship between these places.

We have the figures of animals and trees impressed on the punch-marked coins, *e.g.*, the horse, the elephant, the bull and trees of various kinds within railings. Of the symbols the most important is that of the "Cross and the Balls" known to the Numismatists as 'Ujjain' or rather the 'Mālava' Symbol and this is found in nearly all the coins of Mālwā.[5] The other symbols are 'the Lotus of Eight Leaves', the *Svastika*, the '*triangular-headed*' symbol, and the river symbol with fish which presumably represents the river Bina on which the town was situated. Cunningham's "Tri-ratnas of three points with the *Dharmacakra* wheel" is nothing but the "Three-Umbrellas knotted together" Symbol.[6] This Symbol is very common in the Patna coins. As we know that the Umbrella is associated with the majesty of a king, it may be that this symbol of 'Three-Umbrellas' came to be adopted by the Mauryas as the insignia[7] of their imperial power. The Śuṅgas of Vidiśā were at first the feudatories of the Mauryas, and even when they supplanted them in Magadha, Vidiśā remained their capital. It may be presumed that the coins with the 'Three-Umbrellas' Symbol were issued when the Śuṅgas were on the imperial throne. The 'combined' symbol of the *Tri-ratna* and the Dharmacakra is nothing but an elaborate *Nandipada*.[8] As pointed out by Prof. Rapson,[9] we find the intermediate stages in the evolution of Indian coinage from the punch-marked to the Type System in the coins of Eraṇ. A number of symbols are combined together into a Type and impressed from a die. One of the coins (C. CAL, PI. XI. fig. 10) has 4 symbols—the eight-petalled lotus, the tree within railing, a variety of the 'Mālava' symbol and two fishes enclosed within a straight line, and a semi-circle. Cunningham takes the semicircle to represent the town and he may be right in this identification.

Another coin (No. 11) has the figure of a Bull, the Tree within railing and the Triangular-headed symbol ; the third (No. 12) has on the *Obv.* the Bull, the Tree within railing, and the Lotus of eight leaves and the River Symbol, on the rev, a variety of the 'Mālava' symbol and obscure traces only. Last of all, we come to the Type System. Here prominence is bestowed upon a particular symbol and this becomes the *Type*.

Type No. 1: The *Symbols* Type.[9a], AE.

Obv.: The two Symbols— *Svastika* and *Nandipada*.

Rev. : Conventional (rather rude) representation of a Tree.

Type No. 2: The *Elephant* Type.[9b] AE.

Obv. : Elephant walking to r.

Rev. : A Tree in railing.

Type No. 3 : The Lakṣmī Type.[10] AE

Obv.: The goddess Lakṣmī seated/being anointed by two elephants.'

Rev.: The 'Mālava' Symbol.

Type No. 4 : The *Standing* Man Type.[11] AE.

These coins have a great similarity with the Ujjain coins. The figure of the man is clear : in coins Nos. 16 and 20 (C. CAL, PI. XI), only a portion remains in No. 19 and a little trace in No. 17 on the right of the coin. In the two last cases the figure is very obscure.

Var. a.[12] *Obv.*: The Man standing with a standard in the r. hand facing ; the 'Mālava' symbol to r., Tree in railing to 1. and the river with fish below. A small countermark on the r. near the foot of the man.

Rev. : The 'Three-Umbrellas' knotted together in the middle.

Var. b.[13] *Obv.* : The man standing (?), Tree in railing 1. and a peculiar symbol (cf. S. CCIM, p. 192, No. 3, obv. of Balabhūti of Mathurā) ; the river with fish beneath.

Rev. : 'Mālava' symbol and a countermark obscure.

Var. c.[14] *Obv.* : The Man standing with a standard ; the 'Three-Umbrellas' on the 1., river with fishes shaped like nandipàdas ; a countermark—a five-pointed star above the river.

Rev. : The Svastika with four Nandipàdas at the 4 points (cf.Cun. Ujjain, Pl., X. fig. 11).

Var. d.[15] *Obv.* : The Man (?), only a little trace; the 'Three-Umbrellas' on the 1., the river with fishes shaped like Nandipàdas, and the five-pointed star—the countermark above the river.

Rev. .: An Elaborate *Nandipada*. (cf. Smith—Jain Stūpa and Antiquities of Mathurā. PI. X. and XI.)

Type No. 5 : With the Legend *—Dharmapāla.*[16] AE.

Obv.: *Raño Dhamapālasa* in 'ancient' Brāhmī script ; the letters written from right to left. This is supposed to be the oldest inscribed coin in India of an indigenous origin.[17]

Rev. : Blank.

Type No. 6 : The Legend—*Erak* (eṇa?).18 AE.

It is a cast coin. The traces remain which clearly prove that it was one of a number of coins cast in the mould at the same time. The last letter cannot be properly read. Cunningham wants to restore '*—nya*' or '—na, but Prof. Rapson does not accept the reading. The most probable reading seems to be *Erakeṇa*. The letters are arranged in a peculiar fashion, one above the other. This coin is a *round* one as distinguished from the generality of Eraṇ coins which are square or rectangular in shape.

Obv. : Horse to 1 ; above, the '*Mālava*' symbol.

Rev. : 'In r. and 1. field, a tree within railing' ; between written vertically in Br. characters—*Erak* (eṇa?).

X. Kadasa. (c. 200 B.C.)—

The cast copper coins with the legend Kāḍaśa in Br. have not yet been satisfactorily identified. Cunningham suggested that the legend might have "some reference to the descendants of the serpents called Kāḍru." Buhler explained it 'as the genitive of Kāḍa, the name of a king—a N. Indian form = Sk. Kāla or Pali Kāla, 'black.'[1] As one of these coins was found among the coins of the Kuṇindas, Cunningham was led to infer that they might belong to the ancestors of the present Kaḍaik branch of the Kunets.[2] The identification of the Kunets with the old Kunindas is not accepted by Jayaswal[3] and his view seems to be correct. We have no knowledge of a king named Kaḍa or Kāla. Perhaps the word Kāḍasa refers to the name of a place. In that case, it would mean 'produced in Kaḍasa.'[4] A coin of Ujjain has the legend *Ujeniye* in Br. characters of perhaps the same period[5] and refers to the town of issue. The Kāḍasa coins similarly refer to the town of *Kaḍasa* which can be identified with *Cadrusi* (Koratās ?), one of the towns established by Alexander the Great near his Alexandria-under-the-Caucasus.[6] It is one of the cities of Kapisene and is referred to by Pliny and Solinus. Cunningham suggests that the name of the town was *Cadrusia* and the inhabitants were called Cadrusi.[7] Moreover a "prominent figure" in these coins is a zig-zag line which Cunningham takes to be a 'snake.'[8] But this wavy line may as well stand for a river and as a matter of fact we know that the town Cadrusia stood "in the north bank of the Panjshir river."[9] So it is the river that is symbolised by the zig-zag line. I am, therefore, disposed to accept these coins as attributable to Kaḍasa, the old Cadrusia which is very near to Taxila, the findspot of some of these coins.

A country Karusha is named in the Mahābhārata between Matsya and Bhoja. In the Purāṇas, it is mentioned as a country near the Vindhya range,[10] Mr. Pargiter identifies it with "the region round the modern Rewa and east-wards to the R. Sone."[11] But the long distance from the findspots of these coins which are generally discovered in the Punjab, makes the identification of Karusha with the Kaḍasa of the coins impossible. Consequently Cadrusia seems to be preferable to any other identification.

Obv. and *Rev.* (Similar). Kāḍasa in Br. ; above, river. A cast coin. AE[12]

XI. Kausambi.—

The identification of modern Kosam with the ancient town Kauśāmbī is beyond any doubt.[1] It was the capital of the Vatsas and was generally known as *Vatsa-pattana*, or the "Vatsa City.[2] It is situated 31 miles from the fort at Allahabad above the Jumna river. Ancient Kauśāmbī was not only "a city of great military strength" but "also an important commercial centre, as is indicated by the extraordinary variety of the coins found there."[3] The coins of the Kings of Kauśāmbī perhaps began about the 3rd. cent. B.C. and covered a period of about three hundred years.[4]

The inscribed coins of Bahasatimitra and others belong to the time of the Śuṅgas, of whom perhaps they were feudatories. Bahasatimitra (Bṛhāsvātimitra) lived in c. 123 B.C. and was the contemporary of Balabhūti, the king of Mathura.[5] From the inscriptions of Pabhosa, it has been inferred "that, in the second century B.C., Pañcāla (Ahichtra) and Vatsa (Kauśāmbī) were governed by branches of the same royal family, and that both kingdoms acknowledged the suzerainty of the Śuṅgas."[6]

The coins without inscriptions can safely be assigned to the third cent. B.C. and the others to the two following centuries.[7] The coins of Kauśāmbī have great similarity to the coins of Pañcāla and the later coins of Ayodhyā. The coins of 7 kings—Bahasatimitra, Jeṭhamitra, Devamitra, Aśvaghoṣa, Pavata (Parvata), Śudeva and Dhanadeva have been described by Smith and Cunningham.[8]

Type No. I : The Tree in railing Type. AE.

Obv. : The Tree in railing between two symbols ; one on the 1. has not been identified and the other on the r. was identified as a 'snake' by Cunningham, though the identification does not appear to be correct ; below Brāhmī legend—Aśvaghoṣasa[9] or Jeṭhamitasa.[10]

Rev. : Symbols indistinct.

Type No. 2 : The 'Hill' and 'Mālava' Symbols Type. AE.[11]

Obv. : A small Hill and 'Mālava' symbol with Br. legend—Jeṭhamitasa.

Rev. : Indistinct.

Type No. 3 : The Lakṣmī Type.[12] AE.

Obv. : The goddess Lakṣmī standing in a lotus flower to front ; on each side standing on a small lotus flower, an elephant, with upraised trunk, anointing the goddess.

Rev. : The Tree in railing in the middle with unknown symbols on each side.

Type No. 4 : The *Tree in railing and Bull* Type. AE.

Var. a.[13] *Obv.* : In centre conventional Tree in railing ; below Hill Symbol of six arches ; to 1. eight-rayed wheel and *nandipada* symbol ; to r. 'Mālava' Symbol and *Svastika*.

Rev. : Humped Bull of 'very lanky shape' walking to 1. towards a triangular-headed standard ; an unknown symbol over the Bull. The coin is cast in high relief.

It is the prototype of the coins in Var, b. and is surely of an earlier date.

Var. b. *Obv.* : Tree in railing in the middle, with symbols on each side, the 1. one seems to be a nandipada. The legend in Br.—(i) Bahasatimitasa,[14] 'of Bṛhasvātimitra'; (2) Jeṭhamitasa ;[15] (3) *Raja Dhanadevasa* ;[16] (4) Pavatasa.,[17] 'of Pavata' (Pārvata). In the coins of Pavata the 1. symbol is a three-arched Hill, and the r. one a snake or river.

Rev. : Humped Bull standing r. before a Hill Symbol surrounded by a railing, and 'Mālava' symbol above.

Type No. 5: The Elephant and Tree Type.[19] AE.

Obv.: Elephant standing to 1. between two pillars ; Br. legend above.—*Sudevasa.*

Rev. : Tree to r., unknown symbols 1.

Type No. 6: The *Standing Man* Type.[19] AE.

Obv.—Male figure standing to front, r. hand raised, 1. hand on hip ; Br. legend to r.,—Jeṭhamitasa. *Rev.* Indistinct animal, perhaps a horse. **Type No.** 7 : The Elephant and Horse Type.[20] AE.

Obv.—Horse moving to r. ; Br. legend on top,— *Bahasatimitasa.*

Rev. Elephant with upraised trunk moving to r. ; Tree and Hill symbols behind.

The coins without legends are the Lakṣmī Type and the 'Tree in railing and Bull' Type (Var. a). These coins must be older than the coins with legends ; and it is evident that **Type No.** 4 (Var. a) was adopted by Bahasatimitra, Jeṭhamitra, Aśvaghosha ; and we find 'Tree in railing' on the *Obv.* of the coins of Bahasatimitra, Jeṭhamitra, Pavata, and Dhanadeva. From a consideration of their coins, the kings of Kauśāmbī may be arranged in the following order though no reliance can be placed on the chronological sequence.—I. Bahasatimitra, 2. Jeṭhamitra, 3. Aśvaghosha, 4. Dhanadeva, 5. Sudeva, and 6. Pavata. It is sure that Bahasatimitra and Jethamitra were the two most powerful kings in this list. The coins of Dhanadeva—the 'Tree and Bull' Type are very numerous and this perhaps proves the length of his reign. He had a namesake on the throne of Ayodhya.

XII. Kuluias, The.—

They were 'the eastern neighbours of the Udumbaras' and lived in 'the Kulu valley of the Kangra district'[1] Their coins have been assigned by Prof. Rapson to the first or second cent. A.D. They usually used both Br. and Kh. in the coin legends, as they like the Udumbaras and the Kuṇindas "lived on the border between the regions in which the two ancient alphabets Brāhmi and Kharoṣṭhī prevailed."[2]

They are mentioned in the Mahā-Bhārata, the Bṛhat Saṁhitā and other Sanskrit works, as well as in the inscriptions.[5] Their country was visited by Hiouen Thsang and they are sometimes referred to as *Mlecchas* in the Sanskrit literature, and this perhaps means that they were foreigners. But it is evident from their coins that they had by this time adopted Indian names. The *Obv.* type has great resemblance with Vṛṣṇī coins. (C. CAI., PI. IV., fig. 15).

Type—The *Wheel Type.* AE.

Obv. : The Wheel surrounded by a circle of dots ; Br. legend—Rājña Kolūtasya Vīrayaśasya," (coin) of King Vīrayaśa, the Kolūta.[4]

Rev. : The Hill symbol (the so-called *caitya*) with the *nandipada* above, *Svastika* on 1. and another symbol 'Two S's with a line between' on the r.—the Kh. legend gives only the word Raña. The Br. letters are of the 1st or and cent. A.D. and this conclusion is strengthened by the curtailment of the Kh. legend. As pointed out by Prof. Rapson in the biliteral coin legends 'the importance of the Kh. alphabet tends to diminish as time goes on.' In the earliest known coins of this class which are placed in the first cent. B.C., (in the silver coins of the Kuṇindas and the Audumbaras) the Kh. inscription is full. But in the Kuluta coin the title Rañạ in Kh. is found on the *rev.*

XIII. Kunindas, The.—

They are the Kulindrine of Ptolemy and it is also spelt as Kauliṇḍas or Kauṇiṇḍas. The spelling in the coins is Kuṇinda as also in the Bṛhat Saṁhitā of Varāha Mihira, Kuliṇḍa in the Viṣṇu Purāṇa and Kauliṇḍa in the Markandeya Purāṇa.[1] These coins are found in large numbers "in the country between Ambala and Shahāranpur."[2] and three of the silver coins were found at Jwālamukhi in Kangra associated with the coins of Apollodotos (circ. 150 B.C.)."[3] Cunningham identified the Kuṇindas with the *Kunets* or *Kanets* of the Simla Hills.[4] But Jayaswal rejects this identification and is supported by Sir G. Grierson.[6] They however 'inhabited the country of the Sutlej in the Simla Hill States.'[6] The Udumbaras, the Kulūtas and the Kuṇindas"lived on the border between the regions in which the two ancient alphabets, Brāhmi and Kharoṣṭī prevailed: they accordingly used both of them in their coin legends."[7] In most of the coins of the Kuṇindas, both silver and copper, occur the world *Amoghabhūti*, but these coins "vary much in execution, and probably extend over a considerable period."[8] V. Smith takes the word Amoghabūti to be the name of a king, and was, therefore, forced to the conclusiọn that the name of Amoghabhūti was continued even long after his death. Jayaswal, how ever, has pointed a way out of this difficulty. In his opinion, the Kuṇinda coins refer both to the name of the king and the political community. "Their king, is always mentioned there as *Amoghabhūti, 'of unfailing prosperity,'* and the same appellation appears for centuries (150 B.C. to 100 A.C.). This was an official title and not a personal name."[9] But we have no corroboration of this statement from other sources which would obviate all our doubts. The legends in the an old form of Brāhmī and in some or the coins, these are also repeated in Kharoṣṭhī. The coins with both Br. and Kh. legends are supposed to be of an earlier date by Smith.[10] The later issues were surely influenced by the copper coins of the Kuṣāṇa period. But their attribution to the 3rd and 4th cent. A.D. by Prof. Rapson seems to be too late,[11] though there is practically no doubt that the Hindu states like the Yaudheyas, the Kuṇindas etc. "rose in power as the Greek and Kuṣāṇa supremacies successively declined"[12] The Chatreśvara Type is surely 'later in date than the 'Stag Type' coins with the name of Amoghabuti.'[13] So the period covered is 150 B.C.[14] to 200 A.D.[15]

Type No. I. The Stag Type (2nd cent. B.C.).[16] AR

Obv. : Female with 1. hand on hip with lotus flower in r. hand ; a stag standing to r. and two symbols, one between the horns of the stag and the other above it and this is supposed to be a square Stūpa surmounted by an umbrella ; a mint mark,—a disc surrounded by dots at hindfoot of stag ; the marginal Br. legend—*Amaghabhutasa maharajasa rājña* Kuṇadasa, (Amoghabhūtisa mahārājasa rājña Kuni (n) dasa)—"[coin] of Amoghabūti Mahārāja, Rājā, the Kuṇinda or of the Kuṇindas,"[17] (or of Mahārāja of *unfailing strength*, the king of the Kuṇindas).[18] We also find different symbols in other coins *e.g.* svastika, nandi-pàda or two short curved lines ; and rājña is sometimes spelt as rāña. The so-called Chaitya of three arches (the Hill symbol) also occasionally occurs.

Rev. : A high so-called six-arched chaitya (the Hill Symbol ?) with umbrella (?) in centre ; to r. conventional tree in railing, to 1. *svastika* and a triangular-headed symbol (vajra ?) and above a *nandipada* ; below a curved line (snake or river?) which appears to have been put merely for ornamental purposes ; Kh. legend in the margin —*Raña Kuṇidasa Amoghabhatisa*; below *maharajasa.*[18a]

AE. or Brass—A. With both Br. and Kh. legends.[19]

Obv. : Device and legend in Br. as in silver coins but without mint-mark ; legend generally imperfect.

Rev. : Device as in silver coins ; legend in Kh.

B. With Brāhmi Legend only.[20]

Obv. : Device and legend in Br. as above.

Rev. : Device as above but no legend.

C. With no legend.

Obv. and *Rev.* Device as above.[21]

Type No. 2.—The *Chatreśvara* Type.[22] AE (Later than Amoghabūti).

Obv. : Siva facing with trident battle-axe in r. hand, and leopard skin hanging from 1. arm ; Br. legend— Bhâgavata Chatresvara Mahâtānah.[23] "Of the Almighty Mahâdeva, the lord, *i.e.* the coin dedicated to god Maheśvara." Prof. Rapson identifies the skin on the 1. arm with that of an antelope but as leopard skin is associated with god Siva, so Cunningham's suggestion is more acceptable.

Rev. : Stag standing 1. in the middle ; conventional Tree is railing and a vase with flowers or leaves above, on the r. ; on the 1. the 'triangular-headed' symbol, the Hill symbol (the so-called six-arched chaitya) with a nandipada above and a zigzag line (not a snake) for ornamental purpose 1. ; and a symbol within the horns of the stag.

XIV. Maharaja Janapada.—

Maharaja is the name of a state and is referred to "by Pâṇini in a rule which contemplates a man owing loyalty to it."[1] Jayaswal is of opinion that during the Suṅga period, they had a republican constitution, whatever might have been the system in vogue at the time of Pâṇini. These coins have been found in the Punjab, but the exact locality where this Janapada dwelt cannot be determined. The legends are either in Br. or Kh., and this leads Jayaswal to infer that the original Br. legend was changed into Kh., "when they passed under the influence of the foreign rulers."[2]

Humped Bull and the Standing Figure Type. AE. Var. a. *Obv.* : A Humped Bull to 1., a crescent over the head and a symbol (Vajra?) over the back.

Rev. : A Standing Male Figure to f. and a Kh. legend around the coin—Mahârâja *Janapàdasa*,' Of the Mahārāja Janapada.'[3] In Var. b. occurs the same legend in Br. ; the 'Bull with the crescent' may surely raise a strong presumption that they were Saiva or the worshippers of Śiva.[4]

XV. Mālavas, 'The.—

Alexander, the Great, while marching down the Indus came upon the *Kṣudrakas* and the *Mālavas* or as they were spelt by the Greeks the *Oxydrakai* and the *Malloi* respectively.[1] They had extensive territories and large population. These states had several cities, were very rich and noted for military prowess and had republican constitutions, perhaps formed into one League[1a] as suggested by Mr. Jayaswal. Cunningham places the Mālavas near Multan which he identifies with their capital,[2] or as Jayaswal puts it "their cities were along the Chenab and their capital was near the Ravi"[3] Kauṭilya however does not mention the Kṣudrakas and the Mālavas in his, list of martial republics, and it has therefore been inferred that they had already come under the Imperial Rule of the Mauryas.[4] The two tribes reappear in the Śuṅga times but later on the Kṣudrakas vanish altogether, perhaps they became amalgamated with the Mālavas.[5] In the 2nd cent. B.C., they are found in their new homes at Karkota Nāgar "within the territory of Rājā of Uniyāra, a feudatory of Jaypur," 'a distance of twenty-five miles a little east of south from Tonk in Rajputānā.'[6] They migrated via Bhatinda in Patiala state "where they have left traces of their name (in Mālwāī dialect extending from Ferozpore to Bhatinda)' ;[7] and are found fighting with the Uttamabhadras to the west of Ajmer before 58 B.C. They later on occupied the vast territory to the south of Nāgar 'which permanently bears their name.'[8] There is no doubt that one section of the people remained in North Punjab ; and the two Mālava peoples of Prof. Rapson are surely the two branches of the same tribe.[8a] We find them mentioned among the opponents of Samudragupta along with the Yaudheyas, the Madras, the Arjunāyanas and others. Their subsequent history is lost and they vanish altogether in the later Gupta period. The Mālava coins are generally found in the country "about Ajmer, Tonk and Chitor."

V. Smith rightly points out that "in the vast range of Indian coinages their coins are among the most curious and enigmatical.'[9] The chronology of the series has not yet been precisely determined. Carlleyle and Cunningham assign them to 250 B.C. to 250 A.D. ; Smith and Prof. Rapson are agreed that the initial date is about 150 B.C. but Prof. Rapson pushes them to the 5th cent. A.D. ; Smith however attributes the cessation of this local coinage from Nāgar to "the extension of the power of Chandragupta II about 380 A.D."[10]—and he seems right in his estimate. These two great scholars also differ as regards the dates of the various types. Mr. R. O. Douglas[11] made some suggestions which are very helpful in laying down a few broad principles for classifying the Mālava coins according to chronology. The legends that occur in these coins are—(A) the various forms of the tribal name, (B) and a number of peculiar names of their princes. In class A, we have the following[12] (a) *Mala*, (b) *Malaya or Mālaya*, (c) Mālava or Mālava, (d) Mālava Jaya, "the Mālava Victory," (e) Mālavana jaya and its variants Malavaṇa Jaya, Malavāna Jaya or Malavahna Jaya etc., "Victory of the Mālavas" in Prākrit, (f) Mālavānām Jaya, (Victory of the Mālavas', (g) Mālava ganasya, 'Of the Mālava gana',[13] (h) Mālava Sujaya, 'the well-conquering Mālava (Douglas)". The last legend is read only in one coin ; Mr. Doughlas is however confident that it is not 'na' but 'su'. We however must suspend judgment till the discovery of other similar coins.

Mr. Douglas has correctly shown that , Malaya or Malaya is the earlier form of Mālava ;[13a] the Greek form Malloi stands for Malaya and the correct transliteration for Mālava would have been *Malluoi*.[14] The word 'Mala' he takes to be the name of a king, the founder of the Mālava tribe. The form, *Mālavanā Jaya* is surely of an earlier date than *Mālavānām Jaya*, which may be dated in the 2nd cent. A.D. Another very important datum can be gleaned from the fact that in some of the coins the legends read from right to left. This clearly shows the influence of the *Kharoṣṭhī* alphabet and perhaps the Mālavas brought this practice from their early settlements in the "valleys of the Ravi and the Beas." These coins with very good reasons can be ascribed to an earlier age. The conclusions based on palaeography have to be tested with reference to the form of the legends, the language employed and the way in which the letters are arranged. The adoption of these principles, which are reasonable enough, would necessitate a rearrangment of the different groups of coins in Smith's Catalogue. But the most difficult problem is the chronology of the coins which are generally ascribed to the Mālava kings with peculiar names. The relationship of these coins with those that are unmistakably Mālavan is evinced by some of their legends as well as *provenance*. In Smith's catalogue (No. 70), we have a two-line legend, (a) *Malavā*, (b) *Majupa*, both read from right to left. Here Majupa is the name of a king and he must be connected with the Mālavas.

Jayaswal suggested[15] that the coins with the names of kings belong to the power which superseded the Mālavas. But we cannot accept this view. We find that both the series were contemporaneous from the 2nd cent. B. C. to and cent. A. D. The coins with the tribal names in Prākṛt have to be assigned to the 2nd cent. B. C.; so is the case with the coins of Bhapaṁyana, Yama (Maya?) and others who have to be placed in the same period on palaeographical grounds.[16] Again the coins with their legends in classical Sanskrit.—'*Mālavānāṁ Jaya*'—come down to the and cent. A. D., while V. Smith placeṣ *Maraja, Jāmaka* and *others* in the 2nd cent. A. D. and *Paya* in about 300 A. D. Why two series of coins were simultaneously issued remains an enigma. Only plausible suggestions can be made to explain this state of things. We find in the case of some of the tribal issues that these generally had the names of the tribe and the executive head (or president) side by side, and sometimes bore the name of the Rājanya or executive head only *e.g.* Rājanya' Mahīmitra. In the case of the Mālavas the coins were merely tiny pieces and too small to have the name of the tribe and the head of the state side by side, though we find that on occasions the attempt was made (Smith's coin No. 70). Therefore the Rājanyas issued the coins in their names and also in the name of the tribe of which they were the executive heads. That they were hard-pressed for space is evident from the fact that the word '*Mahārāja*' is generally contracted into one letter '*Ma*'; and in some cases the last letter is not properly drawn.[17] Another suggestion that can be made is that the coins with the names of princes arc those belonging to the feudatory chiefs of Karkota Nāgar who were the subordinate chiefs of the Mālava tribe that had extensive territorial possessions in this region. But this conclusion can be drawn in case the coins with personal names are confined only to that particular town, and the coins with tribal names are found scattered around it.

The matter, however, must be left for further investigation.

The, personal names in the coin legends are very peculiar and "are so many puzzles".[18] Jayaswal's view that these are abbreviations seems to be the only correct interpretation. The names are surely 'odd,' but to take them to be of foreign origin has no justification. The legends are in Brāhmī and in the language of the country ; and if we accept Jayaswal's suggestion many of them, though not all, are found to be of Sanskritic origin and perfectly intelligible. Jayaswal takes the letter 'ma' to be the abbreviation for the word 'Mahārāja' and out of the twenty names in Smith's catalogue, eleven are preceded by this letter. The Mālava coins bear a great deal of resemblance to the coins of the Nāgas ; and there also we find that abbreviations were necessitated by the limited nature of the space for the legends *e.g.* 'Mahārāja Gana' for Mahārāja Gaṇendra.'

The Mālava coins are generally very small. A coin in Smith's catalogue (No. 106) 'is one of the smallest coins in the world" ; it weighs only 1.7 gr. and has a diameter of .2 inch. The small size of these coins and the metal used (copper) clearly testify to the poverty of the community that was served by them. It is also evident that the Mālavas had very little intercourse with the outside world as these coins are obtainable only at Nāgar and its immediate neighbourhood. It was thus a peculiar coinage which merely served the necessities of a community on a low economic level. I follow Smith's classification as the most convenient for reference, though with necessary modifications.

Class A. With the Tribal Name.[19] AE.

Group I. (a) Second Century B. C. (circular).

The eleven coins in this group are assigned to the second century B. C. by V. Smith. In determining the date of these coins, he relies upon Nos. I & II. These two coins may be ascribed to the 2nd cent. B. C. on palaeographical grounds, and they may belong to that early period as the legend is in Prākṛt—*Mālavaṇa Jaya* in coin No. II ; and the legend in No. I also should be read Mālavana instead of Mālava [nāṁ], as proposed. The other coins with legends in Sanskrit of the classical style must be assigned to a very much later date, perhaps 2nd cent. A. D.

(i) *Obv.* : *Mala*, Tree in railing.[20]

Rev. : *Nandipada* Symbol.

The word 'Mala' is taken by Mr. Douglas to be the name of the "original founder of the tribe". So these coins assuredly belong to the earlier series.

(ii) *Obv.* : *Mālaya.*[21]

Rev. : Obscure, irregular dots. 'Mālaya' might have been derived from 'Mala'.—meaning 'the tribe of Mala.'

(iii) *Obv.* : *Hill* Symbol (so-called '*chaitya*' of three arches); above, *Jaya* in large old characters.[22]

Rev. : Radiate sun and another symbol ; legend *Mālavaṇa*, in 2nd cent. B. C. script (Smith).

Group I. (b) 100 B. C.—100 A. D. AE.

Obv. : Legend *Mālavā*.

Rev. : A zigzag line (snake or river?) and a *Nandipada* symbol. (Smith—Nos. 7 & 8).

Group I. (c) 100 A. D.—200 A. D.

(i) *Obv.* : Legend Mālavānāṁ Jaya in classical Sanskrit.

Rev. : Obscure. (Coins Nos. 2, 3, 5, 6 & 9—Smith), (ii) *Obv.* : Conventional tree in railing with *ja 1.* & *ya r.*

Rev. : Perhaps the legend—Mālavānāṁ,

Group 2. With *Vase rev.*[25] (circ.) AE.

Obv. : Mālava jaya, in script of 2nd cent. B. C. (?).

Rev. : Vase in dotted circle.

Group 3. *Tree and Vase* Type. (rec. & circ.) AE.

Obv. : Tree in railing in centre ; legend—Mālavaṇa jaya. The other variants are Mālava jaya, *Mālavaṇā jaya*, *Mālavaṇā jaya* (or jayo), Mālavaṇā jaya or Mala-vahṇa jaya. It is the Prākṛt form and may be dated in the 1st cent. B. C. or A. D. The variants of the legend may supply a chronological clue, if we could only determine the order of these linguistic variations with the lapse of time.

Rev. : Vase in dotted border.

Group4. With Lion rev. (rec.). AE.

Obv. : The legend—*Mālava jaya* and other variants.

Rev. : Lion standing 1.

Group 5. With Bull rev. (rec. & circ.). AE.

Obv. : Mālavahṇa jaya and other variants.

Rev. : Humped Bull walking 1.

These coins seem to be of a later date, perhaps 1st cent. A. D. Coins Nos. 41, 47 & 49 in Smith's catalogue clearly do not belong to this type. In No. 57 the legend is reversed ; it is to be read from right to left, and this is surely of an earlier date, perhaps 2nd cent. B. C.

Group 6. *King's head rev.* (circ.). AE.

Mr. Douglas seems to be correct in his statement that coins Nos. 58, 59, 60 & 72a in Smith's catalogue are really Nāga coins. No. 61 is a Mālava coin but cannot be included in this group, as its rev. is very obscure. The similarity of the coins of this group with the Nāga coins was recognised by Smith also.

'*Obv.* : The legend should be read as—*Mahāgaṇasa jaya*, *i.e.* 'Victory to Mahārāja Gaṇapati'—"distinct points of similarity in design between them and the coins of Mahārāja Gaṇapati of Nāga."

Rev. : King's head r, with curly hair. Prof. Rapson does not accept Smith's identification Really it is very difficult to recognise the type as a 'curly head'; it may be a 'fantail peacock.'

Group 7. Fantail Peacock rev. AE.

These coins are of an early date, perhaps 2nd cent. B. C.; the letters read from right to left.

Obv. : The central device is very obscure. It is not possible to accept Smith's opinion that it stands for a female figure (Smith—No. 63). The legend seems to be Mālava *gaṇasya jaya*.

Rev. : Peacock facing with expanded tail, covering the whole surface of the coin.

Group 8. Miscellaneous Devices. AE

Some of the coins are of an early date. Coin No. 66 is assigned to the 2nd cent. B. C. by Smith ; No. 67 also belongs to the same period at least, as it has the legend '*Mala*' ; Nos. 67a & 67b are of a much later date and No. 64 perhaps belongs to the 2nd cent. A. D. This Group has two coins with tree on the obv. and one with an open lotus flower.

In three other coins, we have only the variants of the 'Mālava' legend. On the *rev*. Smith identified a Nandipada ; but a snake, a peacock and a solar symbol as suggested by him cannot be made out.

Class B.—With the Names of Mālava chiefs (?).[24] AE.

(A) The Early kings—100 B. C. or earlier.

(1) *Bhapaṁyana*, or *Bhaṁpāyana* (Jayaswal), c. 200 B. C. The 'tree in railing' Type. The animal on the rev. seems to be a recumbent Bull and not a lion or tiger as suggested by Smith. (Coin No. 68).

(2) *Yama or Maya.*—2nd cent. B. C.

The 'Tree in railing' Type ; on the *rev*. '*Mālava*' Symbol ; I do not find the snake (Smith No. 69).

(3) *Majupa*, *i.e.* Mahārāja *Jupa* (Yūpa). The legend in two lines—(i) *Malavā*, (ii) *Majupa*, both read from right to left. The *rev*. is obscure, perhaps a lion. It is an early coin (200 B. C.), Jupa was surely a Mālava chief. (Smith—No. 70).

(B) From c. 100 B. C.—100 A. D.

(1) *Mapojaya*. Jayaswal takes it to be Mahājaya *i.e. Mahārāja Jaya*. Two Types of coins—(I) with lion *rev*. (No 71), and (ii) with elephant rev. (No. 72) ; the single line legend on the obv. *Mapojaya* or *Mahājaya* (?).

(2) Mapaya, or Mahārāja Paya, perhaps the same man as Paya and therefore of a later date—acc. to Smith c. 300 A. D. Type—(i) Humped Bull *rev*. and single line legend Mapaya *obv*. (Smith—No. 73—78) ; (ii) the same *obv*. but lion *rev*. (?) (No. 79). No 72a is a Nāga coin kind referred to above.

(3) *Magajaśa* is the abbreviation of Mahārāja Gajasa, of Mahārāja Gaja.' (4) *Magaja* is the identical name— 'Mahārāja, Gaja.' So the coins Nos. 80-—84 (Smith) maybe taken to be the coins of one and the same king. obv. *Magajaśa* ; rev, defaced. (Nos. 80 & 81) ; (ii) *Obv. Magaja ; rev.* elephant or obscure (Nos. 82 — 84).

(5) *Magojava*, or *Magajava* (Jayaswal), *i.e.* Mahārāja Gajava (Gajapa?). Perhaps this name is identical with Gajava ; Legend— *Magojava* obv.; Lion sitting *rev*.

(Nos. 85—87).

(6) *Gajava* (Gajapa?). Perhaps identical with king No. 5 ; Legend *Gajava* on obv.; and Lion (?) rev.

(7) *Gojara*. — Legend Gojara obv.; and animal running *rev*. (No. 88).

(8). *Maśapa*, (or *Maśapa* or Mahārāja Sarpa (Jayaswal) — The Legend Māśapa on the *obv*.; defaced rev.

(9) *Pachha*. Legend *Pachha* on the obv.; and king's head (?) *rev.*

(10) — *Magachha* or Mahārāja Gachha : the Bull Type— the Legend *Magachha* on the *obv*.; and Bull 1. on the *rev*. (No. 94).

(11) *Jamapaya*. — The Legend *Jamapaya* on the *obv*.; the blank or defaced rev. (No. 99).

(C) The Late Period— c. 100 A. D.— 300 A. D.

(1) Yama. — the second of this name. A two-line legend — (a) Yama, (b) illegible ; and a Bull on the rev. about 100 A.D. (No, 92).

(2) *Jāmaka*, — the legend — *Jāmaka* on the *obv*.; and *rev*. defaced. (No. 98).

(3) Mahārāya, — the legend in two lines, — (a) (Ma)h (ā), (b) *rāya* ; rev. blank or defaced — 2nd cent. A. D. (No. 101).

(4) *Maraja* — Legend *Maraja obv.*; Bull rev. No. 102 & 103). It is perhaps an abbreviation for Mahārāja ; and Mahārāya may be the name of the same king, specially as the coin is also dated in the 2nd cent. A. D.

(5) *Mapaka*,—Mahārāja Paka—The Bull *rev.*; and legend *Mapaka* on the *obv.*—2nd cent. A. D.

(6) *Paya*.—The Bull Type with legend *Paya* on the *obv.*, about 300 A. D. For another Paya of an earlier date see Mapaya ; or he may be the same man as the Type is identical, and the characters are of a late date (Mapaya, No. 74).

Class C—Without Legend. AE.

(1) *Peacock and the human figure.*

Obv. : Peacock facing front with expanded tail.

Rev. : Squatted human figure to 1. with obscure marks on the r. (No. 104).

(2) *Vase and Bull.*

Obv, : Vase containing flowers.

Rev. : Bull standing 1. (No. 105).

(3) *Palm-leaf and the Vase.*

Obv. : Pinnate Palm leaf.

Rev. : Vase ; the smallest coin in the collection, only 1.7 gr. in weight and .2 in diameter (No. 106).

(4) *Palm-leaf and the Bull.*

Obv. : Pinnate Palm-leaf ; rev. : Bull standing 1. (Nos. 107 & 108).

(5) *Tree in railing.*

Obv, : Tree in railing, perhaps with legend *Jaya* ; Analogous to coin No. 4 of Smith and similar to coin No. 26 of Douglas. *Rev.*—indistinct.

(6) The *Bull* with large horns.

Obv. : Bull with large horns and speading ears standing l. Rev, : defaced.

(7) *Lotus*- Flower.[25]

(a) *Obv.* : 'Mālava' Symbol ; *Rev.* Conventional Lotus Flower.

(b) *Obv.* : defaced ; *rev.* ; open Lotus Flower.

XVI. Mathura.—

The famous city on the Jumna, the *Modura* of Ptolemy and *Melhoras* of Arrian was the capital of the *Sūrasenas*.[1] It is one of the most ancient places in India and is situated 35 miles to the North of Agra. This sacred city was the "stronghold both of the worship of Kṛṣṇa and of Jainism,"[2] and coins have preserved the names of at least twelve later kings who reigned during the Sunga period."[3] Balabhūti was the contemporary of Bahasatimitra of Kausāmbi (c. 123 B.C.) and was perhaps a feudatory of the Śuṅgas.[4] Another king Brahmamitra who is assigned to the earlier part of the first century B.C. was probably the contemporary of Indramitra of Ahicchatra.[5] In the second half of the first century B.C., Mathurā had passed from the native Indian kings to the foreign Śaka Satraps. It seems that there were three generations of foreign rulers.

The names of the following kings are known to us.— (i) Balabhūti, Puruṣadatta, Bhavadatta, Uttamadatta, Rāmradatta, Śeṣadatta, Kāmadatta, Sivadatta, Śiṣu-chandradatta or —chandrāta and Ghoṣa[6] (? a doubtful name) ; (ii) Gomitra, Viṣṇumitra, Brahmamitra, and Sūrya (? Suya) are later than the previously named princes as is evident from the form of their names in the legends ; and perhaps they ruled after the Śaka Satraps. Probably some of them were contemporary with each other and there is practically no doubt that the first group of kings preceded the foreign rulers. These kings ruled either at Mathurā or in the adjoining territories. Mathurā was however a large kingdom in the 7th century A.D., 833 miles in circuit.[7]

The coins from Mathurā issued by the native Indian princes may be arranged in three groups.—

I. The *Upātikyā* coins of 3rd century B.C.

II. The Indian princes who preceded the Śaka Satraps—Balabhūti and others, from the 2nd cent. B.C. to the middle of the first century B.C.

III. The Indian rulers who followed the foreign kings—Gomitra and others, from the middle of the 2nd cent. A.D. to the 3rd cent. A.D.

Type No. I.——With Legend *Upātikyā*[8] AE

Obv.—Svastika above ; *Upātikyā* in Br. characters of the 3rd cent. B.C. It is a cast coin from a single die. *Rev.*—Blank.

Type No. 2.—*The Standing Figure* Type. AE.

(Cast or die-struck ; brass or copper).

The kings of Mathurā adopted a 'Standing Figure' as the characteristic Type and "it is supposed to represent the god Kṛṣṇa."[9] This Type was also continued by their conquerors and successors, the Śaka Satraps.— Rañubula and Śoḍāsa. On the *Obv.*—The figure standing to front with right hand raised ; legend in Br. with the name of the king in genitive *e.g.* Rājño *Balabhūtisa* etc. These coins may be divided into varieties according to the device on the *rev.*—

Var. a.—Tree in railing rev.[10]

Var. b.—Rows of dots rev.[11]

Var. c.—Elephant l. with 2 rows of dots rev. [12]

Var. d.—*Elephant moving* r. rev.[13]

Var. e.—*Three Elephants with riders rev* ;[14] one to front and others facing to r. and l. each with a man mounted on the neck.

Var. f.—*Horse moving l. rev.*[15]

We have two very peculiar symbols in the coins of Balabhūti and others. Some of the kings have no titles preceding their names in the coins but others have Rājño[16] (*e.g.* Balabhūtisa), Rājā (*e.g.* Utamadatasa), Bhāgavata[18] (*e.g.* Ghoṣathā ?), and Mahārāja.[19] The forms of the names of Gomitra, Viṣṇumitra and Brahmamitra differ from the preceding ones *e.g.*, Gomitrasa, Viṣṇumitrasa etc.[20]

XVII. Panchala (North).—

The ancient kingdom of Pañcāla was divided into two divisions by the Ganges. *Ahichatra* was the capital of North Pañchāla and Kāmpilya of South Pañchāla. Cunningham found these coins "in Rohilkhand, and chiefly at Ahicchatra, Aonla and Bacñaon"[1] and assigned them to North Pañchāla—'the modern Rohilkhand, comprising the Bareilly (Bareli) and other districts between the Ganges and the mountains."[2] These incuse coins are abundantly found at Ahicchatra, the modern Ramnagar which was surely the capital of these kings. But Smith points out that these coins are also found in Oudh and the neighbouring districts, and thinks that the kingdom of these Rājās "must have included eastern Oudh and Bastī, with, perhaps, Gorakhpur—in short, the old kingdom of Kośala";[3] so he calls these kings "the lords of North Pañchāla and Kośala." The kings of Ahicchatra were perhaps feudatory to the Śuṅgas and "in the 2nd cent. B. C. Pañchāla (Ahicchtra) and Vatsa (Kausāmbi) were governed by the branches of the same royal family and both kingdoms acknowledged the suzerainty of the Śuṅgas."[4]

The names of these kings generally end in 'Mitra', and the dynasty is sometimes designated the 'Mitra Dynasty' of Pañcāla. They have been sometimes identified with the Śuṅgas[5] but on insufficient grounds, and there is no doubt that they belonged to a local dynasty. The reasons for and against this identification are noted by Prof. Rapson ;[6] Agnimitra of this dynasty "is supposed to be identical with the second Śuṅga king."[7] But there is no evidence at present, "either to prove or disprove the suggestion. The identity of name may well be, accidental, or, perhaps more probably, it may indicate that the royal families of Vidisā and Ahichatra were related."[8] Indramitra, a king of Ahichatra was the contemporary of Brahmamitra of Mathurā.[9]

The coins found in the neighbourhood of Ahicchatra have thus preserved the names of about a dozen kings who were the contemporaries of the Śuṅgas. The principal characteristic of these coins is a "well-marked obverse incuse containing the ruler's name and certain symbols, usually in a set of three."[10] Their weights "do not correspond with the common Hindu standard of the Paṇa of 80 ratis or 144 grains and its multiples and divisions."[11] Cunningham wanted to identify them with the heavy Paṇa of 100 ratis ; but his view is unacceptable ; and an attempt was made in a previous chapter (on Metrology) to explain this discrepancy. The series is assigned by Smith to the period c. 100 B.C.—100 A.D., but as it is not possible to 'find any sure criterion of relative date' he arranges the names in alphabetical order.

The Pañchāla coins are all of copper. On the *obv*. there are three symbols arranged in a line, with the name of the king in Brāhmī letters below, in a deep incuse square. This is a special characteristic of these coins. On the *rev*. there is either a symbol on an altar with railing, or the figure of some god like Agni or Indra, referring to the name of the king. These three symbols have not yet been satisfactorily interpretated.[12]—(I). On the left, there is a Tree on a square base or in a square railing ; (2), in the centre, according to Carlleyle, a liṅgaṁ guarded by two serpents (Nāgas), which rise up on each side of it ; this is evidently Symbol No. 7 which Prof. Rapson[13] tentatively assumes to be the conventional representation of two Nāgas with expanded hoods ; (3) the right hand symbol is taken by Carlleyle to be two serpents interwined forming a circular knot in the centre. But this view does not seem to be satisfactory.

Below these symbols occur the names of the kings in genitive.—I. Agnimitra; 2. Bhadraghosha ; 3. Bhānumitra ; 4. Bhūmimitra ; 5. Bṛhaspatimitra ; 6. Dhruvamitra ; 7. Indramitra ; 8. Jayamitra ; 9. Phalgunimitra ; 10. Rudramitra (gupta?) ; u. Sūryamitra ; 12. Visvapāla ; 13. Viṣṇumitra ; 14. Yajñajita. On the *rev*. of the coins of Agnimitra[14] occurs a 'Male Figure,' with five-rayed head' standing on an altar with railing ; this figure is identified with Agni, the God of Fire with five flames. The 'standing figures' on the *rev*. of the coins of Bhadra-ghosha[15] have not both been identified ; the female one may be Bhadrā, the celestial Ganges[16] and the other one, if male, may represent Śiva (Ghoṣa). The coins of Bhānumitra have two separate devices on the *rev*.—(a) solar symbol of disc surrounded by eight pellets on a railing with a post at each end flanked by nandipàdas ;[17] or (b) five-pointed flames rising from a nandipada symbol.[18] Bhūmimitra's coins have a figure like that of Agni, as in the coins of Agnimitra ; the railposts have cross-bars.[19] The coins of Dhruvamitra have a 'trident' on a basement of railing on the rev. Dhruva is an epithet of Śiva and perhaps the trident refers to that god.[20] Indramitra had a 'squat figure' seated on (a) a pedestal or low railing,[21] or (b) inside a temple.[22] This figure perhaps represents Indra. The figure on the rev. of the coins of Jayamitra has not been identified ;[23] but there is no doubt that the female figure standing on lotus on the coins of Phalgunimitra represents the constellation Phalguni personified.[24] Rudramitra had a 'trident' on a basement of railing on the rev.[25] and Sūryamitra had the rayed circle of the 'Sun' on the triangular-headed symbol' above a basement of railing.[26] Viṣṇumitra had a four-armed figure on basement with railing on *rev*. ; and this no doubt represents god Viṣṇu.[27] Perhaps the same figure occurs on the rev. of the coin of Viśvapāla, though it is very indistinct.[28] The coin of Yajñajita[29] was found a few years ago in the ancient site of Kurukṣetra, and it is surmised to be a Pañchāla coin by the well-defined incuse on the obv., the special characteristic of the Pañchāla coins. The script of the legend is of the 2nd or 3rd cent. A.D.

From an examination of the coins and their rev. devices, it appears that some sort of close relationship subsisted between Agnimitra, Bhānumitra and Bhūmimitra ; perhaps Bhānumitra and Bhūmimitra were the sons (?) and successors of Agnimitra. The figure of the 'Fire God' is found in the coins of Bhạnumitra[30] and Bhumimitra. They seen to have continued the device of their predecessor Agnimitra to whom it is so appropriate. Similar relationship might have subsisted between Rudramitra and Dhruvamitra ; Dhruva being the successor. The 'Trident was the insignia of both the Kings.

XVIII. Sibis, The *—

The Siboi were the neighhours of the Mālavas (the Malloi) in the Punjab during the time of Alexander.[1] They are referred to as Sivis in the Jātaka and the Śaibyas by Patañjali who took Śibi to be the "name of a, country or state."[2] Later on like the Mālavas, they migrated from the Punjab to Rajputana[3] and their coins are found at Nagarî near Chitor. These coins bear the name of their country or Nation: — Majhimikāya Sibi Janapàdasa—'Of the country (or Nation) of the Sibis of Madhyamikā.'[4] Madhyamikā therefore seems to be their capital and its identification with Nagari is practically certain.[5] These coins are very rare and the metal is copper.

Obv. ; The Upper Part of a Triśūla (Cross'— Cunniūgham) in middle with a small symbol in each angle ; to the r. a straight tree rising from a small circle : Legend in Br.—*Majhimikāya Sibi Janapadasa.*

Rev. : Hill surmounted by the *Nandipada* with a river symbol below. The coins are earlier than the Christian Era.

XIX. Taxila.—

The ruins of Taxila are situated at Shāhdheri about 20 miles North-West of Rawalpindi. It was a very important city in early times on account of its position on the trade-route, connecting India with Central and Western Asia, 'the strength of its natural defences, the fertility of its soil, and a constant supply of good water.'[1] According to Arrian, it was 'a great and flourishing city in the time of Alexander, the Great, the greatest, indeed, of all the cities which lay between the Indus and the Hydaspes (Jihlam).'[2] This is corroborated by Strabo and Plutarch. Takṣasilā was a very old town and is said to have been founded by Bharat, the brother of Rāmchandra after the name of his son Takṣa.[3] At present, the ruins of three distinct cities lie within 3 1/2 miles of each other. The oldest is the Bhir mound. This is "the most ancient of all the sites at Taxila"[4] and "here the old coins are found in greater numbers than in any other part of the ruins."[0] The capital was transferred by the Greeks in the 2nd cent. B.C. to Sirkap in the adjoining region. This Greek town was replaced by the third city at Sirsukh during the time of the Kuṣāṇas, perhaps in the reign of Kaniṣka. From the 5th cent. B.C. to 5th cent. A.D., Taxila passed through the hands of seven nations.—"the Persians, the Macedonians, the Mauryas, the Bactrian Greeks, the Scythians (Sakas), the Parthian and the Kushāns." We are, however, concerned only with the coins of the native dynasties. But it has to be borne in mind that the coins discovered at Taxila might not all belong to that town ; many of them must have come from the neighbouring territories to this commercial centre of antiquity and also a university town. So it is not possible to decide whether these coins should be assigned to Taxila or not, though there is no uncertainty in identification about some of the types *e.g.* the local Taxilian coins of the Lion Type.[6] With this note of caution and subject to future elucidation, the coins discovered at Taxila or near about are grouped under this heading.

In India, the art of striking from a die was at first adopted at Taxila, perhaps under foreign influence. But the method adopted was peculiarly Indian. 'The coins seem to have been impressed with a die while the metal was in a semi-molten state "with the result that the impress of the die was left enclosed in a deep incuse square. The coins of Pañchāla and Tripuri offer other examples of this method."[7] According to V. Smith the single-die coins must have begun not later than 350 B.C. ; perhaps they are of a much earlier date. But there is no doubt that the Taxilian double-die coins must have preceded the coins of the Indo-Greek kings Pantaleon and Agathokles (c, 190—180 B.C.)[8] A. Single-die Coins. AE.

Type No. I. .The Hill Symbol.—The Hill of three-arches (the so-called Chaitya) with a crescent above: — Var. a.—With a monolith to 1., (C. CAI., II., 6). Var. b.—With a Tree in railing to r., (C. CAI., II., 7)

Var. c.—With a *Tree* in middle ; *Nandipada* and *Svastika* to r. (C. CAI., II., 8).

Var. d.—With the plan of a monastery with cells and monolith to 1., and wavy line (river) below (C. CAI., II., 12).

Var. e.—With a *building*, perhaps a temple (C. CAI., II., 13).

Var. f.—With a short limbed square *Cross* to r. in circular incuse (C. CAI., II. 16).

Type No. 2. The *Nandipada* Type. AE. (S. CCIM., XX. 8).—A large Nandipada symbol in the centre ; *rev.* blank.

Type No. 3.—The *Taxila Symbol* Type. AE. (S. CCIM., p. 157, coin No. 20).

A Symbol 'composed of crescents applied to a central boss' ; the 'varieties of this symbol are characteristic of Taxilian coins.'

Type No. 4,—The *Lion Type.*[9] AE.

A Lion standing to 1. with a nandipada in front and svastika above, or without symbols.

B. Double-die Coins. AE.

Type No. I. The *Symbols* Type.

Var. a.—The *Hill and the Cross,*[10]—*Obv.* : The Three arched Hill Symbol with a crescent above ; rev. : A short-limbed Cross.

Var. b.—The *Hill and the Svastika.*[11]—*Obv.* : The Three-arched Hill surmounted by crescent ; rev. : svastika with curved limbs opening 1.

Var. c.—The *Hill and the Nandipada.*[12]—*Obv.* ; The Hill Symbol of Three Arches with crescent above ; and Nandipada ; *rev.* : same as *obv.*

Var. d.—The *Cross and the Stems*[13]—*Obv.* : A short limbed square Cross or quadrilateral with incurved sides above the Hill with crescent ; rev. : A symbol consisting of five stems springing from a railing.

Type No. 2.—The *Lion and Elephant* Type.[14] AE.

Var. a.—(Lion left).—*Obv.* : Lion standing 1., *svastika* above, Hill surmounted by crescent in f.

Rev.: Tusked Elephant standing r., Hill with crescent above.

Var. b.—(Lion right).—*Obv.* Lion standing r., *svastika* above, Hill in front.

Rev. : Elephant L, Hill of Three arches above.

Type No. 3. *Horse and Elephant* Type. AE.[15]

Var. a.—*Obv.* : Galloping horse l, a symbol above, perhaps *svastika.*

Rev, : Elephant standing r., an indistinct object in front of him.

Var. b.[16]—*Obv.* : Horse standing l., a Hill symbol in front, another above, and indistinct traces of another symbol.

Rev. : A tree on the r., Hill with crescent 1. and below it a short-limbed cross ; and in the middle the full front view of an Elephant "with the two ears spread out to the right and the left of the lobes of the head, the trunk hangs down in the middle ; while all four legs are displayed, the hind legs appearing outside the fore legs." (Cunningham).

Type No. 4. The *Rākṣasa* Type[17] AE. (C. CAI., Pl. III., 7)

Obv.: The Head of a Rākṣasa with short ears and protruded tongue ; there are traces of letters above the head.

Rev. : A symbol consisting of five stems springing from a railing flanked by a Hill Symbol on each side.

These coins arc of very rare occurrence and Cunningham possessed only two specimens ; but their importance cannot be over-estimated. There can be no doubt that the head of the Rākṣasa is a very close imitation of the Grecian Gorgon-head tetradrachms of Eretria (cf. Head— Coins of the Ancients, Pl. 5, No. 25) which were not minted after the Persian War.[18] That the particular coin is of Indian origin is evident from its square shape, the metal used, the system of manufacture and the weight. It can be definitely pronounced to be an imitation of a Greek device and the Grecian influence over the die-struck coins has to be taken for granted.

No. 5.—The *Negamā*, (Naigamāḥ) Coins[19]—These coins are figured by Cunningham in his book Coins of Ancient India, Pl. III.

Obvèrse	Revèrse.
No. 8. Br. T (R?) ālima (ta).	Br. Nega (ma).
No. 9. Kh. Dujaka, with ' steelyard' above	Br. Negamā, a 'stroke' or 'bar' above
No. 10. Br. Dojaka.	Br. Nefamā.
No. 11. Br. A (taka ?) takā	Br. Negam (ā).
No. 12. A dancing girl (?)	Kh. * * dare *.
No. 13. A chakra (discus) with Hill symbol above.	Kh. Pancha Nekamma, 'Five Nekamas' with a svasstika and two nandipadas above

These coins were issued on behalf of the mercantile guilds and their relationship with the State had been discussed in a previous chapter. The words on the *Obv.* Tālimata, Dojaka etc. are the names of the capital towns and not of the rulers of the guilds, as suggested by Rapson. The legends are either in Br. or. Kh. ; in Br. it is spelt as Negamā or Nigama, while its Kh. variant is Nekama,

XX. Tripuri or Tripura.—

Modern Tewar, the ancient Tripurī is situated on the river Narmadā, only seven miles to the west of Jabbalpur. The town is said to have been built by the sons of Tarakāsura and according to Matsya Purāṇa, Tripura was the capital of 'Bāna Rājā.' The coins discovered here are of a 'peculiarly Indian[5] manufacture with a deep incuse square, like the coins of Mathurā, Taxila etc.[2]

Type—With *Br.* Legend—*Tripuri*, (3rd cent. B.C.).[3]AE

Obv. : Legend in Br. characters of 3rd cent. B.C.—

Tripuri ; Symbols—Cross, curved line, and *chaitya* (perhaps *Swastika*, *River* and Hill *Symbols*). *Rev.* : *Plain.*

XXI. Vimakas, The[1].—

They are not known from any other source. The coins of their king Rudravarma is included by Cunningham among those of the Audumbaras. It has a great similarity with the 'Mahadeva'[2] coin and bears the same type. There seems to be some sort of relationship between the Vimakas and the Audumbaras ; perhaps they were neighbours.

The Elephant and Bull Type. AE.

Obv. : The Elephant with upraised trunk moving to r. towards trident battle-axe of Śiva ; Br. Legend.

Rev. : Humped Indian Bull to r. and a symbol under head ; it cannot be a flower as suggested by Cunningham. It has a great similarity with the symbol on the rev. of the Vṛṣṇī coin (C. CAI., Pl. IV. fig. 15) : and I take it to be a *Cakra* or discus. Kh. Legend.

The Legend.—

Obv. Br. : rājñavemakisarudravarmasa (v) i ......

Rev. Kh. : rañave .... vu (.) ma—vjjayata (sa)[3] = '(coin of) king Rudravarma, the Vemaki or Vaimaki—the king of the Vimakas, the Conqueror.

XXII. Vrishnis, The.—

The Vṛṣṇīs of old lived at Mathurā. According to the account of the Mahā Bhārata, they went to Dwarakā when hard-pressed by Jarāsandha.[1] But a branch of it must have remained in the original home , and in the Śuṅga times (and cent. B.C.), they issued coins of which perhaps only 'two remain.[2] But shortly afterwards, they fell under the influence of the Śaka invaders, and Jayaswal comes to this conclusion from the fact that the Brāhmi legend of the coin was coupled with the 'script of the invader' *i.e.*, Kharoṣṭhī.[3] The legend on the coins is a peculiar one, different from that of the republican tribes—the Mālavas the Ārjunāyanas, the Yaudheyas and others. It is not merely in the name of the Gaṇa but in the name, of the Rājanya ana Gaṇa of the Vṛṣṇis.[4] Jayaswal tried to clear up this difficulty and showed that in the Vṛṣni Gaṇa, the executive power was vested in two Rājanyas.[5] The coin in Cunningham's book Pl. IV., fig. 15 is in silver.[6]

Type—The *Half-Lion and Half-Elephant.* AR

Ob. : A pillar, with half-lion and half-elephant surmounted by a symbol and surrounded by a railing : legend in Brāhmī[7]

Rev. : The same legend in Kh. and the so-called *Dharmacakra* of Cunningham. Jayaswal has clearly shown that it is the state symbol of the Vṛṣṇis[9]—the weapon "*chakra* or discus, which was their symbol according to tradition as early as the time of Rājanya Kṛsna." Whatever doubt we might have as regards the correctness of the identification is set at rest "by the cutting edges and the projecting points on, the rim."[10] The Legend[11]:—

Obv. : Br. Vṛṣṇir(ā)jajñā ganasyatratarasya.

Rev: : Kh. Vṛṣṇira—nna(ga) . . . (t)ra.— "Of the Vṛṣṇi Rājanya (and) Gaṇa—the protector of the country (Jayaswal)."

XXIII. Uddehikas, The.—

The Audehilkas or Auddehikas are mentioned by Varāha Mihira in his Bṛhat Saṁhitā and are placed in the central Region. Prof. Rapson concludes from 'the general similarity between the coins of Uddehika and Eraṇ' that the "two places were not far apart." The exact determination of the locality must await further research. These coins, however, "mark an interesting stage in the art of coin-making in India.' The symbols instead of being impressed on the coins separately by the different punches are struck from a single die which is made up of a collection of such symbols. The Brāhmī alphabet is of an early period and the coin may safely be assigned to the 3rd cent. B. C. We have the name of only one king Sūryamitra.

Type No. i.—The Humped Butt Type.[2] AE. *Obv.* : Humped Bull to r.; above, tree within railing in a horizontal position.

Rev. : The Legend in old Brāhmī—*Udehaki*, "the Prince of the Uddehikas"; three symbols above,—the 'Mālava' symbol, two *fishes* in a pond, and *tree* within railing.

Type No. 2.—The *Elephant* Type.[3] AE. *Obv.* :

The Elephant to 1.; beneath "five-hooded snake, and (?) tree within railing, both represented horizontally." The coin is almost obliterated ; so the symbols are obscure and doubtful. The countermark is the 'triangular-headed' symbol at top left. This symbol is very common. Prof. Rapson characterises it as a curious symbol' which "occurs so frequently on coins of all kinds—punch-marked, cast and struck—and which no one seems to have explained." Sometimes it is put within a railing as on many of the coins of Bahasatimitra of Kausāmbi. There is no doubt that it is an auspicious sign like the svastika. The equilateral triangle is the 'symbol of God manifested in the cosmos",[4] and when it stands 'on its apex it signifies expansion, or evolution and like the Swastika, the ascending creative force—or life."[5] This may explain its general use but what the two small protruding lines on the right of the triangle represent, cannot yet be determined.

XXIV. Upagauda.[1] —

Prof. Rapson would prefer to take Upagoda as the name of a king but it seems to be a variant of Upagauḍa, the name of a place. Gauḍa in early times was in Uttara Kosala[2] and according to *Matsya*, *Kūrma* and *Liṅga* Purāṇas, Śrāvasti was situated in Gauda. Cunningham takes Gauḍa to be a sub-division of Uttara Kośala and identifies it with "the Gonda of the maps."[3] I presume therefore that the coin under discussion belongs to this province. The question however can be definitely settled by the discovery of more such coins with special reference to their *provenance*. This coin is a cast one and its rev. is blank. It can surely be taken as 'an example of early cast coinage' in which one side was left blank. There is no doubt about its indigenous origin and the Brāhmī script in Buhler's opinion is at least as old as 350—400 EC- *i.e.* pre-Mauryan.

Obv. : The Legend—*Upagodasa* in early Br. script, —"*Of Upagoda (Upagauḍa) ; above, a circle with dot* in centre, and beneath a nandipada (so-called "Taurine") represented horizontally.

Rev. : Blank.

The Nandipada is an auspicious symbol. The circle represents the 'Circle of Life' and the point or dot (parm) is a geometric symbolism of God, the Absolute and Unknowable.[4] So a circle with a dot stands for God as the centre of all life in the universe.

XXV. Yaudheyas, The.—

They are included among the *Ayudhajīvin* Saṅghas and they are referred to as a "*janapada*, a nation or country *i.e.*, a political community." They "considered military art as the vital principle of their constitution",[2] and were "specially noted as warriors."[5] The word *yaudheya* is derived from *yudha*, battle[4] or from a personal name,[5] though the former one seems to be more acceptable. Pāṇini places them in the Vāhika country[6] along with other republican states. There is no doubt that the Vāhīkas were in the Punjab : and Jayaswal takes the word Vāhika to mean 'the country of the rivers',[7] comprising the Sindh valley and the Punjab. Arrian mentions a powerful republic on the east side of the Hyphasis or Beas. Their country was very fertile and the inhabitants were agriculturists but brave in war. Jayaswal suggests with reference to the find-spot of the Yaudheya coins that this unnamed republic on the Beas was probably that of the Yaudheyas.[8] Alexander did not cross the river and had no opportunity of testing the military prowess of this renowned people. The Purāṇas give a monarchical[1] constitution to the Yaudheyas.[9] Perhaps the original monarchy was later on replaced by an aristocracy of 5000 councillors—virtually a republic.[10]

The Yaudheyas survived the Maurya Empire, the Satraps of Mathurā and the Kuṣāṇas. The 2nd cent. A. D. "was full of their military glory"[11] and they are referred to in Rudradāman's (150 A. D.) inscription. In the 4th cent. A. D., the Yaudheyas appear in the inscription of Samudragupta as one of the frontier tribes of the Gupta Empire. Perhaps they left their original home during the Kuṣāṇa period and were in Western Rājputānā during the time of Rudradāmaṇ. Cunningham identified the Yaudheyas with the Johiyas of Bhawalpur who "now occupy the country on both banks of the Sutlej, and the lower Doab between the Sutlej was named after them—the Johiyabār."[12] When the Yaudheyas passed away from history cannot exactly be determined, but it is certain that by the 7th cent. A. D. they were no more.[13] Thus they had a political existence of more than thousand years credited to them.[14]

"The coins of the Yaudheyas are found in the Eastern Punjab, and all over the country between the Sutlej and the Jumna rivers. Two large finds have been made at *Sonpath,* between Delhi and Karnāl."[15] Some of them were found in the Kāṅgrā District and a great many at Jogadheri in the Eastern Punjab ; and Cunningham procured his silver piece[16] and 300 copper pieces 'between the Sutlej and the Jumna rivers'. So it is evident that the Yaudheya territories were extensive ; "the cities of Lahore, Bhawalpur, Bikaner, Ludhiana and Delhi roughly indicate the limits of the tribal territory.[16a]

The Yaudheya coins fall into 3 classes—(a) The earliest,—"the Bull and Elephant Type" coins have been "dated a little before or after the Christian era."[17] These are small copper coins of rough workmanship but have some resemblance "with the earlier coins of the Audumbaras and the Kuṇindas," and on this ground Prof. Rapson assigns them to about 100

B. C.,[18] and these may be as old as the Śuṅga period.[19] (b) The Brahmanya Deva coins are assigned by Smith to the and cent. A. D. This was the period of their great military glory,[30] and it is but natural that they took Karttikeya the war-god for their coin type. So it is not possible to accept Prof. Rapson's view[20a] that these coins are to be dated after the 'warrior' type. (c) The 'warrior' type coins have surely been imitated from Kuṣāṇa models,[21] and we can safely accept Smith's view that these were in circulation upto "the completion of the conquest of Northern India by Chandragupta II about 380 A.D."[22] These copper coins are big in size and better executed than the rude coins of class (b). It appears that the Yaudheyas were divided into 3 distinct clans,[23] and those of the second and third clans were 'distinguished by numeral syllables and special symbols."[24] Some coins have 'dvi' (two) and some 'tri' (three), and these obviously refer to their three sections. The coins of the third class is 'the least numerous.'[25]

Type No. I. The *Bull and Elephant* Type[26] (c. 100 B. C.) AE.

Obv, : Bull standing r. facing a curved object (the national standard ?) within a railing ; 'early' Br. legend— *Yadheyana*, (Yaudheyānāṁ), 'of the Yaudheyas.'[27] In some of the specimens, there is another legend under the Bull which no body has been able to read ; it seems to end in *me*.[28] In other coins of the same type in brass or similar alloy occurs the legend—Kri........ya(dhe)yana ;[2] the second word Yadheyana is certain and for the first word various suggestions are made—(a) Kripadhanaba (Rodgers) ; (b) Bhumidhanusha (Cunningham) ; (c) Bhupadhanuska (Smith) and (d) Bahudhaṅake (Rapson)[29a] Smith is almost positive about the reading Bhupadhanusha and as this word means "of the Lord of the Desert' and seems to fit in with the locality of the Yaudheyas its correctness is beyond doubt. But there may be several varieties of this inscription as pointed out by Prof. Rapson *Rev.* : Elephant walking r.; *nandipada* symbol above and a "scythe-like" object.[30] In some specimens the curved line under the elephant is clear.[31]

Type No. 2. The *Three Symbols* Type.[32] AE.

Two coins are included' by Cunningham among those of the Yaudheyas ; one of them he found at Behat with other Yaudheya coins. These might be earlier than the "Bull and Elephant' Type, but the identification is not absolutely certain. One of them is a single-die coin[33] with only three symbols ; the other is broken, has three symbols, and part of a legend in indistinct Br. characters.[34]

Ovb. : The Three Symbols.—the Tree in railing in the middle is common. In the single-die coin, the symbol to the 1. is one of four circles ('Mālava' Symbol) and the other on the r. is perhaps a conventional tree like the symbol in coin No. 3 of Balabhūti of Mathurā (S CC1M., p. 192). The double-die coin has the 'triangular-headed' symbol on the 1. and a circular object (chakra?) on the r.; an inscription only partly legible—Mahārāja(sa). The rev. indistinct, perhaps a few letters.

Type No. 3.—The *Brahmaṇyadeva* Type.[35] AR & AE

Var. a.—Second Century A.D.

Obv. : *Six-headed* god (Kārttikeya) standing on lotus facing with 1. hand on hip and r. hand raised and a barbed spear on the 1.; the legend completed from a number of coins,—*Bhāgavataḥ svāmino Brahmaṇyadevasya*, "coin of (dedicated to) Almighty Lord Brahmaṇyadeva." Here Brahmaṇyadeva is not the name of a king as presumed by Smith.[36]. It is surely the national god Kārttikeya[37] the war-god, to whom the warlike Yaudheyas dedicated their coins. Whatever doubt we might have is set at rest by the substitution of *Kumārasa,*[38] another name of *Kārttikeya* for Brahmanyadevasya in some of the coins. In a few of these coins, the legends end in words like *drama, dama or darma*. V. Smith was not sure about its meaning and could not explain it ;[39] it is however only a variant of the Greek word drachm, signifing here 'a coin'. In some specimens the god stands on a pedestal,[40] and a vase also occurs in the r. field in a few cases.[41] *Rev.* : Six-headed figure standing on lotus, facing, tree in railing r. and the so-called *chaitya* with umbrella (the Hill symbol) and nandipada above it on the I.[42] In some specimens the figure stands on a bent line,[43] and in others it has only one head radiate.[44] V. Smith takes the figure to be a goddess but his identification does not appear to be correct. It seems to be a male figure and may represent Kārttikeya. But in one of the coins (C. CAI., Pl. VI, fig. 12)[45] the figure is single-headed radiate and is undoubtedly a female, What it stands for cannot be definitely ascertained. It must be a goddess worshipped by the Yaudheyas. Among the symbols, Svastika[46] also appears in some coins.

Var. b. *Obv.* : As in Var. a.

Rev. : Quadruped, perhaps stag standing to r.; above a (?) shrine with curved roof,[48] or a *chaitya*(Hill) to r. and a symbol above and the wavy line (the snake or river).[49]

The Brahmanyadeva Typc II.[50] AE.

Obv. : Single-headed god (Kārttikeya) radiate facing, vase to r.; Legend—Brahmaṇyadevasya drama, 'the coin of Brahmaṇyadeva.'

Rev.: Quadruped (Stag?) standing 1. facing (?) *Tree, Vase* with streamers on the r. and *a dotted circle.*[51] In another coin, we have in the place of 'the vase and circle' a crescent and the zigzag line (river?) below.[52]

Type No. 4. Thc *Warrior* Typc.[53] AE. (2nd cent. A. D.).

Var. a.—No *Obv.* numeral, and no rev. symbol.[54]

Obv. : A Warrior standing, facing f. grasping spear in r. hand with 1. hand on hip ; cock at his 1. foot ; Br. legend—*Yadhayaganasya jaya, (Yaudheyaganasya jaya)*, 'Victory to the Yaudheya tribe.' This figure of a warrior with a spear "in the pose of a dignified 'tri-bhaṅga' represents the type of their citizen-soldier."[55]

Rev. : A robed male figure walking 1. with r. hand extended and 1. hand on hip, like *Miiro* on Kuṣāṇa coins ; dotted circle.

Var. b. Numeral *Dvi* on *obv.* ; Vase on *rev.*[56]

Obv. : As in Var. a.; the numeral '*dvi*' (second) over r. shoulder.

Rev. : As in Var. a.; Vase containing leaves (not flowers) in 1. field and a symbol 'with three points and three dots' in r. field. The 'Vase with leaves' is even now used in Hindu religious ceremonies and is looked upon as an auspicious object.

Var. c.—Numeral '*Tri*' on *obv*.; Shell on *rev*.[57]

Obv. : As in Var. a. & b.; tri (third) over r. shoulder.

Rev. : As in Var. a & b. ; Shell instead of Vase ; Shell is also an auspicious object ; and a symbol composed of two zigzag lines with a line between. The numerals *Dvi* and *Tri* refer to the second and third sections of the Yaudhcya Gana.

XXVI. Rajanya Janapada.—

The identification of Rajanya coins was long delayed due to the wrong reading of the first word as Rājña[1] or Rajña.[2] V. Smith read the three letters as *Rajaña* and took it to be equivalent to Sanskrit *rājañya* or *Kṣatriya*[3] He explained the legend Rajaṅa janapàdasa[4] as meaning "(coin) of the Kṣatriya country." But Mr. Jayaswal was the first to correct this mistake. He takes Rajanya as "the proper name of a political people."[5] They came on the scene about 200-100 B.C. and issued coins in the name of their country. The Rājanyas as a people are referred to in "Pānini, Kātyāyana and Patañjali and also by the Mahā Bhārata."[6] Rājanya coins are procurable in Mathura[7] ; so Smith takes their territory to be not far from that city and locates it "in some part of eastern Rājputānā," perhaps in Dholpur State.[8] But as "coins of this type are found on the Mānaswāl plateau, Hoshyārpur District,"[9] Mr. Jayaswal presumes this to be their home.[10] The type of these coins is closely related to that of the Northern Satraps of Mathurā" and the legends are either in Kh. or Br. Prof. Rapson thinks that the coins with Kh. legends belong to an earlier date[12] and the Raj any a coins are ascribed to 2nd or 1st cent. B.C.

Type No. 1. *Standing Figure* Type.[13] AE.

Var. A. *With Kharoṣṭhī legend* (cast or die-struck).

Obv. : Standing figure, perhaps a deity, with r. hand raised, as on N. Satrap coins ; Kh. legend—Rajaña jana-pàdasa, (coin) of the Rajanya Janapada.

Rev.: Humped Bull standing 1., a symbol above; die-struck and extremely rare.

Var. B. *With Brāhmī legend.*[14] AE.

Obv. : Similar ; same legend in Br.

Rev. : Bull standing 1. in a rayed circle ; cast in high relief (No. 2—Smith), or die-struck (No. 3—Smith).

Type No. 2. *Tree in railing and Lion* Type.[15] AE.

Obv.: Tree in railing Br. legend .... (?) janapada(sa).

Rev. : Lion standing 1., facing (?) a post ; indistinct Br. legend, perhaps including Rājño.

FOOTNOTES

1. * I R. IC., p. 10. 2 *Ibid.* 3 CHI., 529 (Prof. Rapson). 4 *Ibid.*, p. 539. 5 *Ibid.*, Pl. V., fig. 17, p. 539.
* For Abbreviations—see the end of this Chapter.

II. I C. ASR., Vol. XIV., p. 136. 2 D. GDAML, p. 9. 3 C. ASR., Vol. XIV., PL XXXI, (Nos. 3 & 4). 4 R. IC., p. II. 5 C. ASR., Vol. XIV.

III. I J. HP., I., P. 154. 2*Ibid.*, footnote I. 3 CHI., I., p528. 4j. HP.,I.,p. 154;prop. Rapson, however, places them in 4th cent. B.C (CHI., I., p. 528). 5 j.HP., I.,p.132. 5a CHI., I p.528 (Rapson). 6 s. CCIM., p.160 (vol, II). 7 ibid. 8 J. HP., I., p.154; S.CCIM, p.166; CAI, P.106 (Rapson). 9 S. CCIM, p.160; j. HP. I., p.160. 10 C. CAI, p. 90. Ioa R. IC., pl. III., 20.II cf, the Yaudheya coin with soldier standing, holding spear in right hand on the rev., R: IC., pl.III., 14; s. CCIM., pl. XXI, 18,. 19 & 20. 12 S. CCIM., p. 166, pl.XX., 10. 13 ibid., pl. VIII., 4. 14 C. CAI., p. 92, Pl. IX., 9 rev. 15 S. CCIM., Pl. XX., 10 obv. 16 *Ibid.*, p. 180, Pl. XXI, 13 obv.

IV. I C. CAI., Pl. II. 2 R. IC., p. 14. 3 S. CCIM., p. 147. 4 CHI., p. 352. 5 R. 1C., p. 14. 5a C. CAI., Pl, II., fig. 17. 6 *Ibid.*, p. 61. 7 S. CCIM., p. 156, footnote I. 8 C. CAI., Pl II, fig 14. 9 *Ibid.*, fig. II. 10 *Ibid.*, fig. 9. II S. CCIM., p. 156 (No. 4). 12 R. 1C, Pl. I- II; C ASR., XIV PI. X. (No. 10).

V. I D. GDAMI. p. 13. 2 C. CAL, p. 66. 3 J. HP., I., p. 160. 4 C. CAI., p. 66. 5 D. GDAMI, p. 13. 6 S. CCIM., p. 160. 7 J. HP., I., p. 160. 8 *Ibid.*, p. 161. 9S. CCIM., p. 161. 10 J. HP., I., p. 161. II *Ibid.* 12 R. IC., p. II. 13 *Ibid.* 14 C. CAL, p. 67, PI. IV, fig. I; for other specimens see R. 1C., Pl. III, 8; & CHI., p. 539, Pl. V, 14. 15 J. HP. I., p. 161. 16 *Ibid.*, & pp. 42 & 43.—Lakṣana is the 'lāñchaṇa' or heraldic crest. It is usually 'the figure of an animal or river, town or the like.' 17 C. CAL, p. 68, PI. IV, fig. 2. 18 J. HP., L, p. 161. 19 J.A.S.B., 1914; (Numis. Sup. No. XXIII, 247—250.). 20 *Ibid.*, p. 249. 21 C. CAL, p. 68, PI. IV., figs., 5 & 6. 22 *Ibid.*, PI. IV., fig. 5. 23 JRAS, 1900 (A.V. Bergny), p. 411. 24 (a) Kuṇinda coins—Chatresvara Type—Bhagavata Chatresvara MahaMānah (S. CCIM., p. 170). (b) Yaudheya coins—Brahmanyadeva Type— Bhagavatah Svamino Brahmaṇyadevasya. (S. CCIM., p. 181). 25 R. 1C., PI. III., 10. 26 C. CAL, p. 69, PI. IV., figs. 7—9. 27 *Ibid.*, PI. IV, fig. 9. 28 *Ibid.*, PI. IV, figs. 7 & 8. 28a JRAS., 1900, p. 414 (A.V. Bergny), 29J. HP., I., pp. 42 & 160. 30 C. CAL, p. 69, Pl. IV, fig. 10. 31 *Ibid.*, fig. 12. 32 *Ibid.*, fig. 13. 33 JASB., Vol. X, No. 6, 1914. (Numis. Sup. No. XXIII, p. 248).

VI. I D GDAMI., p. 13. 2 S. CCIM., p. 145. 3 C. CAI., p. 95. 4 *Ibid.*, p. 96. 5 S. CCIM., p. 146. 6 R. IC., p. 14; CHI., p. 539. 7 S. CCIM., pp. 153—55 (Nos. 30—33 & 10—11.). 8 *Ibid.*, (No. 10), p. 153. 9 *Ibid.*, No. 32, p. 155. 10 *Ibid.*, No. 33. II *Ibid.* 12 *Ibid.* 13 *Ibid.*, No. 34. 14 *Ibid.*, No. 30. 15 *Ibid.*, No. 33. 16 C. CAL, p. 97, Pl. X, fig. 9. 17 S. CCIM., p. 155 (No. 34). 18 *Ibid.*, No. 35. 19 *Ibid.*, Nos. 21—27, p. 154. 20 *Ibid.*, No. 21. 21 *Ibid.*, No. 23. 22 *Ibid.*, No. 24. 23 C. CAI., PI. X, figs. 16, 17 & 18. 24 *Ibid.*, PL X, fig. 3. 25 S. CCIM., No. 21. 26 *Ibid.*t No. 23. 27 *Ibid.*, No. 22. 28 *Ibid.*, No. 27. 29 *Ibid.*, No. 28. 30 *Ibid.*, No. 29. 31 C. CAI., p. 98, Pl. X, fig. 20; R. 1C., p. 14, PL IV, 5; CHI, I., p. 539. 32 C. CAI., PI. X, fig. 19. 33 S. CCIM., p. 153 (Nos. 19 & 20); C. CAI., PL X, figs. 7, 8 & 20. 34 C. CAI, Pl X, fig. 8. 35 *Ibid.*, Pl. X, fig. 6. 36 CHI, L, p. 532. 37 S. CCIM, Nos. 1-18, pp. 152 & 153; C. CAL, figs. 1-5. 38 S. CCIM., p. 152 (No. I). 39 *Ibid.* 40 *Ibid.*, (No. 2). 41 *Ibid.*, p. 153, (No. 12). 42 *Ibid.* 43 *Ibid.* 44 *Ibid.*, p. 152, (No. 4). 45 C. CAI., p. 97, PL X., fig. 3. 46 S. CCIM., p. 152, (No. I). 47 *Ibid.*, (No. 2). 48 *Ibid.*, (No. 4). 49 *Ibid.*, p. 153, (No. 13). 50 *Ibid.*, (No. 14). 51 *Ibid.* p. 152 (No. 5). 52 C. CAI, Pl. X, fig. II. 53 *Ibid.*, Pl. X, fig. 13. 54 S. CCIM., 152 (Nos 5—8). 55 *Ibid.*, No. 6.
For the History of Avanti—see the Cambridge History of India, Vol. L—Chapters VII, pp. 185—7; XIII, pp. 310—11; XXI, pp. 531—31.

PI. X, figs. 16, 17 & 18. 24 *Ibid.*, PL X, fig. 3. 25 S. CCIM., No. 21. 26 *Ibid.*t No. 23. 27 *Ibid.*, No. 22. 28 *Ibid.*, No. 27. 29 *Ibid.*, No. 28. 30 *Ibid.*, No. 29. 31 C. CAI., p. 98, Pl. X, fig. 20; R. 1C., p. 14, PL IV, 5; CHI, I., p. 539. 32 C. CAI., PI. X, fig. 19. 33 S. CCIM., p. 153 (Nos. 19 & 20); C. CAI., PL X, figs. 7, 8 & 20. 34 C. CAI, Pl X, fig. 8. 35 *Ibid.*, Pl. X, fig. 6. 36 CHI, L, p. 532. 37 S. CCIM, Nos. 1-18, pp. 152 & 153; C. CAL, figs. 1-5. 38 S. CCIM., p. 152 (No. I). 39 *Ibid.* 40 *Ibid.*, (No. 2). 41 *Ibid.*, p. 153, (No. 12). 42 *Ibid.* 43 *Ibid.* 44 *Ibid.*, p. 152, (No. 4). 45 C. CAI., p. 97, PL X., fig. 3. 46 S. CCIM., p. 152, (No. I). 47 *Ibid.*, (No. 2). 48 *Ibid.*, (No. 4). 49 *Ibid.*, p. 153, (No. 13). 50 *Ibid.*, (No. 14). 51 *Ibid.* p. 152 (No. 5). 52 C. CAI, Pl. X, fig. II. 53 *Ibid.*, Pl. X, fig. 13. 54 S. CCIM., 152 (Nos 5—8). 55 *Ibid.*, No. 6.

For the History of Avanti—see the Cambridge History of India, Vol. L—Chapters VII, pp. 185—7; XIII, pp. 310—11; XXI, pp. 531—31.

VII. 1 D. GDAMI, p. 14. 2 S. CCIM, p. 144. 3 *Ibid.* 4 CHI, I, p. 527. 58. CCIM, p. 145. 6C. CAI, p. 91, Pl. IX, fig. I. 7 *Ibid.*, Pl. III, fig. 6. 8 *Ibid.*, Pl. IX. fig. 2. 9 *Ibid.*, fig. 3. 10 *Ibid.*, fig. 18; S. CCIM, p. 151 Nos. 27-29. II *Ibid.*, p. 148, Nos. 1 & 2; C, CAI, Pl. IX, fig. 7, 12 Smith—The Jain Stūpa and other Antiquities of Mathura, Pl. XI; L, fig. 2. 13 S. CCIM, p. 149, (No. 5); C. CAI, p. 92, Pl, IX., fig. 9. 14 S. CCIM, p. 150, (Nos. 14 and 15). 15 *Ibid.*, No. 16. 16C. CAI, Pl. IX., fig. 16. 17 *Ibid.*, Pl. IX., fig. 8; S. CCIM, p. 150, (Nos. 3 and 4). 18 *Ibid.*, p. 144. 19 *Ibid.*, p. 148 (No. aa); C. CAI, Pl. IX., fig. 6, p. 92. 20 *Ibid.*, figs. 4 and 5, 10 and 11, pp. 91-93; S. CCIM, p. 149, (No. 8). 21 CHI, I, p. 539. 22 C. CAI, PI. IX., fig. 10. 23 *Ibid.*, fig. II. 248. CCIM, p. 149 (No. 7). 25 *Ibid.*, p. 150, (No. 17). 26 I accept Smith's reading JRAS, (1900), p. 100. 27 S. CCIM, p. 150, (No. 22). 28 *Ibid.*, p. 151 (No. 28). 29 *Ibid.*, (No. 29).

VIII. 1 C, ASR., Vol. XIV, p. 147 2 R. 1C., p. 11. 3 C. ASR., Vol. XIV. 4C. CAI., p. 88, Pl. VIII, 10; C. ASR.; Vol. XIV., Pl. XXXI, 16.

IX. 1 Old name "*Erakaina*" as written in the Tomara Inscription on the great boar. The semi-circular figure in one of the coins is perhaps a rude representation of the city of Eraṇ. The concentric semi-circular device is a very good representation of the ground-plan of the city of Eraṇ enclosed in a bend of the river Bīna.—Cun. ASR., Vol. XIV.

2 C. CAI., p, 99. 3 *Ibid.* 4 CHI. I, p. 523. 5 C. CAI, p. 100. 6 JBORAS, 1919 (March), pp. 16-72, Pl. IV I; *Ibid.*, 1919 (Decem-ber), pp. 463-494, Pl. III, figs. I-Id. 7J-HP. I. p. 43—"The lakṣana is the 'royal' or 'state' mark." 8 Smith—Jaina Stūpa, PI. VII. 9R. 1C., p. II. 9aC. CAL. PI. XI, fig. 15, 9b *Ibid.*, 13. 10 *Ibid.*, 14. 11 *Ibid.*, 16, 17, 19 and 20. 12 *Ibid.*, 16. 13 *Ibid.*, 19. 14 *Ibid* , 20. 15 *Ibid.*, 17. 16 *Ibid.*, 18. 17 CHI, I, p. 538, PI. V, fig. 1 8 JRAS (1900), p. 108.

X. 1 R. 1C, p. 12. 2 C. CAI, p. 71. 3 J. HP, I, p. 217 and; 82n.

4 ** + ** — ** ace. to Sūtra ** (Pāṇini IV. 3, 53).

5 R. 1C., p. 14. 6 CHI., If, p. 348. 7 C. AGI., p. 37. 8 C. CAI., p. 62. 9C. AGI, p. 36. 10 D. GDAMI, p. 95. II Pargiter, F. E. —"Ancient Indian Historical Tradition, p. 356. 12 R. 1C, P. III, 7.

XI. I ASI-AR, 1921-22 (Meohar Inscription); 1923-24 (Kara Inscription), p. 122. 2 C. CAI, p. 73. 3 CHI, I., p. 524. 4 *Ibid.*, p. 525. 5 *Ibid.*, pp. 525 and 526. 6 *Ibid.* 7 CHI, I., p. 524; R. IC., p. 12. 8 C. CAI, pp. 73-75; S. CCIM, pp. 146 and 155. 9 C. CAI, Pl. V. fig. 14; S. CCIM, No. 2, p. 155. 10 C. CAI, PI. V, fig. 16. 11 *Ibid.*, fig. 17. 12 *Ibid.*, fig. 9. 13 *Ibid.*, fig. 7; S. CCIM, p. 155 (No. 4); R. 1C, P1. III, 12. 14 C. CAI, PI. V, fig. 11-13; R. IC III, II; S, CCIM, p. 155 (No. I). 15 C. CAI, PI. V, fig. 16. 16 *Ibid.*, fig. 18. 17.S. CCIM, p., 155 (No. 3). 18 C. CAI, PI. V, fig. 10. 19 *Ibid.*, fig. 15. 20 *Ibid.*, fig. 8.

XII. I Prof. Rapson in CHI, I., p. 529. 2 *Ibid.* 3 JRAS, 1900—Rapson, Notes on Indian Coins and Seals III—The Kulutas, a people of Northern India. 4 C. CAI, p. 70, PI. IV., fig. 14. Cunningham read

'Koputasya' or 'Koptanasya'; Rapson suggested 'Koputa', 'the very pure'. But it was Mr. Bergny who first correctly read 'Kolutasya'. JRAS, (1900) p. 415.

XIII. IC. CAI, p. 71; J. HP. I., p. 82, footnote I. 2 C. CAI, p. 71. 3 S. CCIM, p. 161. 4 C. CAI, p. 71. 5 J. HP. 1. p. 82, footnote I and 217. 6 CHI, I., p. 529. 7 *Ibid.*, 8 S. CCIM, p. 161. 9 j. HP. I, p. 82, footnote I. 10 S. CCIM, p. 161. II R. 1C, p. 12. 12 *Ibid.* 13 S. CCIM, p. 161. 14—150 B.C.—S. CCIM, p. 161; 100 B.C.—R. 1C, p. 12. 15—100 A.D.—S. CCIM, p. 167, 3rd or 4th cent. A.D.—R. 1C, p. 12. 16 S. CCIM, p. 167. 17 *Ibid.* 18J. HP. I, p. 82, footnote I. 18a S. CCIM, p. 167 (coin No. I). 19 *Ibid.*, p. 168. 20 *Ibid.*, p. 168. 21 *Ibid.*, 169. 22 *Ibid.*, p. 170; R. 1C, PI. III., 10. 23 V. Smith writes mahâMānah which is clearly a misprint for MahâtMānah (âtmâ in the sense of God). MahâtMānah means 'of Mahesvara' and Chatresvara—the lord. (R. 1C, PI. III., 10).

XIV. I J. HP, I., p. 159. 2 *Ibid.* 3 C. CAI, p. 69, Pl. IV, fig. II. 4 J HP. I., p. 159.

XV. 1 J, HP. I, p. 68. Ia "The Mālavas of the Punjab and the Kṣudrakas are associated in Sanskrit literature".—CHI, I., p. 375, footnote I. 2 C. AGI, p. 272. 3 J, HP, I., p. 68. 4 *Ibid.*, p, 149. 5 *Ibid.*, p. 152. 6S. CCIM, p. 162. 7 J, HP, I., p. 152. 8 *Ibid.* 8a ". . . . . is it not just possible that there may really have been two peoples—(i) the Mālava of the north represented the Malloi of the Greek writers, by the coins having the inscription *Mālavānāṁ Jaya*(h), by the Malaya of the Mudrārāksasa, and by the Mo-lo-so (Mo-lo-po) of Hiouen Thsang; and (ii) the better known Mālava of the south-called Mo-lo-po by Hiouen Thsang"— JRAS, (1900), p. 542 (Prof. Rapson). 9 S. CCIM, p. 161. 10 *Ibid.*, p. 162; Numis. Sup. No. 37, p. 43 (ASB, Vol. XIX, No. 6 (New series), II Douglas, R. O.—On some Mālava coins (Numis. Sup. No. 37). 12 S. CCIM.; Douglas—On some Mālava Coins. 13 J. HP. I., p. 153. 14 Douglas—On Some Mālava Coins, pp. 42-47, (Numis. Sup. No. 37). 13a In the Mudrārākṣasa, they are referred to as Malayas. 14 Douglas—On Some Mālava Coins, p. 44. 15 J. HP, I., p. 218. 16 S., CCIM, 174. 17 S. CCIM, Nos, 71, 73, 86, 09 etc. 18 J, IIP, I., p. 218. 19 S. CCIM, pp. 161-64 and 170-78. 20 S. CCIM, p. 174; Douglas, R.O.—On Some Mālava Coins, p. 45 (coin No. 2). 21 *Ibid.*, No. I. 22 S. CCIM, 171 (coin No. II). The coin No. I also belongs to the same type; the legend should be read as *Mālavana* and not *Mālava* [nām]. The other nine coins of this group must be considered to be of a much later date. 23 S. CCIM,' p. 171. 24 J, HP, I, p. 218. 25 Douglas, R.O.—On Some Mālava Coins, (Nos. 29 and 30).

XVI. I C. AGI, p. 429. 2, 3, 4 & 5, CHI, I., p. 526. 6 S. CCIM, p. 190. 7 C. AGI, p. 427. 8 R. IC, p. 13, PL III, 17; C. CAI, p. 86, Pl. VIII, fig. I. 9 CHI, I, p. 526. 10 C. CAI., p. 88, Pl. VIII, fig. .9, II S. CCIM, p. 192 (Nos. 1 & 2 of Balabhuti). 12 *Ibid.*, p. 192 (No. 2, Puruṣadatta). 13 *Ibid.*, p. 193 (No. 1, Bhavadatta). 14 *Ibid.*, p. 193 (No. I, of Rāmadatta, No. 3, uncertain etc.) ; C. CAI, PI. VIII, figs. 13, 14 & 15. 15 C. CCIM, p. 194 (No. I, uncertain). 16 *Ibid.*, pp. 192 & 193. 17 *Ibid.*, p. 193. 18 *Ibid.*, pp 194 & 195. 19 *Ibid.*, p. 194. 20 *Ibid.*

XVII. I C. CAI, p. 79. 2 S. CCIM, p. 184. 3 *Ibid.*, p. 185. 4 CHI, I; p. 526. 5 C. CAI, p. 79. 6 R. 1C, p. 13. 7 CHI, I, p. 525. 8 *Ibid.* 9 *Ibid.* 10 S. CCIM, p. 184. II C. CAI, p. 8o. 12 S.CCIM, p. 186, footnote 2. 13 R. Cat. of 1C, Andhras etc., p. CLXXVI. 14 C. CAI, p. 83, PI. VII, fig. 13; S. CCIM, p. 186. 15 C. CAI, pp. 82 & 83, PL VII, figs. 10 & II. 16 *Ibid.* Pl, VII, fig. II. 17 S, CCIM, p. 187, PL XXII, 4. 18 *Ibid.*, Pl. XXII, 5. 19 *Ibid.*, p. 187, Pl. XXII, 6. 20 C. CAI, Pl. VII, fig. 3. 21 *Ibid*, fig. 19. 22 *Ibid.*, fig. 20. 23 *Ibid.*, Pl VII, fig. 17. 24 *Ibid.*, fig. 5. 25 *Ibid.*, fig. I. 26 *Ibid*,, fig. 4. 27 *Ibid.*, fig. 21. 28 *Ibid.*, fig. 18. 29 Archaeological Survey of India, Annual Report, 1922-23. 30 See Smith's Catalogue—Coin No. 4 '(Bhānumitra), Coins Nos. I & 2 (Bhūmimitra), PL XXII, figs. 5 & 6, p. 187.

* C. ASR, Vol. XIV; p. 146, PL XXXI (Nos. 13 & 14)—The reproduction is very indistinct.

XVIII. I J. HP, I, p. 68. 2 *Ibid.*, p. 153, footnote 3. 3 *Ibid.*, p. 153. 51). GDAMI, p. 116.

XIX. 1 Marshall, Sir John—A Guide to Taxila, p. 2. 2 *Ibid.* 3 D. GDAMI., p. 200. 4 Marshall—A Guide to Taxila, p. 3. 5 C. AGI, p. 129. 6 Marshall—A Guide to Taxila, Pl. II. 3 & 4. 7 R. 1C, p. 14. 8 S. CCIM, p. 147. 9 *Ibid.*, Pl. XX, 7 (Coins 14-18), p. 157. 10 C. CAI, Pl. II, fig. 15. II *Ibid.*, fig. 19. 12 S. CCIM, p. 157 (No. 37). 13 C. CAI, PI. III, fig. 6; S. CCIM, p. 159 (No. 36). 14 S. CCIM, p. 158 (Nos. 22-32); C. CAI, PI. III. figs, 1 & 2. 15 S. CCIM, p. 158 (No. 33). 16 *Ibid.*, (No. 34). 17 *Ibid.*, p. 159 (No. 35); C. CAI, PI. III, fig. 7. 18 Head, B. V.—Coins of the Antlents, p. 10, Pl. 5, figs. 24 & 25; Gardner, Percy.—The Earliest Coins of Greece Proper, pp. 18-20. 19 JRAS, (1900), p. 99; J. HP, II, p. 78; ASR, Vol. XIV.

XX. ID. GDAMI, p. 206. 2 JRAS, (1894), p. 553. 3 *Ibid.*, Pl. 15; R. IC, p. 14.

XXI. I JRAS, 1900 (Prof. Rapson), p. 429, footnote 2; C. CAI, p. 68, Pl. IV, fig. 6. 2 *Ibid.*, fig. 5. 3 JRAS, 1900, p. 412 (Bergny) and pp. 428 & 429 (Prof. Rapson).

XXII. 1 D. GDAMI, p. 58 (Dvāravati) ; J. HP, I, p. 77. 2 *Ibid.*, p. 157. 3 *Ibid.* 4 *Ibid.*, p. 40. 5 *Ibid.*, p 41. 6 C. CAI, p. 70. 7 *Ibid.*, J. HP, I, p. 157. 8C. CAI, p. 70. 9 J. HP, I, p. 157. 8C. CAI, p. 70. 9J. HP, I, p. 157. 10 *Ibid.*, footnote 2. II JRAS, 1900, p. 416 (A.V. Bergny).

XXIII. I JRAS, (1900), pp. 98-102. 2 *Ibid.*, Indian Coins and Seals, I, fig. 1. 3 *Ibid.*, fig. 2. 4 Havell, E. B.—The ideals of Indian Art, p. 86. 5 *Ibid.*

XXIV. 1 JRAS, 1900 (Prof. Rapson), pp. 102-03. 2 D. GDAMI, p. 63. 3 C. AGI, p. 467. 4 Havell, E. B.—The Ideals of Indian Art, pp. 73 & 86.—"As the spokes of a wheel are attached to the nave, so are all things attached to Life."—quoted by Havell.

XXV. J. HP, I, pp. 35 & 36. 2 *Ibid.*, p. 37. 3 C. CAI., p. 75, 1 *Ibid.* 5 J. HP. I, p. 134. 6 *Ibid.*, p. 38. 7 *Ibid.* 8. *Ibid.*, p. 67. 9 J. HP, I, p 74. 10 *Ibid.*, pp. 67 & 74. II *Ibid.*, p. 149. 12 C. CAI., p. 76. 13 J. HP, I, p. 151. 14 *Ibid.*, p. 174. 15 C. CAI., p. 76. 16 *Ibid.*, p. 79. 16a S. Majumdar—Notes on C. AGI, p. 690. 17 S. CCIM., p. 165. 18 R. 1C, p. 15. 19 J. HP. I, p. 150. 20 *Ibid.*, p. 149. 20a R. 1C., p. 15 (sec. 60). 21 *Ibid.*; S. CCIM, p. 105. 22 *Ibid.* 23 J. HP. I., pp. 145 & 160. 24 S. CCIM., p. 165. 25 *Ibid.* 26 S. CCIM., Pl. XXI, 13 & 14, pp. 180 & 181; C. CAI., Pl. VI, figs. 2-4; R. 1C., Pl. III, 13. 27 S. CCIM., p. 180 (No. I). 28 *Ibid.*, (No. 2) 29 *Ibid.*, p. 181 (No. 5). 29 JRAS, (1900), p. 107, footnote I. 30 *Ibid.*, p. 180 (No. 3), Pl. XXI, 13. 31 C. CAI., Pl. VI., fig. 3. 32 C. CAI., p. 77, Pl. VI., figs., I & 5. 33 *Ibid.*, Pl. VI, fig. I. 34 *Ibid.*, Pl. VI. fig. 5. 35 S. CCIM., pp. 181-82, Pl. XXI, 15-17; C. CAI., p-78, Pl. VI, figs. 9-12, R. IC., PL III, 15. 36 S. CCIM., p. 181, footnote I. 37 R. 1C., Pl. III, 15; J. HP. I., p. 150 & 218 "On the second type they give the representation of God Kārttikeya, the presiding deity of Heroism and War and name him on the coin. In fact the coin itself is significantly dedicated to the Deity of Heroism. In other words the figure is their La Liberte'. 38 S. CCIM., p. 182 (Coin Nos. 15-17). 39 *Ibid.*, p. 182, footnote I. 40 S. CCIM., pp. 181-82 (Nos. 9 & 17). 41 *Ibid.*, p. 182 (No. 15). 42 *Ibid.*, p. 181, (No. 81, 43 *Ibid.*, (No. 9). 44 *Ibid*,, (No. 16). 45 C. CAI. p. 78. 46 S. CCIM., p. 181 (No. 9). 47 *Ibid.*, p. 182 (No. 20) ;C. CAI., Pl VI, fig. 13. 48 S. CCIM., p. 182 (No. 20). 49 C. CAI., Pl. VI., fig. 13. 50 S. CCIM., p. 182 (Nos 18a, 18b, & 19). 51 *Ibid.*, (No. 18b),. 52 *Ibid.*, (No. 19). 53 *Ibid.*, pp. 182-83, Pl. XXI, 18-20; C. CAI., Pl. VI, 6-8; R. 1C., Pl. III, 14. 54 S. CCIM., Pl. XXI, 18. 55 J. HP. I., p. 150. 56 S. CCIM., Pl. XXI, 19; C. CAI., Pl. VI, 7, R. 1C., Pl III, 14. 57 S. CCIM., Pl. XXI. 20; C. CAI., Pl. VI, S.

XXVI. I R. IC., p. 12(Sec. 47) 2C. CAI., p. 89. 3 S. CCIM., p. 164. 4 *Ibid.* 5 J. HP. I., p. 158. 6 *Ibid.* 7 S. CCIM., p. 164. 8 *Ibid.*, p. 165. 9 *Ibid.* 10 J. HP. I., p. 159. II. R. I.C., p. 12; S. CCIM., p. 165. 12R. IC., p. 12. 13 S. CCIM., p. 179 (No. 1). 14 *Ibid.* 15 *Ibid.*, p. 180 (No. 8).

BIBLIOGRAPHY

Allan, John.—Catalogue of the Coins of the Gupta Dynasties and of Sasāñka, king of Gauḍa, (A catalogue of the Indian Coins in the British Museum). 1914.

Anderson, B. M. Jr.—The Value of Honey. 1917.

Archaeological Survey of India, Annual Report for 1905-6, 1913-14, 1922-23, 1923-24, 1924-25.

Arthaśāstra of Kauṭilya—Translated by R. Shamasastry, 1915 (Bangalore).

Avebury, Lord.—The Origin of Civilisation.

Babelon, E.—Les Origines de la Monnaie etc.

Barker, D. A.—The Theory of Money, 1913. (The Cambridge Manuals of Science and Literature).

Banerjee, G.—India as known to the Western World.

Banerji, R. D.—Annual Basumati of 1333 B.S.

—— A New Type of Audambara Coinage. (Nums. Sup. No. XXIII—J.A.S.B. Vol. X. No. 6, 1914.)

—— Prāchin Mudrā, (Calcutta, 1322 B.S.)

Bhandarkar, D. R.—Lectures on Ancient Indian Numismatics, (The Carmichael Lectures, 1921—Calcutta University).

—— The Carmichael Lectures, 1918.

BrāhMāna—Aitareya.

—— Śatapatha.

—— Taittirïya.

Brown, C. J.—The Coins of India, 1922, (The Heritage of India Series).

Cambridge Ancient History, The.—Vol. IV (Persian Empire).

Cambridge History of India, The.—Vol. I. Ancient India—edited by E. J. Rapson, 1922.

Carmichael Lectures, The—1918 and 1921.

* For Bibliography see Rapson, Indian Coins and Cambridge History of India, Vol. I, p. 683 & 688.

Cunningham, Sir Alexander—The Ancient Geography of India (London, 1871); edited by S. N, Majumder Sastri, 1924, Calcutta.

——— Coins of Ancient India from the earliest times down to the 7th century A.D. 1891 (London).

——— Coins of Medieval India, 1893 (London).

——— Numismatic Chronicle, 1873.

——— The Stūpa of Bhārhut, a Buddhist Monument, 1879, (London).

——— Archaeological Survey of India, Vol. IV, IX, and XIV.

Das, A. C.— Ṛgvedic Culture, 1925 (Calcutta).

Dey, Nundo Lal.—The Geographical Dictionary of Ancient and Medieval India, Second Edition, 1927, (Calcutta Oriental Series, No. 21. E. 13).

Douglas, R. O.—On Some Mālava Coins, (Numis. Supp. No. XXXVII, J.A.S.B. (New Series), Vol. XIX, 1923, No. 6).

Elliot, Sir Walter.—Coins of Southern India, (The International Numismata Orientalia), 1886.

Encyclopaedia Britannica, The.—Vol XVII, Ninth Edition.

Gardner, Percy.—The Earliest Coins of Greece Proper, (From the Proceedings of the British Academy, Vol. V).

Gṛhya Sūtra—Gobhila.

——— Hiraṇyakeśi, etc.

Havell, E. B.—The Ideals of Indian Art, 1920.

Head, B V.—A Guide to the Principal Gold and Silver Coins of the Ancients, from Circ. B.C. 700 to A.D. I, (Department of Coins and Medals, British Museum), 1895.

——— Historia Numorum (Oxford, Clarendon Press, 1887)

Jayaswal, K. P.—Hindu Polity, Parts I & II (1914).

Jevons, W. S.—Money and The Mechanism of Exchange (London, 1910).

Journal, The.—Of the Royal Asiatic Society of Great Britain and Ireland, 1895, 1900, 1903, 1924 (Cent. Supplement, October).

Journal, The.—Of the Asiatic Society of Bengal, 1911, 1914, & 1924.

Journal, The.—Of the Bihar and Orissa Research Society, Vol. V, parts I & IV (1919).

Kauṭilya's Arthaśāstra—Trans. by R. Samasastry, (1915).

Macdonald, Arthur, A.—A History of Sanskrit Literature, (1913).

Macdonald, George.—The Evolution of Coinage, 1916. (The Cambridge Manuals of Science and Literature).

Malcolm, Sir John.—Central India (1832).

Marshall, Sir John.—A Guide to Taxila, (1918).

—— Statement to the Press on the Pre-historic Civilisation of the Indus Valley.

Maspero, Gaston.—The Dawn of Civilisation, (1910), (Edited by A. H. Sayce & Trails, by M. L. McClure). Reprint : Fifth Edition).

Maspero, Gaston.—The Struggle of the Nations, 1910, (Second Edition).

—— The Passing of the Empires, 850 B.C.—330 B.C. (1910).

Manu—Mānava Dharma Śāstra.

Max Muller, F.—History of Ancient Sanskrit Literature, 1860.

Mitra, Panchanan.—Prehistoric India, 1923.

Mookerji, Radhakumud.—Local Government in Ancient India, 2nd edition, 1920.

Numismata Orientalia, Part I.

Pānini's Aṣṭādhyāyi.

Palgrave, Sir R. H. Inglis.—The Dictionary of Political Economy, Vol. II, (1917).

Pargiter, F. E.—Ancient Indian Historical Tradition.

Periplus of the Erythraean Sea, The.—Trans. & Annot. by Wilfred H. Schoff, (1912).

Prāyascittatattvam of Raghunandana.

Rapson, E. J.—Ancient India from the earliest times to the first century A.D. Cambridge, 1914.

—— Catalogue of the Coins of the Andhra Dynasty The Western Ksatrapas etc. 1908.—(A Catalogue of the Indian Coins in the British Museum).

—— Indian Coins, 1898. (Encyclopaedia of Indo-Aryan Research, Vol. II, Part 3, B.)

Rawlinson, G.—The History of Herodotus, (Everyman's Library).

Rawlinson, H. G.—Intercourse between India and the Western World.

Samhitā— Ṛgveda.

—— Taittirīya.

Schoff, W. H.—The Periplus of the Erythraean Sea, 1922.

Sewell, R.—A Forgotten Empire (Vijayanagar).

Seyd, Ernest.—Bullion and Foreign Exchanges, (London, 1868).

Skeat, W. W.—The Etymological Dictionary of the English Language.

Smith, V. A.—Catalogue of the Coins in the Indian Museum, Calcutta, Vol. I, 1906.

—— The Early History of India from 600 B. C. to me Muhammadan Conquest, 1914 (3rd edn.).

—— The Jaina Stūpa and other Antiquities of Mathurā, (1901).

—— Oxford History of India from the earliest times to the end of 1911 (Oxford, 1919).

Spencer, Herbert.—The Principles of Sociology, Vols. I & II, 1906.

Thomas, Edward.—Ancient Indian Weights, 1874. (Marsden's Numismata Orientalia, Part I).

Todd, J. A.—The Mechanism of Exchange, 1917.

Tylor, E. B.—Anthropology, 1913.

Walsh, E. H. C. Indian Punch-marked Coins.—Cent. Suppl. to the J.R.A.S. 1924.

—— Punch-marked Coins, J.B.O.R.S., Parts I & IV, 1919.

Watt, Sir George.—The Commercial Products of India, 1908.

Whitehead, R. B.—Catatogue of Coins in the Punjab Museum, Lahore, Vol. I.

—— The Pre-Mohammedan 'Coinage of North western India, 1922. (Numismatic Notes and Monograms, No. 13).

Yājñavalkya—Dharma Śāstra.

Yajurveda—Kṛṣṇa.

INDEX

A

B

C

D

E

G

H

I

J

K

L

M

N

O

P

Q

R

S

T

U

V

W

Y

Z

★★★

PLATES

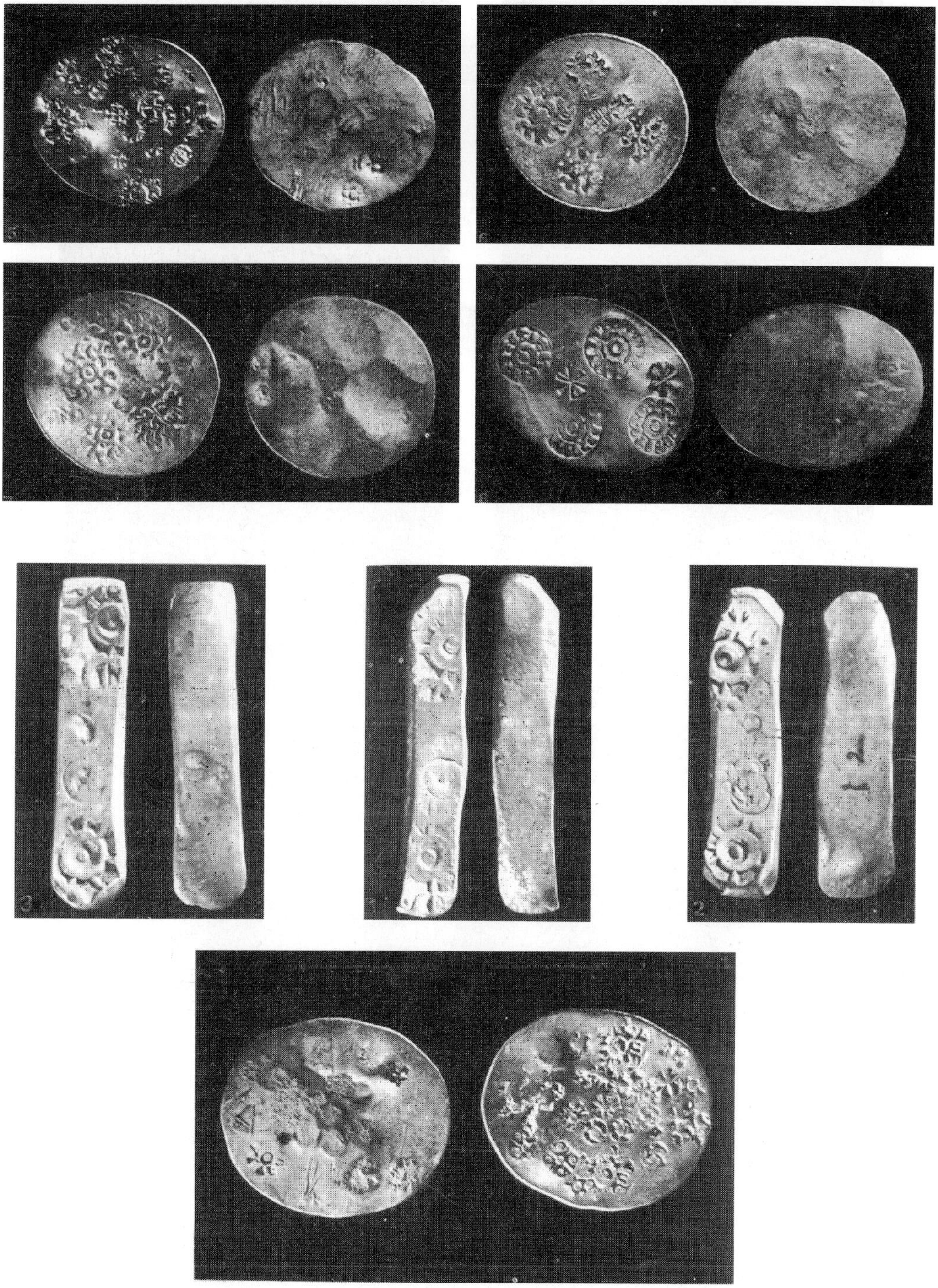

Pl. 1.Punch Marked Silver Coin, 4th and 6th century B.C.

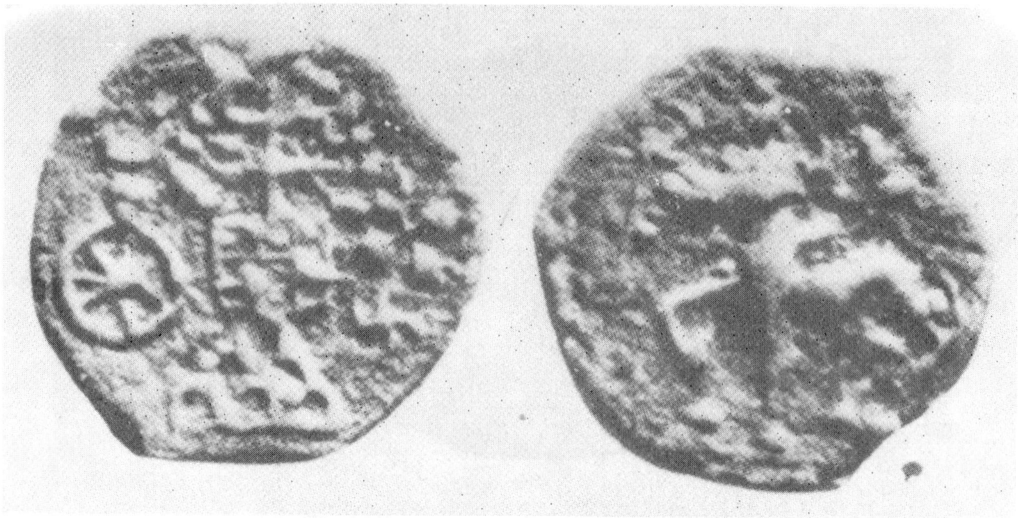

Pl. 5.Hill and Kalpa Tree on Coin, Tribal, Ist century B.C., Kausambi.

Pl. 6.Early Pandya Copper coin showing the asvamedha horse Ist and IInd century A.D., B.C., National Museum.

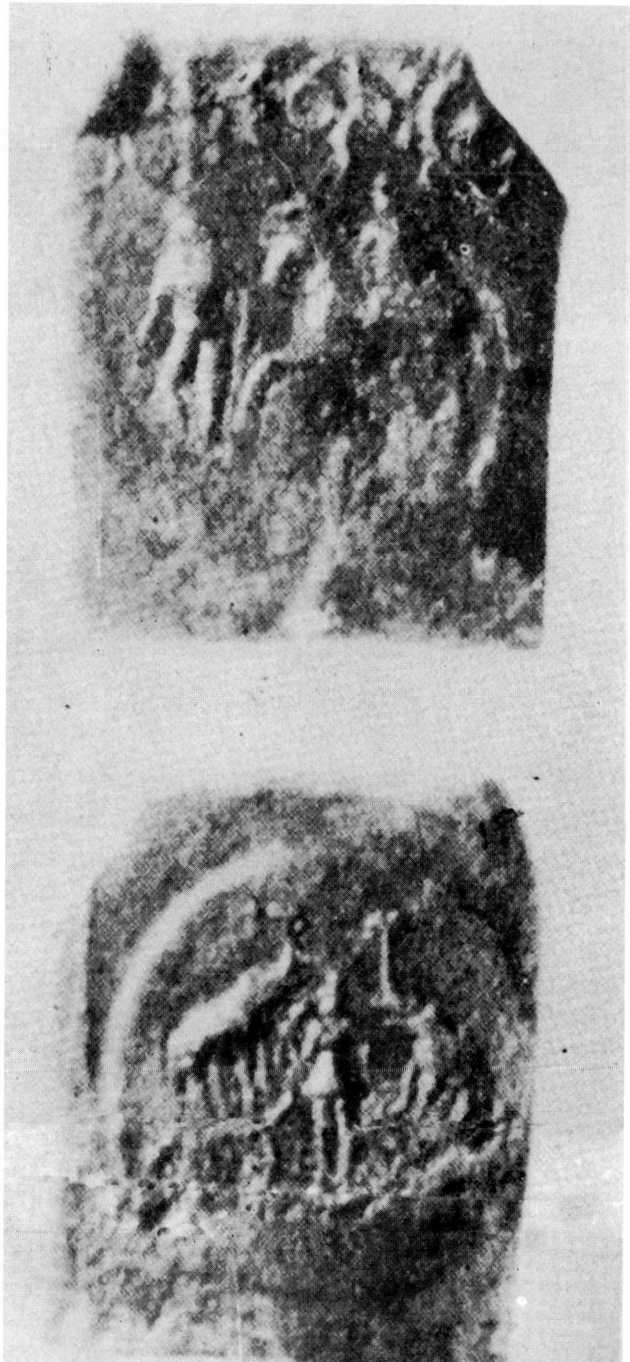

Pl. 7.Lakshmi bathed by elephants on reverse of Sujyeshtha's Coins, IInd century B.C.

Pl. 11.Anthropomorphic, Zoomorphic and Symbolic representation of Sri on Tribal coin Kuninda Amoghabhuti, Ist century A.D.

Pl. 12.Coin of Gautamiputra Satakarni, Ist century A.D., National Museum.

Pl. 13.Gold coin of Kanishka, Ist century A.D.

Pl. 14.Gold coins of Havishka, Ist century A.D.

Pl. 15.Gold coin of Kushan.

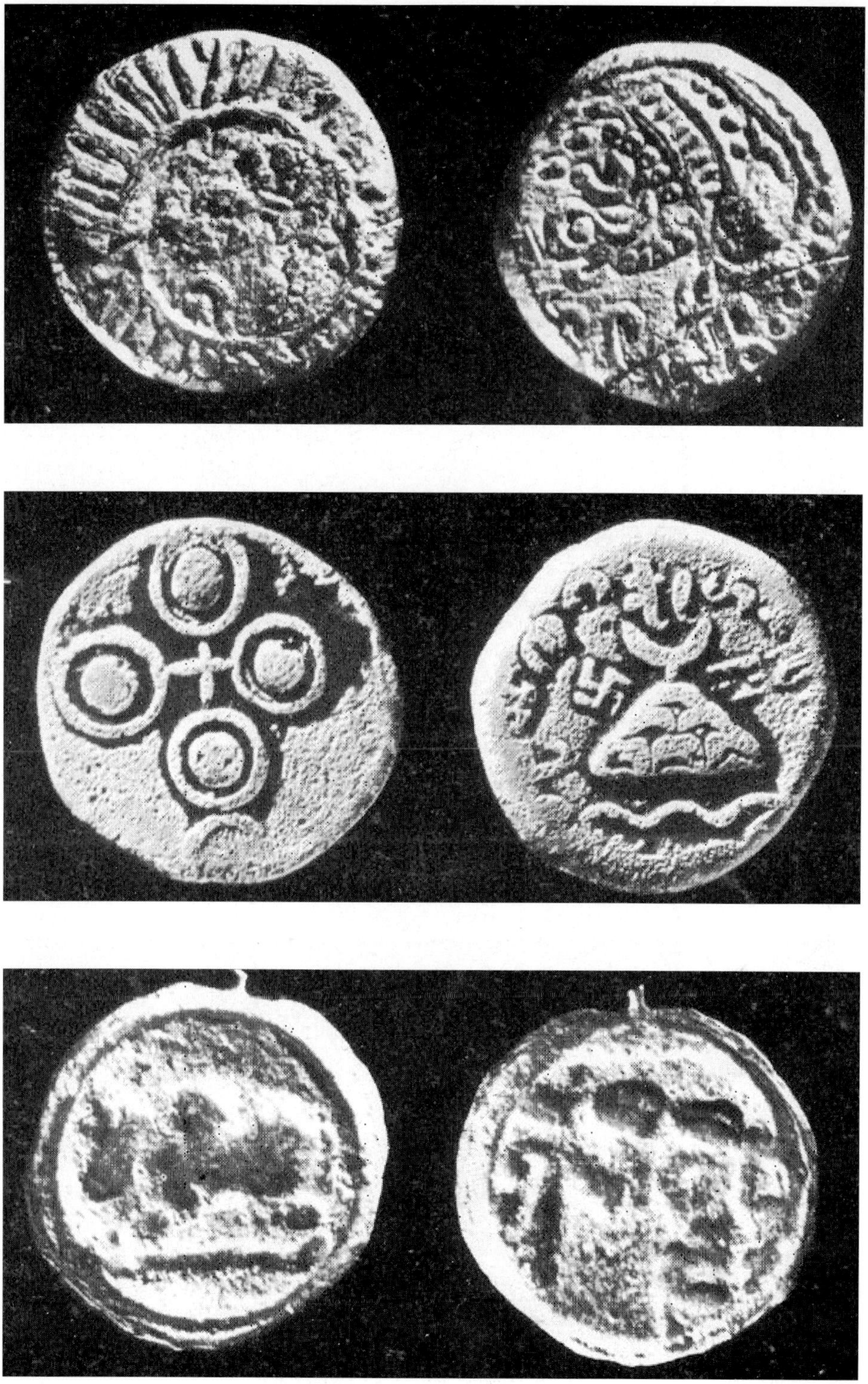

Pl. 16-A.Copper and Silver coin Satavahana, Ist century A.D.

Pl. 16-B.Copper and Silver coin Satavahana, Ist century A.D.

Pl. 17.Coin of Sri Yana Satakarni (Satavahana), IInd century A.D.

Pl. 18.Coin of Damasena reverse, Kshatrapa, 3rd century A.D., National Museum.

Pl. 19.Coins of Chandra Satakarni, IInd century A.D., National Museum.

Pl. 20.Yaudheya coin showing Kartikeya, IInd century A.D., National Museum.